THE POTENTIALITY OF 'DEVELOPMENTAL STATES' IN AFRICA
Botswana and Uganda Compared

Edited by
Pamela Mbabazi & Ian Taylor

COUNCIL FOR THE DEVELOPMENT OF
SOCIAL SCIENCE RESEARCH IN AFRICA

© Council for the Development of Social Science Research in Africa 2005
Avenue Cheikh Anta Diop Angle Canal IV, BP 3304 Dakar, 18524 Senegal.
http://www.codesria.org
All rights reserved

ISBN: 2-86978-164-4

Page Layout: Djibril Fall
Cover Design: Ibrahima Fofana
Printing: Imprimerie Graphiplus Dakar, Senegal

The Council for the Development of Social Science Research in Africa (CODESRIA) is an independent organisation whose principal objectives are facilitating research, promoting research-based publishing and creating multiple forums geared towards the exchange of views and information among African researchers. It challenges the fragmentation of research through the creation of thematic research networks that cut across linguistic and regional boundaries.

CODESRIA publishes a quarterly journal, *Africa Development*, the longest standing Africa-based social science journal; *Afrika Zamani*, a journal of history; the *African Sociological Review*, *African Journal of International Affairs (AJIA)*, *Africa Review of Books* and *Identity, Culture and Politics: An Afro-Asian Dialogue*. It co-publishes the *Journal of Higher Education in Africa* and *Africa Media Review*. Research results and other activities of the institution are disseminated through 'Working Papers', 'Monograph Series', 'CODESRIA Book Series', and the *CODESRIA Bulletin*.

CODESRIA would like to express its gratitude to African Governments, the Swedish Development Co-operation Agency (SIDA/SAREC), the International Development Research Centre (IDRC), OXFAM GB/I, the MacArthur Foundation, the Carnegie Corporation, the Norwegian Ministry of Foreign Affairs, the Danish Agency for International Development (DANIDA), the French Ministry of Cooperation, the Ford Foundation, the United Nations Development Programme (UNDP), the Rockefeller Foundation, the Prince Claus Fund and the Government of Senegal for support of its research, publication and training activities.

This book is dedicated to the memory of Patrick Bazaara Nyangabyaki, who was part of this project from the start and attended the initial workshop in Gaborone. Sadly, he passed away whilst the project was underway.

May his soul rest in peace.

Contents

Dedication iii
Acknowledgements vii
Abbreviations viii
About the Contributors x

1. **Botswana and Uganda as Developmental States (?)**
   Pamela Mbabazi and Ian Taylor 1

2. **Success or Failure of Developmental States in Africa: Exploring Africa's Experimentation at Developmentalism**
   Francis Nyamnjoh and Ignasio Malizani-Jimu 16

3. **Uganda as an African "Democratic Developmental State?": HIPC Governance at the Turn of the Century**
   Timothy Shaw 33

4. **The Developmental State in Africa: The Case of Botswana**
   Ian Taylor 44

5. **Uganda's Institutional Framework for Development Since Colonialism: Challenges of a Developmental State**
   James Akampumuza 57

6. **The Institutional Framework of the Developmental State in Botswana**
   David Sebudubudu 79

7. **Decentralization in African Developmental States: Experiences from Uganda and Botswana**
   Neema Murembe, Gladys Mokhawa and David Sebudubudu 90

8. **Gender and Developmental States: Botswana and Uganda**
   Pamela Mbabazi, Godisang Mookodi and Jane Parpart 104

9. **The Privatization Experience in Uganda: Prospects and Challenges of Its Implementation**
Muriisa Roberts 122

10. **The Developmental State and Manufacturing in Uganda and Botswana: The Textile Industries Compared**
Pamela Mbabazi and Gladys Mokhawa 133

11. **Conclusion: Developmental States and Africa in the Twenty-First Century**
Pamela Mbabazi and Ian Taylor 147

References 153

Acknowledgements

This project was funded by the Council for the Development of Social Science Research in Africa (CODESRIA), as part of its Comparative Research Network programme. The editors and contributors express sincere gratitude to the following members of staff of CODESRIA for their support during the project: Professor Adebayo Olukoshi, the Executive Director, Professor Francis Nyamnjoh, Head of the Department of Publications and Dissemination (formerly of University of Botswana), Bruno Sonko and Abdou Ndao, Programme Assistants for their excellent administrative and technical help.

Sincere thanks and appreciation go to the Vice Chancellor for his support in organizing the second CODESRIA Workshop at MUST in February and opening the workshop, and Professor Timothy Shaw, Bank of Uganda Chair in Development Studies at MUST who initiated the link between MUST and Botswana and encouraged the embryonic Faculty to be a part of this project.

We thank David Witty, a lecturer in the Faculty, for ably coordinating the February CODESRIA workshop, Mr. Steven Karuhanga (Faculty Administrator), Mr Andrew Ainomugisha and Ms Clare Karooma (M.A Students at MUST) who worked tirelessly with David to ensure that the workshop was a success.

Finally, we thank the various contributors to this project for their involvement, academic input and friendship. Part of the whole rationale behind this project was to bring institutions and people in Africa together and academic links between Botswana and Uganda have now been firmly established—particularly between the University of Botswana and Mbarara University of Science and Technology. MUST's motto is "Succeed we Must". We feel that this has been achieved.

Pamela Mbabazi and Ian Taylor

Abbreviations

AG	Attorney General
BoP	Balance of Payment
BOU	Bank of Uganda.
CA	Court of Appeal
CID	Criminal Investigations Department.
DA	District Administrator
DC	District Commissioner
DRIC	Divestiture Reform and Implementation Committee
ERC	Economic Recovery Credit.
ERP	Economic Recovery Program
ESAF	Enhanced Structural Adjustment Facility
HIPC	Highly Indebted Poor Countries Initiative (HIPIC
IBRD	International Bank For Reconstruction and Development.
IDA	International Development Association.
IFIs	International Financial Institutions
IGG	Inspector General of Government
IMF	International Monetary Fund
JVA	Joint Venture Agreement
LCs	Local Councils
LEGCO	Legislative Council.
MOPED	Ministry of Planning and Economic Development.
MPs	Members of Parliament
MTN	Mobile Telephone Networks (MTN) Uganda Ltd
NRA	National Resistance Army, now Uganda Peoples Defence Forces (UPDF).
NRC	National Resistance Council.
NRM	National Resistance Movement.
PAC	Public Accounts Committee
PERD	Public Enterprises Reform and Divestiture (PERD) statute 1993 (Act) 2000.
PU	Privatisation Unit
RTA	Registration of Titles Act
SAC	Structural Adjustment Credit.
SAF	Structural Adjustment Facility.
SAP(s)	Structural Adjustment Programs
SAPRI	Structural Adjustment Policy Participatory Review Initiative
SDA	Special District Administrator.

SDR	Special Drawing Rights.
SI	Statutory Instrument
SOE	State Owned Enterprise
SWIPCO	Swiss Procurement Company
UAC	Uganda Airways Corporation
UCB	Uganda Commercial Bank.
UDC	Uganda Development Corporation.
UIA	Uganda Investment Authority
UPC	Uganda Peoples Congress.

About the Contributors

James Akampumuza is the Dean, Faculty of Commerce, Makerere University Business School (MUBS), Uganda. He is also a Practising Advocate.

Ignasio Malizani-Jimu is a Lecturer in Economic Geography at Mzuzu University, Malawi.

Pamela Mbabazi is a Development Planner by training and has been teaching various courses in Development Planning and Rural Development at Mbarara University of Science and Technology in Uganda over the last eight years. She is currently the Dean of the Faculty of Development Studies. Her research interests include governance issues, the impact of globalization on third world countries and peacebuilding. Her publications include *Supply Chain and Liberalisation of the Milk Industry in Uganda* (2005) and articles in *Global Networks; A Journal of Transnational Affairs*.

Gladys Mokhawa is a Lecturer in Public Administration, Department of Political and Administrative Studies, University of Botswana.

Godisang Mookodi is a Lecturer in Gender Studies, Department of Sociology, University of Botswana.

Neema Murembe is Associate Dean and Head of Department, Development Studies, Mbarara University, Uganda.

Francis Nyamnjoh is currently Head of Publications and Dissemination at CODESRIA, Dakar, Senegal, which he joined from the University of Botswana in 2003.

Jane Parpart is the Lester Pearson Professor of International Development Studies at Dalhousie University, Canada and a Visiting Professor at both MUST, Uganda and the University of Stellenbosch, South Africa.

Muriisa Roberts is a lecturer in Development Studies, Mbarara University, Uganda.

David Sebudubudu is a Lecturer in Politics, Department of Political and Administrative Studies, University of Botswana. He is also a member of the Democracy Research Project (DRP), University of Botswana?

Timothy M, Shaw is Director, Institute for Commonwealth Studies, School of Advanced Study, University of London, England and a Visiting Professor at Mbarara University, Uganda and the University of Stellenbosh, South Africa.

Ian Taylor is a Lecturer in the School of International Relations, University of St Andrews and a Visiting Research Fellow at the University of Stellenbosch, South Africa. He previously worked at the University of Botswana for four years. He is the author of *Stuck in Middle GEAR: South Africa's Post-Apartheid Foreign Relations* (2001) and is the co-editor of *Africa in International Politics: External Involvement on the Continent* (2004), as well as other work on broad development issues in Africa.

1

Botswana and Uganda as Developmental States(?)

Pamela Mbabazi and Ian Taylor

The construction of democratic developmental states in Africa must now be seen as one of the most urgent tasks facing the continent in the new millennium. The Structural Adjustment Programmes of the last two decades have plainly not worked to the benefit of the average African. This is not to say that a strong dirigiste project is the necessary counter-weight to neo-liberalism. Instead, it is probable that the state's role is best suited devising broad developmental programmes and then implementing such projects. The success of this hinges upon the involvement of individual homes, entrepreneurs and private—as well as public—institutions. As Mkandawire and Soludo (1999) have written:

> Two important lessons from Africa's development experience have been that failure to mobilize the resource-allocative functions of the market can only contribute to the inflexibility of the economy; and failure to recognize the weakness of market forces in a number of fundamental areas can lead to failed adjustment. Development policies will therefore have to be keenly responsive to the capacities and weaknesses of both states and markets in Africa and seek to mobilize the former while correcting the latter. Dogmatic faith in either planning or markets will simply not do.

There is of course a major problem in defining a developmental state simply from its economic performance: not all countries with good growth rates are developmental states. The definition of the 'developmental state' runs the risk of being tautological since evidence that the state is developmental is often drawn deductively from the performance of the economy. This produces a definition of a state as developmental if the economy is 'developing', and equates economic success to state strength while measuring the latter by the presumed outcomes of its policies. In Africa, there have been many examples of states whose performance up until the mid-1970s would have qualified them as 'developmental states' in the sense conveyed by current definitions, but which now seem anti-developmental because the hard times and especially political turmoil, brought the economic expansion of their countries to a halt. Recognition of episodes and possibilities of failure leads us to a definition of a developmental state as one whose ideological underpinnings are developmental and one that seriously attempts to deploy its administrative and political resources to the task of economic development. We will discuss this definition in greater detail below but at this point we state that the purpose of this book is to critically interrogate the whys and wherefores of Botswana and Uganda as 'developmental states'.

At the same time, this study will cross-examine the dominant discourse vis-à-vis development namely, the idea that the market is the be-all and end-all of all discussions pertaining to economic progress and that, concomitant with this line of thinking, the role of the state must be curtailed from involvement in economic planning and management (Shaw 1997). The liberalisation mantra, so intricately bound up with certain, arguably dominant, readings of globalisation, negates any active role for the public sector in promoting development, except perhaps as a minimalist regulator. This particular understanding of globalisation is highly problematic, particularly as it is precisely those administrations that have maintained a role for the state in promoting social and economic development— the so-called 'developmental states'—that have the most impressive track records vis-à-vis growth and economic progress.

Despite this, there has been an attempt to re-interpret and re-frame the notion of the developmental state in order to justify the form of globalisation favoured by transnational capital viz. neo-liberalism. We can see this as a 'transnational process of consensus formation among the official caretakers of the global economy…generat[ing] guidelines that are transmitted into the policy-making channels of national governments and big corporations' (Cox 1994: 49).

This project is immensely important when discussing the role of the state in Africa in promoting development in the era of globalisation as there has been a concerted attempt to assert that the course best suited for Africa is an active stripping away of the state and its role in African economies. Official bodies like the Organization for Economic Co-operation and Development (OECD), the World Bank, the IMF, and the G-7 'shape the discourse within which policies are defined, the terms and concepts that circumscribe what can be thought and done [and] also tighten the transnational networks that link policy-making from country to country' (Cox 1994: 49). Attacking the developmental state is part and parcel of this. As Gosovic remarks, very accurately in our minds:

> The discrediting of the 'developmental state'…of public institutions and endeavours (that are deemed a 'bad', and in contrast to the private and hence privatization which are considered an unmitigated 'good'), and of the development record of earlier decades have, together with the delegitimization,

and making into an anathema key aspects of the UN's development work and of the traditional North-South agenda, contributed to and constituted the outcomes of the current intellectual hegemony (Gosovic 2000: 453).

Yet, many other post-independence states have had an 'activist' role for the state in the economy making them relatively successful. This study aims to identify the nature and quality of this role, comparing it to Botswana and Uganda, in order to distinguish the differences (and perhaps similarities) that stake out the two countries' developmental record and the comparative role and style of state activity. Indeed, a further purpose of this book is to discuss the debate over the developmental state and its potential in fostering growth and development within the constraints of a globalised world and with particular reference to Africa, focused on Botswana and Uganda.

At the same time, this study will naturally recognise that within the 'practice of development', there now exists states but also increasingly civil societies and private companies—both directly and indirectly. The 'triangle' or 'tri-sector' of this trio of actor types, as encouraged by the World Bank (1999) et al, exists at all levels, from the local to global and constitutes the prevailing contemporary form of 'governance' (MacLean, Quadir and Shaw 2001). These triangles can be managed and directed to enhance sustainable long-term human development as well as for shorter-term profit or image. Such 'trilateral partnerships' became increasingly popular in the 1990s as states and other actors sought to rebalance their relationships in the interests of democracy and sustainability as well as development and add an interesting and novel dimension to the notion of an African developmental state, as Shaw in his chapter amply demonstrates.

For Africa, the various international financial institutions have argued that African states lack the capacity to pursue policies similar to the developmental states of East Asia, whilst being far too susceptible to vested interests in the political realm. Known as the 'impossibility thesis', African states that remained in the business of guiding development threatened to bring disaster and had to be reined in by SAPs. Elites in Africa have frequently taken on board such advice and have come to believe that a minimalist role for the state is required. Whilst recognising the problematic nature of a great deal of African state formations, across the board liberalisation and state rollback has been similarly dubious. It is thus extremely important to challenge the thesis that state involvement inexorably leads to economic decline and that developmental states in Africa are an impossibility. Examples do exist in Africa that contradict to a large degree this position. Botswana is one such case and some of the developmental efforts promoted in Uganda by the state are of interest.

For sure, there is a definite need to challenge the current dominant rubbishing of the state's role in facilitating development. Even in Tanzania, which is often held up as an African 'basket case' and an example of what the African state should not do, recent research has found the orthodox condemnation of Tanzania's development trajectory misplaced. As Mathew Costello has written:

> [I]n nations with scant industry and thin capital markets, such as Tanzania, state-led investment is necessary to establish conditions under which private investment can generate growth. Where there is little expectation of investment, and where the conditions for private sector investment appear weak, the state may have a role to play in strengthening the market and providing initial investment (Costello 1994: 1518).

Yet before we go into greater detail vis-à-vis 'developmental states' in Africa, we briefly turn to the wider global context of the debate over development policy and the role of the state, initially concentrating on East Asia, the region where 'developmental states' were ostensibly born.

Developmental states and the East Asian experience: Rewriting history

To talk of an 'East Asian model' may appear quixotic as there is a variety of forms that the developmental state in Asia has exhibited. Clearly, the type of interventions aimed at promoting the economy and at sharing the benefits across the wider society have been varied. Having said that, it seems clear that if we are to speak of a lesson learned from the recent past in Asia, it is that government intervention can and has played a crucial role in propitiating the development of factors that facilitate some form of auspicious participation in the global market. The regulation of foreign direct investment (FDI) in the service of building up local capacity and employment has been a key to this strategy. The literature on the developmental state is immense and multifaceted and space precludes an in-depth interrogation.

The first major study on the developmental state was produced by Chalmers Johnson in his 1982 book MITI and the Japanese Miracle (Johnson 1982). In this important book, Johnson drew up four constituent parts of a model of what became termed 'the developmental state'. These four segments were: the presence of a small but professional and efficient state bureaucracy; a political milieu where this bureaucracy has enough space to operate and take policy initiatives independent of overly intrusive interventions by vested interests; the crafting of methods of state intervention in the economy without sabotaging the market principle i.e. the concept of 'market-conforming'; a pilot organisation such as Chalmers found in MITI. The notion of what market-conforming means is not simply where a government makes sure there is enough investment in people, fosters a competitive climate for the private sector or maintains on 'open economy'. Rather, Johnson saw the market as a device that could be utilised for advancing a developmental agenda whereby the state involved itself in 'setting...substantive social and economic goals' (ibid.: 19). As Öni writes, 'it is the "synergy" between the state and the market which provides the basis for outstanding development experience' (Öni 1991: 110).

This understanding undermines those who see the state as being in opposition to the market and rather points in the direction of the successful developmental state:

> Industrial policy is not an alternative to the market but what the state does when it intentionally alters incentives within markets in order to influence the behaviour of civilian producers, consumers and investors…Altering market incentives, reducing risks, offering entrepreneurial visions and managing conflicts are some of the functions of the developmental state (Johnson 1999: 48).

As Mbabazi and Mokhawa demonstrate in their chapter in this book, this is indeed reflected in government policies in both Botswana and Uganda.

Although various authors have questioned aspects of Johnson's work, particularly the historic uniqueness surrounding Japanese development at the time which lay the foundation for the attainment of the developmental state, the success of other Asian states that used strategic interventions and achieved high growth periods (Singapore, South Korea, Taiwan etc.) arguably demonstrates the conceptual purchase of the developmental state. Leftwich (1995: 401) asserts that:

> Developmental states may be defined as states whose politics have concentrated sufficient power, autonomy and capacity at the centre to shape, pursue and encourage the achievement of explicit developmental objectives, whether by establishing and promoting the conditions and direction of economic growth, or by organising it directly, or a varying combination of both.

Part of the rationale for this book is to explore the applicability of these comments to concrete examples in Africa, a continent which is usually thought of as the last place where 'sufficient power, autonomy and capacity at the centre' is said to exist.

It should be noted that in talking of 'developmental states' we really mean 'state capitalist' developmental states, following Gordon White's three typologies: state capitalist, intermediate and state socialist (White 1984).

Some authors have argued that the developmental state is unique to East Asia (Öni 1991: 13). Cline (1982) has asserted that the Asian model cannot be generalised because of its inherent constraints on international markets i.e. that only a certain number of states can pursue the export-oriented growth model side of the developmental state otherwise everyone else would introduce protectionist barriers to them. The problem with Cline's argument is that it contradicts our experience after he wrote his paper: the barriers he envisioned actually came down, rather than were erected in the 1980 and 1990s. And as

Mbabazi and Mokhawa demonstrate in their chapter, this is not wholly the case in either Botswana or Uganda, particularly taking advantage of AGOA. In fact, other recent work has demonstrated that developmental states are not limited to East Asia but have been achieved elsewhere. In his study of Mauritius, Richard Kearney found that 'continuation of NIC (and Mauritian) development presumes effective government macro-economic policy leadership in both monetary and fiscal areas. It further presumes the maintenance of an entrepreneurial climate so that diversification and exploitation of new manufacturing niches, can proceed in the private sector. Government policy choices are critical to development' (1990: 8). Other authors have indeed concluded that Mauritius is a developmental state (Meisenhelder 1997).

What hasn't worked has also been held up as evidence of the existence of a broad model associated with features of the developmental state. In his study of India, Ronald Herring points out that the aspirations of India's developmental trajectory were derailed by the very conditions that contributed to success elsewhere: New Delhi was committed to planning and strategic intervention but the state was too soft and embedded to govern the market. State bureaucrats, although generally competent, were too estranged from the business of the market whilst at the same time equally estranged from the broader, poorer population and thus contributed to an erosion of legitimacy that opened the way for economic populists (Herring 1999: 309). In their study of Burkina Faso, Kevane and Englebert (1999) found that Ouagadougou lacked any notable entrepreneurial class of sufficient size, whether domestic or international, to create wealth and generate growth, from which development might be advanced. Looking at Brazil and Mexico, Schneider found that the bureaucracy was a major impediment to the implementation of the developmental state, despite an official ideology proclaiming a commitment to development, as the bureaucracy was a political player in itself and could not act in an administrative fashion á la Weber (Schneider 1999).

Leftwich has arrived at some defining characteristics of a typical developmental state, which have been kept in mid by all authors in this book as they researched their chapters. According to him, six major components define the developmental state model:

- a determined developmental elite;
- relative autonomy;
- a powerful, competent and insulated bureaucracy;
- a weak and subordinated civil society;
- the effective management of non-state economic interests; and
- legitimacy and performance (Leftwich 1995: 405).

We can say that there appears some form of consensus on the ingredients for a successful developmental state. Evans, in his influential work, agrees that a capable and autonomous bureaucracy that makes use of the market and formulates national goals and one that has the competence and resources to implement these goals is crucial (Evans 1995). In a comprehensive review of neo-liberal objections to the developmental state, Ha-Joon Chang argues that successful developmental states have pursued policies that co-ordinate investment plans; have a national development vision implying that the state is an entrepreneurial agent; that engage in institution building to promote growth and development; and that finally, play a role in conflict management, mediating in conflicts that arise out of reactions and counteractions to the development trajectory: between the winners and losers as it were (Chang 1999: 192–99). In their chapters, contributors touch on some of these themes when evaluating different aspects of development policy in Botswana and Uganda.

Clearly, there are degrees of success. And acknowledging this we have to be careful vis-à-vis the purpose and intentions of this book. We do not advance the idea that developmental states in Africa can be or will be similar to those found in Asia. This would be ridiculous and empirically impossible. Nor are we trying to argue that the experiences in Botswana or even Uganda are comparable in scope or practice to those found in the East. The point of this book is to critically examine whether or not any elements of the developmental state model, as outlined by Leftwich above and as commented on by other analysts, has any purchase in Africa, by examining the cases of Botswana and Uganda. Our book is thus quite modest and is certainly not making any grand claims that Botswana or Uganda can be considered *in toto* 'developmental states'. Nor is it trying to promote Botswana or Uganda as 'models' that we think the rest of Africa should be followed. No, the prime purpose of this book is to thoughtfully interrogate the developmental experiences of the two countries, in comparative perspective, to see if any commonalities can be identified that have contributed to development. In doing so, we aver that elements that contributors identify throughout the book show that in the context of Africa, a state that is purposefully-driven to promote development and that utilises the offices of the state in order to facilitate improvement, alongside other actors such as the private sector and civil society can, in the particular circumstances the content finds itself, be regarded as 'developmental'. By examining Botswana and Uganda, we are not seeking to privilege these two states over others, though the track record of Botswana in particular does stand out from much of the rest of the continent (though we of course acknowledge its failings and problems).

Having acknowledged the above caveats, we note that the hegemonic discourse suggests that state intervention in Africa was disastrous in the 1970s (the Berg Report has been particularly influential in this regard). But is this true? Firstly, relatively high levels of growth, savings and investment rates were achieved. In addition, the dirigiste policies pursued at the time reflected contemporary theory (and, it should be added, were supported by IFIs). Import-substitution policies were approved of as common sense, particularly as the local African bourgeoisie was quite weak. But it is not as if the developmental state has been tried across Africa and has failed. Sure, many states in the 1970s (i.e. before the lost decade of debt peonage) had developmental agendas (Ujamaa, Afro-Marxism etc), but the developmental state model as is widely regarded, was not efficiently executed. In most states on the continent, due to a weak local bourgeoisie, there was very little—or even none—involvement by the capitalist class in formulating policy.

In addition, during the 1970s comparative advantage in the global economy was seen as the key to Africa's development, encouraging single-commodity economies and effectively inhibiting real diversification, thus closing off space for any sort of strategy akin to the developmental states of East Asia who constructed fresh comparative advantages as they transformed their export portfolios. Yet, examples do exist in Africa that contradicts to a large degree the globalisation mantra of the hegemonic guardians, as well as the impossibility thesis.

Selection of the two case studies

Botswana has, since independence in 1966, been governed uninterruptedly by the Botswana Democratic Party. This party has pursued state capitalist policies, even during the heyday of African experimentations with socialism. Both the growth and developmental record of independent Botswana has been impressive. From being one of the poorest countries in the world at independence, Botswana has enjoyed rapid economic growth and is now classified by the World Bank as an Upper Middle Country, with a per capita GDP of more than $6000. Yet, when it became independent, it had a per capita income equivalent then to roughly US$80.

Uganda though still a poor country, has made tremendous strides over the recent past and by the dawn of the new millennium it could well be considered an emerging economy. Uganda is now often referred to as a useful example for countries in Africa experiencing rebuilding, having reversed decades of maldevelopment and now with an average annual growth rate of approximately 6 percent for the last six years or so. Uganda, which was once torn by civil war, has developed into an almost 'stable' nation in East Africa, although there are still pockets of insecurity in the north and south-west (Kabwegyere 1995; Karugire 1996; Kasozi 1999). There is no more talk of the bloody deeds of dictator Idi Amin, but plenty about the economic successes of President Yoweri Museveni. Uganda is now largely seen by the international community—of non-governmental organisations and corporations as well as states—to be doing good things, for example: liberalisation of the economy, tax collection, the fight against AIDS, the 'Movement' system of governance, relatively clean leadership, women's empowerment, inaugurating a Ministry of Ethics and Integrity etc (Dicklitch 1998; Hansen and Twaddle 1998).

Conversely, many other African countries have experienced economic decline and a retreat from most developmental indices post-independence, as Nyamnjoh and Malizani-Jimu detail in their chapter. Although this has not been a linear process and many countries experienced relative 'golden periods', the history of many post-independence states in Africa has been comparatively disappointing. However, discussion of the nature of the state in Africa has tended to be captured within the normative framework of traditionally Western models. As one analyst remarks, 'what needs to be recognised is that the African state is not failing as much as our understanding of the state' (Dunn 2001: 49).

The source of Botswana's development trajectory has been the use of fortuitous deposits of diamonds and minerals, a welcoming posture towards Foreign Direct Investment and a tourism policy that has courted the top-end of the market (see Taylor, this volume). A beef export industry that has preferred status with Europe further contributes to state receipts. But, an abundance of natural resources such as diamonds or cattle is no guarantee of success and does not explain Botswana's developmental record, as Taylor and also Sebudubudu point out in their chapters. In the immediate aftermath of independence, Zambia enjoyed high prices for its mono-export, copper, and yet from the mid-1970s onwards has experienced rapid economic decline, with severe implications for the country's development. Similarly, Zimbabwe was blessed with a burgeoning agricultural sector and, at independence, had the most developed and diversified economy in the region outside of South Africa. Unlike Zambia, Botswana has largely avoided the pitfalls of the 'Dutch Disease' i.e. the effect of a large change in wealth resulting from a sudden and dramatic change in the price of a primary product or of a sudden and dramatic discovery of a primary resource. Certainly, the growth of the Botswana economy is not simply a story of a mineral enclave with an ever-growing government, attached to a stagnating traditional economy, as Sebudubudu remarks in his chapter.

Uganda, as mentioned above, experienced a turbulent past particularly in the 1970s and 1980s and has undoubtedly come a long way to its present state of relative calm and quite impressive levels of economic progress. Uganda has laboured under the legacy of slavery and colonialism, economic backwardness, past corrupt and oppressive leaderships, and to some extent, a brutal geography and an unforgiving climate (e.g. in northern Uganda). Much of these elements are commented on in Akampumuza's chapter. To date, however, as a result of relatively committed leadership, aided by an engaged world, Uganda—that is, the state, civil society and private companies—has made tremendous improvements which have had reverberating effects in the country and region as a whole (Bigsten and Kayizzi-Mugerwa 2001; Mbabazi and Shaw 2000). The NRM government of Yoweri Museveni, in particular, has in many ways tried to empower Ugandans to take charge of their economic fate (Brett 1997; Onyango 2000). There is some degree of freedom of expression and a much greater rule of law in comparison to previous regimes. Indeed, contrary to past regimes, this government at least recognises that the most valuable resource is the Ugandan population and investment in basic education has been substantial with the introduction of Universal Primary Education (UPE), and so have been improvements in health care provision. These have had important ramifications vis-à-vis gender, as Mbabazi, Mookodi and Parpart point out.

It is worth mentioning though that the country is still faced by numerous challenges that have impacted on human development and one area that the present NRM government has tended to focus on is the promotion of agro-processing industries as well as commodities for export. These have no doubt made a significant impact on the progress of the economy. Mbabazi and Mokhawa's comparative chapter on the case of the textile industry in both countries covers this in some detail.

On the whole therefore, Uganda's 'success story' can be largely attributed to, among other factors, the visionary leadership of the NRM government, favourable policies pursued by the government which have created an enabling environment for the thriving of the private sector (as Roberts points out in his chapter), and the support by the international financial institutions and a host of donors. The decentralisation process, as outlined by Murembe, Mokhawa and Sebudubudu, has also facilitated movement in this direction, empowering local communities and using the state as an agent of grassroots development.

The key to the differences between 'successful' states and the experiences of others, is seen as the effective construction of a 'developmental state', as opposed to the development in other countries of a rapacious and inefficient state which has hampered development. Identifying the comparative reasons why this has occurred and seeking out lessons that other African countries could learn from Botswana and perhaps Uganda (or conversely, if any lessons can be taught in the other direction) is the main thrust of this book. In all, this book seeks to analyse the developmental record of Botswana and Uganda and seek to examine this record, with reference to the notion of a 'developmental state'. In doing so we try to compare and contrast this developmental state with the types of state structures inherited and developed by selected African states in the post-independence period and to explain how and why the type of state structures in other African states developed and how these hampered development in these countries.

In doing so we hope to contribute to an investigation into the economic and social development of Botswana and Uganda and provide a comparative perspective of development in African countries. This may help policymakers identify, for potential future development strategies, key aspects that may be utilised by other African states, although we are cautious of this and advise reflection upon the particular historical contexts within which both countries spring from. But certainly, the study aims to interrogate what has been happening in Uganda and put it into comparative perspective through an analysis of Botswana's trajectory. In doing so, we wish to refute the one-size-fits-all prescription of the International Financial Institutions, whilst flagging the need to move away from dirigiste preoccupations. It is hoped that our study will help the discipline of Development Studies move away from isolated case studies on particular countries and rather mesh together in a methodologically comparative fashion, studies from different parts of Africa that will inform analysts in a rich comparative manner.

Methodology

The project consisted of collecting secondary literature on the two countries economic and political development. This was the methodological first step and was done in support of individual scholarly research (in practical terms, this meant that individual researchers were required to collate as much data as possible within their own countries). Once created, this data was then brought together and decisions were made, initially at a workshop held in Gaborone in April 2003, as to which features allowed for comparative analysis. Once the basic structure and arguments had been developed during this workshop, the project then began to systematically develop a comparative study on the historical, political, social and economic nature of the developmental states under review. Primary sources and interviews were then utilised to construct each individual chapter's contents.

It should be noted that many of the contributors had already conducted a fair amount of preliminary work on their topics; in deed most contributors were recruited due to their expertise and previous knowledge, although the project was committed to empowering and helping advance the careers of junior academics in both countries (something which we hope this book will help facilitate). Because of the comparative nature of this study, a discussion of the theoretical problems the research team faced was conducted, mostly over electronic mail, although a second workshop in Mbarara (in February 2004) was very helpful in this regard. Essentially, the first methodological workshop produced a great deal of analysis and discussion with the other writers and this was then built upon as the project unfolded.

As noted above, the initial literature was evaluated in the light of primary information gleaned from interviews and the collection of government and non-government (e.g. Chambers of Commerce, think-tanks, NGO consortiums etc) data in Gaborone, Kampala and Mbarara. The study followed the comparative method and seeks to help contribute to the construction of a specifically Africa-oriented comparative methodology of use to further research into the development processes in Africa.

Lay-out and overview of the book

The following chapter, by Nyamnjoh and Malizani-Jimu, looks at the past experiences of Africa in pursuing development. They outline the continent's historical encounter over the past four to five decades with the pursuit of development and provide an overview and analysis vis-à-vis economic and social policies and the political and global context which the two authors see as circumscribing Africa's development experience. In doing so, Nyamnjoh and Malizani-Jimu quite correctly and succinctly urge cautious optimism about the applicability of the developmental state model. Indeed, the two assert that what Africa needs is not a strong state but rather a capable one able to chart a path to sustainable development. But in advocating this position, the chapter notes that African states currently have to grapple with two simultaneous dilemmas: how to develop economically and how to build nation-states. Resolving this tension is a key problematic faced by all countries on the continent.

Shaw's chapter seeks to look at Uganda as a democratic developmental state but by rethinking what we mean in an era where contracting-out, flexibilisation/feminisation, regionalisms, the privatisation of security, supply chains etc. stake out the modern state. In doing so, he pushes us to rethink some key assumptions, stressing the need to broaden our definition of the state and—in the context of this volume—the developmental state. Certainly, the features Shaw mentions are no longer aberrations but rather central features of the political cultures and economies of the majority of the world's states and are typical of Africa. Indeed, such distinctive forms of capitalisms confirm that there are important differences around the world and it is unhelpful to try and fit the world into one single model of development. Thus the current political culture/economy of 'Africa' has to be situated in a range of interrelated contexts, from global to local. Certainly, definitions of and relations among states, economies and civil societies are everywhere in flux, not least in Uganda, as Shaw notes. In doing so, he provides us with an interesting 'take' on what an African developmental state may look like, one outside the usual parameters outlined in most literature.

In his chapter, Taylor argues that in Botswana the commitment to development by both the political and bureaucratic elites has been central, but that this has been put into practice by the strategy of putting into place institutions which have helped sustain long-term growth as part of a broader national developmental vision. With the state acting as an entrepreneurial agent, there has been, to varying degrees, a co-ordination between the private and the public sectors, with the developmental state being based on a foundation of capitalism in which the government, through a wide variety of incentives, actively promotes private investments by national and multinational corporations. Taylor argues that this has been facilitated by an efficient and well-trained bureaucracy that has resisted the descent into corruption that has been the hallmark of much of the civil service in other parts of the continent. Indeed, skills development, not only in the bureaucracy but also in the wider private sphere have been an important aspect of Botswana's success. Taylor details some of the criticism, particularly with regard to inequality in the country, that has been levelled at the country, but maintains that Botswana perhaps proves that capable state intervention can play a vital role in creating conditions for sustained trade growth. In this he shares with Nyamnjoh and Malizani-Jimu 'cautious optimism'. Certainly, the Botswana developmental state has achieved respectable accomplishments, whatever the downside to this story. But perhaps the key thing that Taylor notes is that for a developmental state to 'succeed' or even exist, the primacy of politics in the complex process of development is fundamental and decisive. In other words, it is not how much state intervention should take place, but rather what kind.

The following chapter, by Akampumuza, looks at Uganda's institutional framework, arguing that it was consciously underdeveloped by colonialism and further weakened by postcolonial regimes, particularly their ill-advised policies and chronic instability. The results of this still inform the developmental agenda in Uganda today. Trying to recuperate, Uganda has through a wide variety of incentives, actively promoted private investments by liberalising and privatising public enterprises, embedding these initiatives in the various policy frameworks adopted, often under donor-inspired development schemes. The Asian question and the government negotiating framework for promoting Foreign Direct investment are used to illustrate the challenges facing Uganda's institutional framework for development. Although enforcement and monitoring institutions supposed to facilitate the realization of these policy objectives are found structurally and operationally weak, they have nevertheless facilitated positive economic developments, though some pointed out reforms could even help achieve more. Akampumuza's chapter essentially stresses that institutions matter and that, as with Taylor's findings, is not how much state intervention should take place, but rather what kind and in what context. Sound institutions competently managed help provide this favourable context.

In a similar vein, Sebudubudu discusses the institutional framework of Botswana's developmental state. According to Sebudubudu, and echoing Taylor, the Botswana state has since independence established a number of institutions to drive the economy forward. It is through these institutions that the Botswana state has played a leading role in economic development. The focus of this chapter is on these key institutions that were put in place by the Botswana state to promote economic growth and development. In particular, the chapter examines pilot institutions such as the Ministry of Finance and Development Planning (MFDP), a powerful ministry, and service organisations such as the Botswana Development Corporation (BDC), the Financial Assistance Policy (FAP) / Citizen Entrepreneurial Development Agency (CEDA), the Botswana Export Development and Investment Authority (BEDIA) and the Directorate on Corruption and Economic Crime (DCEC), amongst others. The chapter examines the reasons for creating them as well as the role they have played in Botswana's economic development.

Murembe, Mokhawa and Sebudubudu then discuss in a comparative chapter how the state in Uganda and Botswana has sought, through decentralisation, to promote development. In Uganda, despite the threats to the system of decentralisation, and unlike in other developing countries such as Nigeria, Uganda's experience has brought benefits to the ordinary person, arguably leading to participatory and collective responsibility in the development of the country, particularly in the rural areas. The authors emphasise the context, whereby any recovery process has had to take place after a massive degeneration of public service provisions. In this light the authors argue that the benefits from the decentralisation process in Uganda are surely visible, highlighting that the involvement of women and the disabled is institutionalised—something which even in the developed world is rare to find. Resource mobilisation has equally increased and this is now matching the area covered in service provision and quality of service given. In Botswana, although local authorities are allowed to make an input in the development process through district development plans, the final decision as to what goes into the National Development Plan rests with the central government. Nevertheless, local authorities play an important role in Botswana's developmental process and have aided the development trajectory of the country. They have not only brought services such as basic education, roads, health facilities etc closer to the electorate but have also played a key role in their provision. However, the authors assert that a lack of resources is one of the major hurdles local authorities face, as they are overly dependent on central government for resources. But in both cases, the authors argue that decentralisation has been used as a tool by the government to improve service delivery and also, and this is contentious, to open up democratic space for input into both policy planning and implementation. In doing so, decentralisation can be said to help legitimise the regimes in both countries, visibly demonstrating to the populace that 'their' governments are delivering. As delivery is key to any notion of a developmental state, this can be said to be of high importance.

In their chapter on gender and the 'developmental state', Mbabazi, Mookodi and Parpart provide a comprehensive overview of the situation concerning gender and the state in both countries. They ask whether the ostensible benefits of 'developmental states' are gendered and in what ways. Bearing in mind the importance of institutions in such states, the authors ask whether or not there is more gender equality in Botswana and Uganda and whether or not women are more able to access political and economic opportunities and institutions. Indeed, are relations between the sexes more tolerant and flexible in developmental states? Certainly, as the chapter makes clear, both Botswana and Uganda have demonstrated a strong commitment to improving the lives of women and both countries have also been influenced by the demands of local women's associations, though in Botswana such groups are more closely tied to the state than is the case in Uganda. However, as the chapter shows, patriarchal assumptions and practices continue to hold sway in many arenas, and in both countries issues of domestic violence and HIV/AIDs remain crucial. Ultimately, both cases remind us that economic development is not in and of itself a panacea for women's problems and that patriarchy and paternalism are difficult to change. A truly gendered approach within a developmental state must take history and culture seriously. As the authors argue, this is a prerequisite before even the most successful 'developmental states' in Africa can claim to be truly developmental for all.

Following on from this, Roberts argues in his chapter that policy implementation is one of the crucial elements in the success of every state's economic programme. The chapter examines the challenges and prospects Uganda's privatisation policy has met, especially in its implementation process, arguing that Uganda as a nascent 'developmental state' has had some weaknesses as well as some strengths in facilitating privatisation. This chapter seeks to document the factors which have hindered the implementation of privatisation policy in Uganda and discusses its' prospects in today's Uganda. The chapter does not address in detail the question whether or not Uganda is a developmental state, but rather stresses the challenges state policies have met in their implementation. It highlights the challenges that should be addressed by the state in its development initiative and hence draws lessons for other countries based on Uganda's experiences.

Finally, Mbabazi and Mokhawa examine the role of the state in promoting the development of the textile industry in both Botswana and Uganda. According to the chapter, in Botswana the state has been strategically interventionist and as such been able to formulate a series of policies aimed directly at infrastructural development and economic growth within the country. As for Uganda, the authors argue that the state is in many ways trying to be developmental and is struggling to industrialise. That it faces numerous challenges is undeniable, but attempts at such policies are evident. In both cases, the relative successes enjoyed in Botswana and Uganda has been due to state intervention. Certainly, in both countries, the state has consistently intervened in the development of the textile industry. But, as the authors note, given global neo-liberal pressures for limiting state involvement in industry this is difficult and under constant criticism. However, developmental activism is regarded as not optional but vital. The authors suggest that both countries need to practice developmental state activism to produce goods that have a potential to penetrate global markets. In both Botswana and Uganda emphasis on high-level bureaucratic competency and a conducive institutional framework are vital. Concluding, the authors argue that both countries need to recognise the potentiality that the textile industry offers for national development. Finding the appropriate measures, involving both the state and the private sector, will remain one of the greatest challenges for the textile industry and the government in both countries.

2

Success or Failure of Developmental States in Africa: Exploration of the Development Experiences in a Global Context

Francis B. Nyamnjoh & Ignasio M. Jimu

Implicit or explicit in all rhetoric on development in African countries is undeniably a desire to improve the socio-economic aspects of all people by ensuring among other things a reasonable access to the necessary goods and services for a modest living. Lack of development implies a denial of choices and opportunities for living a tolerable life (UNDP 1997). Yet, in every African country the poor outnumber those who can claim to have security to the basic needs of life. Statistics indicate a rise of poverty, unemployment and inequality in many African countries, which is a nude manifestation that development in its broadest sense is an illusive ideal to many African states. This is more than a scandal considering numerous commitments by African states to alleviate poverty since it is tantamount to betrayal of the hopes for better life for all. It is not a secret even to the ardent optimists of Africa's development that nearly a half-century of post-colonial economic endeavour has not been enough for Africa to realize positive and substantive change in the socio-economic aspects of the peoples. The paradox is that nationalist struggles in the early years preceding and after independence in many African states drew strength from the socio-economic agenda and upliftment of the African peoples beleaguered by decades of colonialism.

Why so much poverty despite decades of preoccupation to achieve development by state and non-state actors alike (cf. Ferguson 1990, 1999)? We note that for most African leaders 'development' has been certainly a central preoccupation, which means that African states have been in one way or another developmentalist (Mkandawire 1998). Development is everywhere in Africa a hot general election issue. Lack of development, ill-development in some instances, is carrot to woo voters, a rallying call for mass mobilisation and political conscientisation of peoples from diverse ethnic, cultural, religious and regional traditions. Independence from colonial rule was indeed a starting point for concerted indigenous action to engender development. After four to five decades of post-colonial development experience the capacity and drive of African countries and leaders to eradicate poverty and achieve meaningful development remains a far-fetched dream.

The question that often fascinates African poor, scholars and oftentimes the leader is whether Africa can make significant progress worth mentioning. What has come of United Nations development decades? While other regions, for instance East Asia, have registered significant development achievements and emerged from the quagmire of underdevelopment, African states too many to recount remain typical basket cases and lessons of failed development. While the so called Asian Tigers or newly industrialising Countries (NICs)-Korea, Thailand, Malaysia, Taiwan for example, have managed to reverse the crippling effects of poverty, through export oriented manufacturing industries strategy, many African states have failed in their import substitution and in many cases have slide back to the extent that at the turn of the 21st century in many African states there are more poor people than there were in the late 1960s (*The Economist* 2004:3-4). With development becoming ever more elusive, is it not time for Africans to rethink their development dream? In doing so, what lessons could Africa learn from the East Asian experience? Could Africa's salvation lie in the now acclaimed East Asian model of the developmental state? Just how good is the developmental state model as an analytical tool for assessing and predicting socio-economic and political failure or success of the Africa states? These issues are particularly crucial at this day and age when the global and the local are increasingly interconnected in the way events occur and the perspectives they elicit.

We pursue these issues by outlining Africa's development experience over the past four to five decades with an analysis of economic and social policies and the political and global context circumscribing Africa's development experience. We are very much interested in analyzing the domestic and external impediments to protracted growth and sustainable development in Africa and unlike others, advocate for cautious optimism about the applicability of the developmental state model, by showing that what Africa needs is not so much a strong state as a state that is capable of charting the path to sustainable development. As we argue below, at independence African leaders could argue that their greatest challenges were 'how to develop economically, and build nation-states' in a bipolar polar world where being non-aligned was often more imagined than real. The significance of the two challenges indeed made African states a unique group in the developing world. New challenges have assumed great prominence with the passage of time, including how to promote and protect national interests in a world that is unequally affected by the globalisation of poverty and marginality, and how to deal with the scourge of HIV/AIDS which has affected Africa more than anywhere else (Nyamnjoh 2005).

Empirical indicators of Africa's failed development

In a recent publication, the United Nations Conference on Trade and Development (UNCTAD) summarised the economic situation in Africa thus:

> African countries remain by and large dependent on the export of a few commodities, and terms of trade losses have further aggravated their capacity to invest in human and physical infrastructure. Present levels of national savings and investment are insufficient to ensure a process of accumulation necessary to place Africa on a sustainable growth path. Despite commitments by the international community to assist Africa in its efforts to achieve accelerated growth, the support provided has fallen far short of expectations. Indeed, official development assistance has suffered a continuous downturn trend, representing less than one third of the internationally agreed targets. Furthermore, despite recent action for the reduction of African debt, including the HIPC initiative, a permanent exit from debt problems is proving elusive (UNCTAD 2001).

This assessment underscores the fact that Africa is a continent of paradoxes. With abundant mineral wealth and other natural resources including abundant cheap labour supplies (all essential for a sound agricultural and industrial development strategy), African states and leadership are dismally failing to harness the continent's potential into meaningful development. The debate today revolves on prospects for Africa ever claiming the 21st century (The International Bank for Reconstruction and Development/The World Bank 2000). Africa's poverty, unemployment and inequality rates are undeniably the highest in the world. Average income per capita in most countries is lower than it was at the end of the 1960s (IBRD/WB 2002:2). Like the rest of the developing world, Africa's development challenges at independence are far from over. The continent is laden with hostile foreign exchange regimes, famines, civil wars, trade imbalances, low productivity in agriculture and industry, diseases such as cholera, tuberculosis and recently HIV/AIDS that are taking their toll on Africa's fragile and poverty stricken populations. Africa's participation in world trade has been declining steadily with export shares falling even in the traditional primary products (*The Economist* 2004).

In Africa where only 6 countries are in the upper middle-income category, at least 38 countries are classified as low-income (The World Bank Rankings 1998; Meier and Rauch 2000; African Development Bank 2003). Our discussion is centred on sub-Saharan Africa (SSA), where the bulk of the low-income countries are found. With the exception of North and Mediterranean Africa and South Africa, some have argued that 'Africa' is SSA, which comprises some forty countries, including the islands of Madagascar, Mauritius, Sao Tome and Principe (Iheduru

1995). The countries of SSA share some politico-economic characteristics such as low level of socio-economic development, dualistic economy (one rational economy and the other rural-informal), and state dominated structures. Politically, except for Ethiopia and Liberia, all have been colonies. Most African states have at one time or another come under authoritarian rule, for instance, Uganda under Idi Amin, Moi's Kenya, Banda's Malawi, Ahidjo and Biya's Cameroon, Eyadema's Togo, Mobutu's Zaire (now the Democratic Republic of Congo) and the military dictatorships of Nigeria. Almost all African states have dependent economies that are severely indebted externally. Foreign indebtedness at 10 percent of total developing countries debt is a serious problem in Africa reaching crisis level not because its total debt is greater than that of any region, but rather because the ratio of debt to the gross domestic product (GDP) is quite high. African foreign debt has been growing over the years, from US$ 6 billion in 1970 to US$ 9 billion in 1980 and US$ 186 billion by 1987 (Iheduru 1995:47). In 2000, sub-Saharan Africa's external debt stood at $206 billion (United Nations Conference on trade and Development 2001).

Some analysts argue that four to five decades of independence have brought Africans few economic benefits and in most instances the economic situation has worsened (Smith 1997; *The Economist* 2004). The worsening of the economic situation in postcolonial Africa is all the more striking when one considers the fact that during Africa's decade of independence, some countries like Uganda, Kenya and Ghana were at the same level of economic development like some Asian Tigers, and that despite possessing strong natural resource bases, trade, growth and development in these countries have failed to be impressive. For example, in 1965, Ghana's incomes and exports per capita were higher than South Korea's. However, by 1972 South Korea's exports per capita overtook Ghana's and its income level surpassed that of Ghana by 1976. Differential growth patterns account for the disparities in incomes per capita between these states. For example, during the thirty years between 1965 and 1995, South Korea's exports increased by 400 times while Ghana's increased only by 4 times, as real earnings per capita fell to a fraction of their earlier value (International Bank for Reconstruction and Development 2000:19). Ghana's experiences are indicative of the general trend in Africa, slow growth in exports and falling income levels per capita. As the World Bank further posits, the effect has been lack of development of the sort experienced in East Asia. With these statistics is it surprising that by 1995 economic and social indicators in many African countries were not any different from those of South Korea in 1960 or Indonesia, Malaysia and Thailand in 1975.

In World Bank terms, Africa is today caught in a low-equilibrium development trap, just as Asia was in the 1960s. With the exception of Botswana which has emerged 'from rags to riches', the lot of countries and peoples in Africa remains a precarious existence. Meier and Rauch (2000) note that, on average, incomes in many African states are now less than what they were two decades ago (see also

The Economist 2004). The rate of growth of gross domestic product (GDP) for low-income countries in Africa declined from 3.5 percent per annum between 1960 and 1973 to 1.4 percent between 1978 and 1980 and further to 0.5 percent in the 1982-1995 periods (Diejomaoh 1998). With the exception of South Africa, Sub Saharan Africa's average income per capita averaged just US$315 million in 1997. The income for 48 Sub-Saharan African countries stood at less than that of Belgium, one of Europe's smallest economies. Worse still, Africa's average output per capita in the 1990s was less than 30 years before – with some countries having fallen by more than 50 percent (The World Bank 2000).

Other paradoxes of Africa's development experience are declining savings and investment per capita since 1970. With low savings rate in the region of 13 percent of GDP, investment rates are comparatively lower than other regions of the world and productivity on investments is diametrically disappointing. However, population growth has continued to rise with devastating effects on the environment and resource use, implying that it is difficult if not impossible for Africa to sustain a major long-term economic growth. Worse still, income inequality is as high as in Latin America, making Africa's poor the poorest of the poor with more than 40 percent of its 700 million people living below the internationally recognised poverty line of $ 1 per day, with incomes averaging just $ 0.65 a day in purchasing power parity terms (International bank for Reconstruction and Development/ The World Bank 2000:10; *The Economist* 2004:3-4).

Africa's share of world trade has also plummeted to less than 2 percent, resulting in high and persistent balance of payment and inflation problems crippling and effectively worsening prospects of a quick economic recovery. Consequently, some commentators talk of an 'African crisis', of multifarious dimensions characterised by declining food production, trade imbalances, rapid population growth and its implications, declining net inflows of external resources, rising external indebtedness, political instability and social disorders (Ayittey 1992, 1999; Samir Amin 1996; Hope and Kayira 1996; Hountondji 1992). Our own analysis traces the failure of Africa's development to two sources – unfavourable domestic and international economic and political environments, and suggest, metaphorically, that, development plans and rhetoric notwithstanding, Africa's lack of development is due largely to the fact that the continent's development potential is doubly crippled by two parasites, one internal, the other external. We now turn to a detailed appraisal of the domestic impediments to sustained and rapid growth in Africa.

Domestic economic, social and political policies

Economic and social policies pursued by most African countries are counter-productive and inimical to rapid economic growth (Schatz 1988). Policy means economic, social and political principles and priorities, which inform economic decision in the productive areas of the economy and society (Todaro 1992).

Generally speaking, policies that offer little or no incentive or which encourage courses of action that strain economic growth and defy sound social and political rationality are counter-productive and a danger to sustained economic growth and development. A typical case would be policies ostensibly designed to promote economic progress and benefit the rural and urban poor, but which ultimately benefit mostly the urban elite. In many cases, the policies pursued by African governments in the areas of agriculture, industry, foreign exchange and population have not been effective in the sense of bringing meaningful development to all and sundry.

Although the majority of Africans live in rural areas and agriculture is the main source of their livelihood, government policies have often served to constrain the growth of this sector. Throughout the 1960s and 1970s, African governments, with the exception of a few, neglected agriculture in favour of import substitution industries, which were biased in favour of urban-centred manufacturing industries (Meier and Rauch 2000). The zeal of farmers to produce enough food for subsistence and also for export to finance industry, was weakened by taxation of cash crops, controls of prices of food stuffs and low prices paid to farmers, under resourced, inefficient research and extension services and general under-investment in rural infrastructure. The proliferation of parasitic marketing boards also constrained agricultural development, as the marketing monopolies and price controls enjoyed by the marketing boards were a disincentive to the agricultural sector, as often, the higher prices on the international market never trickle down to the producers (Meier and Rauch 2000). On the other hand, government sponsored import substitution industries enjoyed monopolies or were protected from foreign competition by tariffs, import controls and other measures that constrained the development of a competitive spirit and appeared in many ways to legitimise inefficiency. It is now acknowledged that strong government involvement in the economy in many cases (of especially weak, dependent states under structural adjustment) prevents the evolution of a strong enterprising economic sector (Mkandawire and Olukoshi 1995). The hidden hand of global capital and its concerns, for example, through the IMF, World Bank and national interests of Western partners, make it possible for autocracy to pay lip service to democracy and development in exchange for guaranteeing the political stability needed by investors to venture into the periphery. In exchange for having weak foreign relations, autocratic regimes in Africa are afforded the ability and protection to flex their muscles vis-à-vis the development needs and expectations of their own populations, in a perplexing and mystical manner. Hence, instead of development for ordinary Africans who thirst for it, people's rights, dignities and expectations were bargained away in myriad ways in the name of development (Nyamnjoh 2001). Economic problems have only worsened in recent times thanks to decades of stifling structural adjustment programmes facilitated by local dictatorships that have seldom hesitated to embezzle and bank abroad (Bayart et al. 1999; Mbaku 2004; Hope & Chikulo 2000; Nzongola-Ntalaja 2002).

The state and its technocrats substituted or prevented the emergence of an entrepreneurial class. This scenario reduced the state to an avenue for capital accumulation for those with access to state resources through 'blind forces' or serious mistakes in management decision, which, according to Hountondji (1992), culminated in a 'deliberate policy of spoils and plundering of public coffers by the ruling elite'. For two or more decades, Amin (1996) argues, African governments of both leftist and rightist ideological orientations assumed greater control over economic affairs, often advancing policies that facilitated governmental corruption. The effect of governmental corruption 'is not just crippling African societies: it is bleeding their potential' (Washington 1988). Hence, Nyamnjoh's argument that in most cases, 'The state-owned businesses are everything short of profit-making enterprises, they are in fact run as 'public private businesses for the benefit of patrons and clients in power, and more often than not, instead of making money for the state, the state is forced to borrow to keep them going, for what matters at the end of the day is patronage not prosperity' (Nyamnjoh 2000:25). And dishearteningly, Nyamnjoh further observes that if the African state is more often than not keener on patronage, this is more to check against popular modes of politics than intended to encourage economic policies committed to the eradication of misery.

There is adequate awareness that economic growth can only be meaningful if the population is not growing faster than the economy and individuals are less keen to monopolise the fruits of personal success (The South Commission 1990). Over the last four to five decades, African population growth rates have always been higher than growth rates in the economy (Abraham 1995; The South Commission 1990), and successful individuals have been keener to celebrate autonomy than to redistribute their wealth to those at the margins of the narrow regime of personal success. The net effect has been that the benefits of economic growth are absorbed by a growing population, but with few graduating into a life of comfort and dignity. In most instances population growth has exceeded that of food production. For instance, in the 1950s annual population growth rate was 2.1 percent. By 1970 it jumped to 2.7 percent and in the 1980s it was 3.0 percent. In contrast, food production grew by 1.8 percent (Abraham 1995), leading to food deficits and the need for food imports and aid and increasing malnutrition and famine (Diejomaoh 1988; FAO 2000). These aspects have a debilitating effect on Africa's overall economic performance not to say about prospects of sustainable development.

It is informative to realise that there are certain domestic elements, which though non-economic, have influenced Africa's harsh economic realities. Such factors as political instability, authoritarian regimes and unprogressive attitudes have impacted negatively on economic growth (Ayittey 1992). Fragile political institutions for instance create insurmountable barriers to economic prosperity, especially in warfare situations. Myriad military coups and dictatorships partly account for Nigeria's and Ghana's economic crisis, while civil wars in Mozambique, Democratic Republic of Congo (DRC), Sierra Leone, Angola, Somalia and Liberia have paralyzed or prevented growth of their economies (Ray 1998). In Sudan the GDP fell almost two percent in 1988 due to the combined effect of civil war and drought (Abrahim 1995). In countries with authoritarian regimes like Malawi under Banda, long term economic objectives and strategies were replaced by myopic, short-term policies like large public sector deficits to support politically determined projects (Hope and Kayira 1996), while in the multiparty political dispensation lending decisions are based on political and other non-financial criteria. This scenario reflects conflict between economic and political rationality, which according to Schatz (1988), enshrines government schemes providing opportunities for graft, and political patronage.

For many African states, the production of primary products like agricultural raw materials does not encourage technological innovation, particularly where peasant or smallholder cultivation prevails. It tends to freeze technical initiative, which Kindleberger terms technological 'fossilization' (Kindleberger 1958: 301). On the other hand, the production of primary products in plantations or technologically advanced plants encourages disparities in the distribution of wealth by concentrating the benefits of comparative advantage to few elites or firms or international companies originating from advanced countries, which end up repatriating the profits. In practice the developed nations, through their economic power, extract the greater benefits (Griffiths 1999: 169) and within African countries, export earnings tend to be distributed very unevenly among the rural population (Todaro 1992: 373).

International political economy

The world economy is more integrated now than it was two centuries ago. Decisions made in one part of the world have an impact on other countries because of ever growing economic linkages and interdependency on the basis of comparative advantage. The theory of comparative advantage recognises that countries have different economic opportunities and capabilities and developing those capabilities for the market is the logical way for maximising economic returns through trade. This implies that countries should specialise in the production of commodities in which they have comparative advantage that is relatively more efficient, and exchange for commodities of their comparative disadvantage (Salvatore and Dowling 1977: 63). The most important normative aspect of the law of comparative advantage is the contention that any resources should be invested in the export products rather than in the import competing or substituting industry; on the basis that a country would be more efficient in the production of the export good which could then be exchanged for desirable import goods.

Inherent in the theory of comparative advantage is the firm belief in market efficiency and therefore it is also a call for free trade, liberalisation of markets and competitive market ethic espoused by the classical theorists like Adam Smith and David Ricardo and the neo-classical economists epitomised by the Washington consensus. The links were mainly trade, investment flows and labour movements. However, Africa has historically been at the margins of the global economy (Ayittey 1999), experiencing unfavourable terms of trade, investment flows and labour movements.

The international division of labour between the industrialised centre (rich countries) and the non-industrialised periphery means that African countries participate in trade through exports of products in which they have advantages derived from nature and tradition rather than from the productive skills of their labour and desire (Amin 1997). This trend has its antecedence in the colonial era, when the colonial administration in Africa deliberately inhibited industrial development and promoted heavy reliance on the export of primary products, with the result being low prices and price fluctuations. The perpetuation of this trend is responsible for Africa's plight, particularly the failure to diversify economies after independence. The World Bank acknowledges that Africa's slow economic growth is a reflection of poor export performance, especially the very low and unreliable prices paid for African commodities. The terms of trade as governed by the theory of comparative advantage are unequal, thus international distribution of income has become more unequal; and the differences in economic structure among countries bias the gains from trade in favour of the technologically advanced and industrialised countries (Meier 1989: 384). The specialisation in the production and export of primary products therefore compromises the development potential of African countries. In fact, for a number of reasons, few African countries have benefited from the international division of labour.

First, the price elasticity of demand for most non-fuel raw materials appears to be relatively low (Todaro 1992: 372). For instance, the income elasticity of demand in developed countries for Africa's agricultural raw materials, food stuffs and beverages supplied is less than one, that is, an increase in income of one per cent leads to a less than one per cent increase in expenditure on these products. This implies that in the long run the share of African countries in the world economy declines (Salvatore and Dowling 1977: 173). Apart from declining share in world trade over time, prices of primary products are far from being stable, which implies uncertainties in revenue from exports. For example, between June 1980 and June 1982, the price of sugar fell by 78 per cent, rubber by 37 per cent and copper by 35 per cent, a trend that has continued till date, for all primary products, with the exception of oil and diamonds. As the value of exports fluctuate widely, a specialised country lacks control over national income, money supply and hence over its rate of development. This captures the plight of Zambia, for example, whose economic downturns have been occasioned by its excessive dependence on copper exports (Ferguson 1999). The declining terms of trade against producers of raw materials condemn African countries into worsening poverty, underdevelopment and dependency on developed countries and the Monetary Fund (IMF) and the World Bank for development assistance and balancing of budget deficits. Unequal exchange increases inequality between countries, thereby making the poor poorer and the rich richer (Emmanuel 1976). Prevailing unfavourable terms of trade drain Africa of scarce resources. According to UNCTAD (2001) 'unchanged terms of trade' could have made available resources for domestic uses and investment which under optimum productive levels could lead to economic growth at a much faster rate and raised income by as much as 50 percent.

African states are victims of their own specialisation in primary production, which is subject to ever declining terms of trade. As wealth per head at a global level increases, African countries should not expect fair prices for raw material exports. Even if the physical output of raw materials and manufactured goods grow at equal rates, the terms of trade will still shift against raw materials. Unlike the developed world where increased efficiency takes the form of higher prices for factors of production and constant prices for goods, in developing countries, factor returns are low in spite of increased productivity, and implies that the benefits go abroad due to lower factor prices in developing countries (Kindleberger 1958: 298). Ultimately, the international trade in raw materials serves to transfer wealth from poor African states to wealthy ones via the price mechanism.

The failure of African producers of primary products to control over production is another weakness. Price declines are not duly due to unfair practices of the rich countries rather over production in developing countries. The competition among the producers of primary products to out bid each other aggravates the downturn pressure on prices, resulting in additional transfers of resources to the rich countries, the 'North' (The South Commission 1990: 178-9). However, the tendency of the terms of trade to turn against African countries is not an argument against specialisation in foreign trade. Rather, there is need for greater flexibility in the allocation of resources so as to take advantage of the benefits in foreign trade and to limit loses when demand shrinks or competitors out do African producers. Although this argument shifts the blame back to the African countries, it is important to realize that resources of these countries are relatively fixed such that it becomes easy to respond to an opportunity or improvement of trade but extremely difficult to respond to a decline by shifting resources to other sectors. Zambia is a typical case in this regard. Over investment in the copper mining sector attracted a lot of other economic activities but when the mining sector started to decline the government could not adjust immediately into non-mining activities as easily as a developed country could have done. The effects on Zambia's higher than average urban population have been illusive expectations of modernity (Ferguson 1999).

The development of synthetic substitutes for instance reduce the demand for primary commodities or raw materials such as synthetic rubber for natural rubber, orlon for wool, nylon for jute and cotton, plastic for hides and skins and many others (Salvatore and Dowling 1977: 173). As agricultural commodities and raw materials originating from African states are being displaced by man-made substitutes produced in the industrialised countries (The South Commission 1990: 178), the share of the world market export earnings for synthetic products rise over time while the share of primary products falls (Todaro 1992:372). The beneficiaries of this trend tend to be the developed countries rather than the African states. In addition, owing to technological advances in the developed countries, new technological breakthroughs increase efficient utilisation of raw materials which means the raw material content of many manufactured goods tend to diminish (Salvatore and Dowling 1977: 173). Over time the demand for raw materials declines because of improved efficiency and this implies a market loss to exporters of primary commodities (The South Commission 1990: 178). Declining consumption of raw materials is not only a function of technological efficiency in the use of raw materials but also a reflection of structural changes in the economies of developed countries as the service sector develops. Salvatore and Dowling, for instance, note that rapid increase in the output of services than commodities in developed countries results in declining consumption of primary products since services have generally less raw material content per dollar or per Euro of out put than manufactured commodities (Salvatore and Dowling 1977: 173). In the case of agricultural food stuffs like sugar, wheat, fruits, vegetables and oil seeds, which are also produced in developed countries, trade barriers or protectionism in the form of tariffs, quotas and non-tariff barriers – such as sanitary laws regulating food and fibre imports – have a devastating effect on developing countries (Salvatore and Dowling 1977: 173). For instance, the common agricultural policy of the European Union (EU) is more discriminatory against food exports from developing countries. To Todaro this is much more discriminatory than the policies that had formerly prevailed in the individual EU nations (Todaro 1992: 372).

In the area of investment flows, African states have benefited from investment decisions and technology transfers of multinational corporations and bilateral agencies. However, it is pertinent to point out that the level of international investment is low compared to regions such as South and East Asia, which have benefited more from Western capital, particularly from the USA (Ayittey 1999). Given a chance Africa would benefit accordingly, but geopolitical considerations work against the realization of such a vision, since power relations determine the dynamics of investment flows (Abraham 1995). Ironically, compounding this apathy for Africa by international investors, is the brain drain by some of Africa's best brains. Although brain drain has sometimes been noted to yield brain gain, in general, Africans in the Diaspora contribute more to the development of other continents while Africa is languishing, devoid of proper leadership, skills and other specialised knowledge (Abraham 1995; Odhiambo 2004).

Is there hope for Africa?

What we have shown so far is that the slow growth of Africa's economies and apparent dismal development can best be understood by disentangling the complex interaction of specific internal conditions and the logic of the world expansion of capitalism. The need for analysis of this kind cannot be overemphasised if Africa is to achieve its poverty reduction millennium objective by the year 2015. The opposite is to ignore these interactions. This is what African leaders and academics who legitimate their positions with doctored statistics and uncritical conceptual noises advocate, ignoring internal shortfalls and focusing overly and exclusively on colonialism, imperialism, slavery, the unjust international economic system and exploitation by multinational corporations as if domestic environments were totally beyond impeachment (Ayittey 1992). Any analysis which ignores corruption of Africa's political class, the fragility of Africa's economic base, the low productivity of Africa's agriculture, ethnic belonging, and other factors that render Africa uncompetitive and risky for investment, is in every sense counter-productive. The success or failure of Africa's political economy could only be appreciated by analyzing its structures, underpinnings and directions within its own history and that of the international capitalist system (Ayittey 1992; Iheduru 1999). There is need for long-term and interim development objectives for each Africa country (South Commission 1990: 14-15).

With the failures highlighted above, one is bound to interrogate the extent to which African states are able to achieve development on the model of the developmental state (Mkandawire 1998; Taylor 2001, 2003; Stein 2000). At independence in the 1950s and 1960s, mainstream development and political theory, multilateral organisations and donor practice emphasised the importance of the state in the development process. Since then change has essentially been unidirectional, continuously shifting the frontier between developed and developing countries (Bigsten 1999). Throughout the period from independence, nowhere in Africa can it be said that the state assumed a back seat role in development discourses. Many African states adopted structural adjustment programmes (SAPs) supported by the IMF and the World Bank. SAPs encompassed rapid and extensive liberalisation, deregulation and privatisation of economic activity as a way of overcoming economic stagnation and decline. While the SAPs have been applied more intensely and frequently in Africa than in any other developing region (UNCTAD 2001), hardly has any African country graduated from such programmes with success, establishing the conditions for rapid, sustained economic growth (Mkandawire and Olukoshi 1995).

De-industrialisation is one remarkable effect of trade liberalisation in a good number of countries. Yet, only a few African countries – for example, Botswana since independence and Uganda lately – are making substantive progress (Taylor 2003b). These states have a semblance of the developmental state whose main characteristic is a strong and sufficiently autonomous government. In the words of Ha-Joon Chang (1999: 192) 'this state takes the goals of long-term growth and structural change seriously, 'politically' manages the economy to ease the conflicts inevitable during the process of such change (but with a firm eye on the long-term goals), and engages in institutional adaptation and innovation to achieve those goals'. Botswana's ruling party, the Botswana Democratic Party (BDP) and Uganda's National Revolutionary Movement (NRM) government of Yoweri Museveni appear to offer such a vision. Botswana's success story is attributed to her dynamic, democratic and development-oriented policies. Similarly, Uganda's recovery is attributed to the efforts by Yoweri Museveni's National Revolutionary Movement (NRM) to re-introduce law and order, providing conditions for favourable change, and a vision and environment for effective institutional building and conflict management. These adjustments are notable because in essence they provide a good environment for the growth of the private sector. In the case of Uganda these conditions have also win back the support of international financial institutions and donor countries. Uganda is further noted for successfully containing the spread of HIV/AIDS, a rare and remarkable achievement on the African continent. Such successes, limited though they are, would suggest not only the need of a strong state to transform economies of Africa, but also the responsibility and commitment to vision of development in the service of human dignity. This notwithstanding, the debate is far from ended, over the role of the state in development, and the extent to which the state can legitimately regulate the involvement of private initiative in national development. Whatever position one takes in this debate, it is obvious that development is only possible with a reduction in policy distortions at the macro level and in investment risks, and with an improvement in public services and infrastructures, greater efficiency (Bigsten 1999: 25).

Although liberalisation of economies is resented in many African states, in some cases it is the only way of relieving the state of unhonoured responsibilities. Elites have seemed the most creative not at mobilising and conscientising the masses for collective interests, but to curb mass involvement, controlling and strengthening their own omnipotence in national socio-economic and politico-cultural life (Nyamnjoh 2000:24; Mbaku and Saxena 2004). It is hardly surprising therefore that scarce resources and donor funds are not invested in human, rural, urban or industrial development but in consumer luxuries. African elite excels in foreign consumption while the masses they govern are starving. Democratic change in the 1990s has not in many cases reoriented the consumption of African leaders.

In Malawi, the government spends millions on maintaining several state residences, numerous presidential trips within and outside the country, media institutions catering for the affluent, and many more senseless endeavours while the people are dying of hunger and curable diseases (Englund 2002, 2004). The plight of poor Zimbabweans has not eluded the grasp of international media. While attention has been on the big people in government, as politics is often taken to be the serious business of big people, it is the ordinary people who are paying the price with their own lives and dignity (Mate 2005). The situation is so dehumanising that to some, African states has reached a dead end. Ordinary people seeking nothing more than their daily bread are increasingly dehumanised and it is not uncommon for the desperate poor to wish for a return to the colonial era when their humanity was greatly devalued but life was at the same time much better (Nyamnjoh 2000).

African states may not have the advantages and conducive environment of the East Asian Tigers, but this has not stopped their governments from endorsing the rhetoric of the developmental state. The few who have made some success as developmental states, Botswana for example, there has been failure to diversify the economy by developing a vibrant industrial base despite the determination of the ruling elite and in spite of a competent bureaucracy (Taylor 2001). The end of the Cold War and the rise in importance of the states of Central Europe has meant fewer Western donor funds for African states (McGraw 1992: 267).

It is time for the development of new thinking informed both by African specificities and the success stories of East Asia. Intensified globalisation has increased the challenges to the political capacity of African states to determine their destinies, as political borders have become more porous to the flows of goods and capital, passage of people, communication through the airwaves, airborne traffic and space satellites, which were not a threat to the same degree when the East Asian states registered record economic growth. As the vulnerability of the African state to outside influences grows, the capacity to forge centralised polity as the model of developmental states postulates becomes difficult to attain. The context in which African states have to operate is increasingly difficult for any government to pursue autonomous foreign and domestic policy (McGraw 1992). The vulnerability of the African state is worsened by the readiness of powerful actors such as western governments, international non-governmental organisations (NGOs) and multinational corporations to bypass the so called 'inefficient and corrupt state structures'. That Africa's institutional structures need reform to win the trust of the donor nations need not be overemphasised since experience indicates that African states cannot do without foreign aid, just as they cannot forge an indigenous or homegrown economic system autonomous from the West. However, there is need to guard against the tendency of donors dictating economic policies that only compound the marginality of local actors and structures. Development in Africa would remain largely an illusion, because of the weaknesses of African states to the 'perceived exigencies of a global economy' (Taylor 2003a), compelling Africa states to perpetually adjust to the demands of accumulation in the rich states by further marginalising the very people they are supposed to protect (Amin 1997).

There are advantages of being late developers, as Africa's underdeveloped states can afford themselves the advantage of being able to draw lessons from the few success stories on the continent and elsewhere. The economic strategies that have made Botswana an enclave and epitome of what Africa can achieve with sound economic management can be of benefit to the countries in the Southern Africa Development Community (SADC) and beyond. African states may as well learn from the technologically advanced industrial societies of the West and the new industrialising countries of East Asia. One of the major lessons could be that while short-term growth may be heavily influenced by the international business cycle and global economic environment, long-term development trends are more directly the result of economic fundamentals – savings, investment, population growth, trade and productivity improvements as well as policy reforms in various African states (IBRD/The World Bank 2002: 27).

Africans needs to emerge from the quagmire of classic Marxist – dependency syndrome of explaining the lack of development in Africa. Pre-occupation with the leading scholars of the dependency tradition that western development was possible only as a result of the creation of a capitalist world economy – the central mechanism for exploiting non-Western areas and preventing them from developing, thus ensuring they remained economically 'underdeveloped' (Haynes 1996:9) need to be replaced with a balanced world view. Overemphasis on the negative effects of imperialism and the international economic system without a concrete course of action has retarded the development of Africa. Even if the development of the industrialised countries was possible only because of the underdevelopment of the Third World, decades of experimentation have shown that Africa cannot achieve sustainable development through policies of disengagement from the global capitalist system. Self-sufficiency, socialism and calls for increased trade between African states and with 'progressive' states elsewhere have not yielded the intended results. The economic rise of the East Asian newly industrialising countries – South Korea, Thailand, Hong Kong, Malaysia and Taiwan – since the 1970s could have been unimaginable without a negotiated or nuanced understanding of dependency.

It must be understood that compelling though it might be, an over focus upon the international capitalist system can only neglect domestic factors such politics, culture, inter-ethnic tensions and all the divergences that affect the development chances of Africa (Rangel 1986: 42). Enriching though divergences are supposed to be, their impact on the development prospects of different African states has largely been negative, for various reasons internal and external to Africa.

The scenario is compounded by geographical factors like population/resource ration and global location of states involving specific geopolitical and core-periphery relationships that may encourage but largely appear to hinder development prospects (Wallace 1990: 222).

Basic geographical and demographic differences have significant effects on the policy options of many African states. For instance, territorial extent is important because it is associated with the quantity and variety of natural resource endowments available to be harnessed. States such as the Democratic Republic of Congo (DRC) and Malawi are bound to develop economies that differ in their internal diversity and dependence on foreign trade simply because of the sheer territorial extent. Industrialisation in small states like Botswana appears to be constrained by technological and market requirements. The low levels of per capita income undermine the potential benefits of a policy of import-substituting industrialisation. Plants are either too small to achieve economies of scale, or else plants of the minimum economic size are grossly under-utilised (Wallace 1990: 231).

If we take into account the cultural, political and economic diversity of the African states, the result is a diversity that makes comparative analysis of development along a single trajectory highly problematic. Experiences from some West African states like Nigeria, Côte d'Ivoire, Liberia and the Great Lakes states of Burundi and Rwanda reveal the indisputable fact that higher rates of politicised ethnic diversity reduces development by raising risk of conflict and difficulties of cooperation in commerce as well as development policy formulation. The breakdown of law and order in Somalia, a nearly mono-ethnic state, manifests the politics of poverty and accumulation hinged on appropriation, growth and distribution of state resources.

It is now widely accepted that corruption has large costs for economic development. Higher levels of certain forms of corruption are associated with lower growth and lower levels of per capita income. Corruption also undermines the competitive forces that are central to well functioning of markets in the sense that it distorts the choice between activities and lowers the returns to public and private investments (The World Bank 2002b: 106). In situations where new firms have to pay bribes to get registered and begin operations, some may well decide simply not to enter. Common forms of corruption are also associated with low public spending on health and education, which in turn limits opportunities for poor people to participate in the economic life of their countries. At a deeper level corruption weakens the legitimacy of the state (The World Bank 2002b: 106).

The policy environment needs serious consideration, especially in light of the temptation for politicians to use tax policies to reward their friends and supporters with exemptions and other loopholes. Politicians can also use the institutions of tax administration to persecute their enemies with repeated audits and harassments by tax inspectors. Such arbitrary actions have the consequences of encouraging perceptions of unfairness that feed taxpayer non-compliance. Institutional reform is a necessary change, especially the creation of autonomous tax administration from the ministry of finance to improve fairness and depoliticisation of tax administration. However, often, the potential benefits of autonomy are not always realized because of lack of sustained political autonomy (The World Bank 2002b: 111).

Africa cannot afford to ignore the development of financial institutions if at all development is to take root. Sound and efficient banking and insurance systems are crucial for poverty reduction efforts. Development of banking and financial institutions played crucial if not essential roles in the development of industrialisation in England in the eighteenth century, the United States in the nineteenth century and much earlier in the Netherlands in the seventeenth century. Banking facilitated the mobilisation of capital for large investments (World Bank 2002b:75-6), hence financial development contributes significantly to economic growth and through a strong effect on economic growth, poverty reduction and income distribution.

The challenge of development is not solely one of dismantling the economic, or political, or financial conditions prevailing in Africa. It is a tangle involving a complex web of interacting elements both local and global that hinder development in Africa while facilitating progress in other pats of the world, and the diversities all over African making it problematic for a single prescription even among neighbouring countries with similar common ethnic make up, political system and resource endowments. The hope for Africa does not lie in ideology rather pragmatic approach to the enduring challenges and emerging consequences of the ever shrinking global polity which paradoxically is engendering a widening of disparities between nations and among people within nations. We are optimistic that just as the world has been able to halve poverty in the twentieth century in other continents, the twenty-first century will be Africa's century subject to realistic internal adjustments and negotiated global capital and political imperatives to Africa's dream of halving poverty by 2015. There is a strong case for Africans to work within real life situations to make things better. Idealised version of a developmental state in a global polity that privileges the market imperatives make this all a castle in the air. Africa is not bankrupt of development ideologies, what is missing are not mere development ideologies rather concrete steps to effect economic growth, reduce poverty and achieve significant development.

3

Uganda as an African 'Democratic Developmental State'? HIPC Governance at the Turn of the 21st Century

Timothy Shaw

This chapter argues that, informed by the demise of the Asian developmental state in the mid-1990s and the *possible* rise of an African variant in the early-2000s (Mkandawire 2001), we need to rethink the assumptions and analyses of 'comparative politics' to accommodate a range of irrefutable current phenomena such as contracting-out, corruption, flexibilisation/feminisation, fundamentalisms, money-laundering, narco-diplomacy, regionalisms, smuggling, the privatisation of security, supply chains etc. These are no longer aberrations but rather central features of the political cultures and economies of the majority of the world's states and are typical of regions like Africa, Central America, Central Asia and Eastern Europe. Furthermore, such distinctive forms of capitalisms confirm that there are important differences amongst its major regional variants, not just in the trilateral world i.e. between liberal trans-Atlantic Anglo-America, corporatist continental Europe and Japan (Cox 1999), but also among and between overseas Chinese, Latino, Islamic and African diasporas. Thus the current political culture/economy of 'Africa' has to be situated in a range of interrelated contexts, from global to local (Shaw 1999), as presented in the first half of this chapter.

Definitions of and relations among states, economies and civil societies are everywhere in flux, given globalisations, regionalisms, migrations, neo-liberalism etc. Yet, as indicated below, contemporary texts on government, international relations and/or political science rarely appreciate this. Likewise, the post-bipolar world community now consists of some two hundred mainly poor, small and weak countries. But most orthodox studies of foreign policy fail to recognise their tenuousness or vulnerability (Khadiagala and Lyons 2001) unlike the state of analysis in the less ominous/global world of the 1960s. Today, only a minority of critical analysts focus on the other side of globalisations (Broad 2002, Gills 2000, Klein 2000, Mittelman 2000) or on the regional and global networks of informal/illegal trade in people and products, mafias/militias, drugs and guns etc (Cox 1999). Yet the formal governmental regimes of over half the members of the United Nations and World Bank exert at best a tenuous control over their territories, economies and civil societies.

In the aftermath of the erstwhile Asian miracle/model, we need to reflect on resulting analytic and policy insights. Were 'Asian values'/the 'Singapore School' merely an intellectual disguise or subterfuge for Asian (essentially overseas Chinese) cronyism (Crawford 2000)? Might the African renaissance supersede that in Asia a decade later? Is Thandika Mkandawire's (2001) formulation of an African democratic developmental state a chimera? Could the juxtaposition of Asia 1990s and Africa 2000s throw creative light on developmental experiences/lessons/policies? In particular, are HIPC and NEPAD compatible, leading to an original framework for an innovative form of local to continental African developmental governance?

I turn first to the global-local dimensions of Uganda as an emerging democratic developmental state, before turning to an analysis of its current HIPC governance.

Global

First, just as states are highly heterogeneous—from Switzerland and Singapore to Somalia and Sierra Leone—so likewise are non-state actors. The two non-state corners of the 'governance triangle' (Commonwealth Foundation 1999: 16) include global corporations and local micro-enterprises along with informal and illegal enterprises as well as formal and legal.

Thus it is imperative to recognise that global capitalisms are in fact heterogeneous rather than homogeneous. Indeed, relationships around the governance triangle vary between liberal Anglo-America, corporatist Europe,

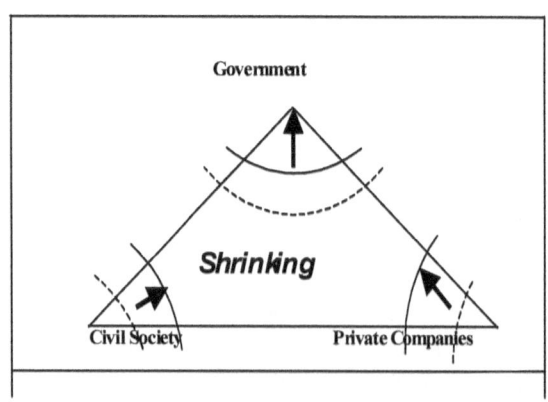

welfarist Scandinavia and Asian varieties, notably Chinese (mainland *and* overseas) versus Japanese. Africa has its own distinctive form of for-profit structures, increasingly impacted by South African capital and brands.

Similarly, NGOs vary from familiar global INGOs to very local grassroots organisations (Desai 2002; Van Rooy 2002). In particular, NGOs can be distinguished in terms of whether they are primarily engaged in policy advocacy as think tanks or service delivery as subcontractors although most do both in varying proportions. Major INGOs have become increasingly engaged with international agencies in the UN and IFI nexuses in terms of both advocacy and subcontracting (Nelson 1995 and 2002). And such legal arrangements are matched by illegal transnational networks amongst mafias, militias, private armies etc (Cox 1999; Mittelman 2000).

'Global civil society' is very heterogeneous (Anheier, Glasius and Kaldor 2001; Glasius, Kaldor and Anheier 2002) with global social movements coming to play increasingly salient yet quite incompatible roles. On the one hand, many contemporary INGOs have been the sources of new global issues, such as ecology, genetic engineering, gender, global warming, international criminal court, landmines, ozone-depletion, small arms etc (Van Rooy 2001) and now blood diamonds (Smillie, Gberie and Hazelton 2000). These have led to major global coalitions such as the International Campaign to Ban Landmines (ICBL) which resulted in the Ottawa Process (Hubert 2000, Tomlin 1998), now replicated in the Kimberley Process. But they have also advanced anti-globalisation sentiments as reflected in the battle of Seattle against the MAI and subsequent alternative summits and counter-demonstrations at major global and regional summits (Klein 2000; Van Rooy 2001).

In turn, major global corporations increasingly seek to insulate themselves from popular pressures/boycotts through a variety of strategies: from association with the UN Global Compact to corporate codes of conduct, ethical as well as fair trade initiatives, strategic alliances with certain IOs or NGOs etc. Thus many of the MNCs which feature in Naomi Klein's *No Logo* (2000) in terms of being targets of anti-corporate campaigns, e.g. McDonald's, Nestle, Nike, Shell etc, are most active in the UN Global Compact (Parpart and Shaw 2002).

One novel aspect of South-North trade in the new global political economy is supply chains which link local producers to global markets in novel ways in a variety of sectors, including new horticultures etc, in a form of partnership (Bendell 2000; Murphy and Bendell 1997). Typically these link producers of fresh flowers, fruits and vegetables to major supermarket chains and use IT for communication and airfreight/containers for transportation (Ponte and Gibbon 2003). These in turn are open to pressure from advocacy groups over ecology, gender, labour etc, leading to Ethical Trade Initiatives and Extractive Industries Transparency Initiative (EITI) as well as Fair Trade, conditionalities over gender, housing and labour practices etc, as is apparent in thumb-print sketches of sources of specialised coffee beans in Aroma, Costa, Second Cup, Starbucks: 'chain governance'.

There is a growing revisionist debate about whether the three corners of the governance triangle are really separate or are rather different points along a continuum. Certainly, there is continuous communication and interaction along the three sides of the triangle, yet there is also some autonomy at particular times in particular instances over particular issues. In short, notwithstanding the continual possibility of co-optation, many actors at all levels in the governance nexus do maintain a degree of independence, as increasingly demanded by their stakeholders. Thus, the state is not entirely diminished: in some sectors, at certain times, under specific regimes and conditions, it can be 'strong', albeit in association with other state and non-state actors.

Continental

According to Mkandawire (2001: 310), 'The first few examples of developmental states were authoritarian. The new ones will have to be democratic, and it is encouraging that the two most cited examples of such 'democratic developmental states' are both African – Botswana and Mauritius' (Mkandawire 2001: 310). Inter- and non-state relations in Africa are changing at the turn of the century (Khadiagala and Lyons 2001) because of globalisation/neo-liberalism extra-continentally but also because of new threats/leaders intra-continentally, now advocated in terms of an African Renaissance, from the African Union and African Economic Community to the New African Initiative (NAI) and the New Partnership for Africa's Development (NEPAD). These have resonance within the G8 community Africa Action Plan, reinforced by bilateral Blair and Chretien initiatives for the continent. These may inform and legitimise regional peace-keeping responses to resilient regional conflicts and they might even facilitate, perhaps unintentionally, non-state definitions of 'new' regionalisms such as ecology, ethnicity, brands, religions, sports etc (Parpart and Shaw 2002). These may extend legitimacy to new African developmental states and their related NEPAD ideology (Taylor and Nel 2001).

Coinciding with such promising developments are moves away from orthodox structural adjustment programmes (SAPs) and conditionalities towards poverty-reduction programmes. SAPs were widely criticised as being onerous and ineffective. Given the pressures on the IFIs, as well as the sequence of Asian, Russian and Argentinean crises, the IFIs have moved towards special programmes for Heavily Indebted Poor Countries (HIPC I and II). To qualify, African regimes had to meet SAP terms and design acceptable poverty reduction strategies in association with civil society.

In the case of Uganda, one of the few currently successful HIPC cases, in the late-1990s the Uganda Debt Network (UDN) acted as an intermediary between the state and private sector on the one hand and civil society on the other at both design and implementation stages, moving from policy advocates to policy agents or subcontractors, achieving the status of an authoritative epistemic community (Callaghy 2002). As UNCTAD (2000: 148) indicated on the Uganda case, the latter's Poverty Eradication Action Plan (PEAP) was founded on four pillars:

i) creating a framework for economic growth and transformation;
ii) ensuring good governance and security;
iii) directly increasing the ability of the poor to raise their income; and
iv) directly increasing the quality of life of the poor.

Thus Uganda is something of a model in terms of designing a Policy Framework Paper (PFP) and then maintaining momentum through Poverty Reduction Strategy Papers (PRSPs) in collaboration with a wide network of ministries, international organisations and NGOs, both local and global. According to UNCTAD (2000: 143):

> The PRSP is intended to be a country-owned document prepared through a participatory process which elicits the involvement of civil society, other national stakeholders and elected institutions. 'Ownership' in this context refers to the Government's taking the lead in the preparation of PRSP, including the animation of the participatory process (which is expected to increase public accountability) and the drafting of the action plan.

Such a poverty reduction network constitutes an example of partnership for rural development as advocated by IFAD in its *Rural Poverty Report 2001: The Challenge of Ending Rural Poverty*: a mix of state-NGO-private sector governance facilitated by decentralisation.

Similarly, given its recent espousal of 'human security', countries like Canada commit more resources to the continent than national interest alone would justify, in part because of notions of human security and in part given concerned diasporas. As Chris Brown (2001: 194) suggested, at the turn of the century:

> As a continent where human security is manifestly at risk, Africa came to figure more prominently in Canada's foreign policy during 2000 than a narrow examination of national interests might suggest.

National

Patterns of governance in Africa, increasingly inseparable from the notion of a democratic developmental state, are in flux at all levels: local to continental, and all sectors, from state and corporate to non-governmental organisations (NGOs); i.e. the three corners of the governance triangle. Contemporary notions of governance have a variety of conceptual, ideological, institutional, political and theoretical sources and correlates (Jenkins 2002; Quadir, MacLean and Shaw 2001). Governance on the African continent, as with others, varies over time and between regions (Reinikka and Collier 2001; Shaw and Nyang'oro 2000). And it reveals similarities and dissimilarities with other continents. As elsewhere, notions of comparative politics/development have evolved profoundly over the last decade as the mix of globalisations and liberalisations have impacted in cumulative ways. The focus on the state has been superseded by a recognition of diverse and changeable patterns of governance reflected in concepts like public-private partnerships, networks, coalitions etc (Fowler 2002; Mbabazi, MacLean and Shaw 2002).

The debate continues over whether globalisation does offer some opportunities for some African states, civil societies and companies at all levels, with the more optimistic liberals insisting that it does, despite all the negative evidence and press over the last two decades (Makhan 2002; Nsouli and Le Gall 2001; Reinikka and Collier 2001) Nevertheless, if SAPs generated much scepticism, even defeatism on the continent, then their *de facto* successor, offering a distinctive form of globalisation, negotiated debt relief for Heavily Indebted Poor Countries (HIPC) (Anena 2001; Gariyo 2001), is leading to a novel form of governance. As Callaghy (2001: 138 and 142) suggests:

> All HIPC debt relief is now to be tied directly to poverty reduction. This is to be ensured by the creation of Poverty Reduction Strategy Papers (PRSPs) put together by debtor countries in consultation with civil society groups…If seriously implemented, this new process could be an important change in international governance on debt, aid and development more generally and may have major implications for the unfolding of democratization processes in Africa and elsewhere.
>
> The UDN continued to grow and increase its capabilities. By 2000 it had more than sixty members as well as strong ties to the Uganda Joint Christian Council and business, student and labour organizations…it was becoming very active in coordinating civil society participation in the PRSP process, which it was doing with the help of Northern NGOs. Lastly, it had improved its own organizational capabilities and was running its own independent website.

'HIPC governance' by definition involves the state negotiating Poverty Reduction Strategy Programmes with a range of non-state actors at local to global levels, in the Uganda case facilitated by the Uganda Debt Network, itself a heterogeneous coalition of (I)NGOs, think tanks, religious groups etc. In the process of so negotiating and facilitating HIPC governance, the UDN has itself been somewhat transformed not only in status, but also in practice: not just advocacy but also delivery, raising issues about co-optation etc (Nelson 1995 and 2002). And certainly, redevelopment has not been evenly distributed across Uganda: the north (61 percent support for multiparty politics) remains more impoverished and alienated than the south (39 percent support for multiparty politics in the West) as reflected in opinion polls, as well as support for opposition parties and guerrilla movements (*Sunday Monitor* Kampala, 3 February 2002). Conversely, Museveni gets most support for his handling of the political debate from the West (52 percent) and least from the North (30 percent). In short, there are profound limits to 'democracy' even in today's Uganda, yet these may be increasingly excused in relation to developmental success, i.e. the trade-off between economic and political liberalisations.

Further, given the influential role which the donors play in today's Uganda, there may be a danger in them tending to divide NGOs into delivery or advocacy types as both varieties are needed to make governance more efficacious and accountable (Lister and Nyamugasira 2003). Moreover, there may also be a danger in privileging civil society overly to the detriment of formal, multi-party politics: civil society, especially when legitimated or reinforced by global donors/media, can effectively squeeze out other democratic processes like elections.

The distinctively Ugandan debate about Movement versus multiparty politics is not separable from the parallel discourse about occasional formal elections versus continuous civil society activity/advocacy. As John Makumbe (1998: 305) suggests: 'For most of Africa,...civil society would include trade unions; professional associations; church and para-church organizations; resident, student, business and other special interest associations; the media; and various types of NGOs'.

Whilst he recognises the weakness of contemporary civil society in much of the continent, including its tenuous democratic features, Makumbe (1998: 317) concludes that with extra-continental support it can continue to develop:

> The resurgence of civic protest in virtually all sub-Saharan African countries since the late-1980s has resulted, inter alia, in the transformation of the continent's governance and political systems, with civic groups in most of these countries demanding that their governments be democratic, transparent and accountable to the people. Although much has already been achieved, much also remains to be done if Africa is to have an effective and vibrant civil society.

Similarly, extra-continental actors are also increasingly concerned about the continent in part because of a variety of non-state connections, from diasporas/refugees to biodiversity, conflicts, drugs and guns, sustainability; hence the debates in Canada at the turn of the millennium about Angola, Congo, Sierra Leone, Sudan etc involving civil societies, communities, companies, media etc as well as the government (Brown 2001; Van Rooy 2001).

Local

Finally, given decentralisation and urbanisation, the local level of governance—city and community—is of growing importance for human development/security and reveals similar patterns of partnership to the other levels; i.e. increasing roles of non-state actors in terms of service delivery etc. As we will see in the case of

Mbarara municipality and county, subcontracting to local companies for education or to local NGOs for AIDS hospices etc has become commonplace. Over the last decade there has been +/-10 percent growth in Western Uganda, albeit from a very weak base post-Amin/Obote II regimes. This has advanced both human development and human security. The former is defined by the UNDP (1994: 13) as expanding human capabilities and choices whilst minimising vulnerabilities, and the latter (UNDP 1994: 24) as 'freedom from fear and freedom from want': human security is not a concern with weapons – it is a concern with human life and dignity' (UNDP 1994: 22).

This chapter draws, then, from a variety of interrelated disciplines and debates: from political science/economy and international relations to African, development and security studies, to which I return at the end. It seeks to juxtapose generic concepts like 'civil society' and 'governance' with cases drawn from Africa. While it concentrates on the Great Lakes Region (GLR), it reflects analyses and debates from Sub-Saharan Africa as a whole (Villalon and Huxtable 1998). In particular, I juxtapose notions drawn from the overlapping HIPC, African developmental state and NEPAD genres. I also bring in notions of human development/security given their salience in the contemporary continent (Hampson, Hillmer and Molot 2001; UNDP 1994 and 1999). And I particularly reflect on peace-building and reconstruction in today's Uganda: the roles of NGOs and think tanks.

Civil society and the state in contemporary Africa: Beyond liberalisation

At the start of the twenty-first century, NGOs are engaged in service delivery and/ or policy advocacy from local to global levels (Clark 2002; Desai 2002; Nelson 2002) leading to partnerships of multiple types (Fowler 2002) which impact the state, whether it seeks such links or not: 'NGOs create alliances and networks to place pressure on the state' (Desai 2002: 497).

One side of the governance triangle—that between the state and civil society—is focused on democratisation or political liberalisation. By contrast, the other side—that between the state and the private sector—is preoccupied with economic liberalisation or privatisation. How compatible are these two forms of liberalisation? Furthermore, both impact the bottom, horizontal axis of the triangle, that between the two non-state elements: i.e. civil society and private companies. In short, there appears to be something of a stand-off (contradiction?) between global competitiveness and a democratic deficit: which is primary for local and global interests/institutions?

In such a fluid context, the roles of think tanks as well as NGOs (e.g. the spectrum in Uganda from Private Sector Foundation and Economic Policy Research Centre (see more below) to Centre for Basic Research (CBR) and UDN versus old, established research institutions like the Makerere Institute for Social

Research (MISR) at Makerere, are in flux, as indicated in the broad-based coalition supporting the PRSP process (UNCTAD 2000).

HIV/AIDS has also led to innovative civil society-state/corporate relations in Uganda as elsewhere on the continent. NGOs have been active in financing hospices for the dying, prevention campaigns, orphanages for children without parents etc; and MNCs are increasingly active in terms of infected workers. The stand-off between civil society and the state over HIV/AIDS in South Africa is not replicated in Uganda as the Museveni regime has been in the vanguard of straightforward communication/education (Barnett and Whiteside 2002), leading to the regional Great Lakes Initiative for AIDS.

Civil society and the economy in contemporary Africa: Beyond privatisation

'African capitalism' in contemporary Uganda is quite distinctive and different from that elsewhere. It includes not only traditional and contemporary ex-colonial commodities and supply chains but also informal (and illegal?) and formal regional exchanges. It thus now includes fruit, horticultural and vegetable exports as well as coffee and tea; and to the region it includes electricity, Coca Cola, Mukwano soap products, UHT milk etc. And in addition to serving as an entreport for Central African resources, it also serves as a conduit for informal coltan, diamonds and gold out, and guns and other basic needs in. The mix of legal and illegal is problematic and controversial, with the UN contributing to the debates. But clearly, the Ugandan economy as a whole has gained from the Congolese conflict/expeditionary force.

In addition, the termination of apartheid has enabled South African capital, franchises, links, technologies etc to enter Uganda, so competing with local (African and Asian), British/European and Asian capitals: Century Bottlers' Coca Cola franchise, MTN cell-phones, MNet cable and satellite TV, Nandos and Steer fastfood franchises, Woolworths upmarket shopping (two branches in the 'new' Kampala), Shoprite Checkers supermarkets and Metro Cash-and Carry wholesaling, South African Breweries etc.

Such alternatives lead towards new opportunities and to new regionalisms: beyond established inter-state East African Community (EAC), now augmented by the East African Legislature and onto new security provisions, and Great Lakes Region (GLR) to flexible non-state forms of regionalisms defined by ecologies, ethnicities, infrastructures, technologies etc.

Governance in contemporary Uganda: Beyond peace-building to human development/security?

According to Ajulu (2001) 'For Uganda, the future looks too ghastly to contemplate. The elections have not only confirmed the traditional divide between the south and the north but, more critically, opened another internal divide within the NRM. These are very sensitive issues which will require delicate handling if Uganda is to avoid a return to the lawlessness of the 1970s and 1980s. The wild card in this whole question remains the generals returning from the DRC'.

Human development/security at the turn of the millennium in a small 'fourth world' state like Uganda at the periphery is a function of the balance between the local/national and the global/regional (Shaw 1999). And at all levels, governance is dynamic rather than static: the balance among state, economy and civil society varies between levels and over time. Uganda has made a remarkable comeback in the last 15 years in terms of basic human development/security, at least for most of its regions (Baker 2001, UNDP 1998). But the sustainability of such an African renaissance is problematic unless a judicious balance is maintained among patterns of governance at all levels. In particular, the notion of national development is problematic when the gap between, say, Kitgum to Kabale is rather wide (Baker 2001; UNDP 2000) as indicated in the continued tensions and violence (Erhart and Ayoo 2000; UNDP 2000)

Local governance offers a variety of advantages over centralised government but accountability, transparency etc need to be continually demanded/monitored: onto democratic decentralisation? And governance at the local level may require a continually changing mix of state and non-state resources and relationships (Kasfir 1998 and 2000) as work on Mbarara suggests (Mbabazi and Shaw 2000; Mbabazi, MacLean and Shaw 2002).

Lessons from/for governance in Africa at the start of the twenty-first century

The official, optimistic scenario emerging from Uganda in the early twenty-first century in terms of African or HIPC governance is that of a continuous negotiation among corporations, NGOs/networks, state and partnerships involving new capital/franchises/technologies and commodity/supply chains etc. By contrast, the critical, pessimistic preview suggests arbitrary decision-making, exponential corruption, state violence etc, as reflected in growing concerns regarding accountability, transparency etc (Lewis and Wallace 2000). Nevertheless, given Uganda's comeback in the 1990s, are there lessons to be learned for local to global decision-makers?

Here, I look briefly into possible lessons for established disciplines such as political science, international relations and political economy as well as for interdisciplinary fields such as African/Development/Security Studies. In terms of orthodox cannons, case studies like contemporary Uganda suggest the imperative of going beyond the state and formal economy and examining myriad links between these and the non-state/-formal: real triangular forms of mixed actor governance. And in terms of more recent interdisciplinary perspectives, there is a need to reflect on new issues/relations around developing countries and communities, so questions of traditional and 'new' security cannot be separated from the GLR etc. Indeed, Uganda in the 21st century as in the 19th and 20th centuries suggests the imperative of situating external challenges and opportunities in the context of state-society relations: what we now know as globalisation. The place of new, poor, small, weak states in a globalising, let alone turbulent, world is crucial for analysts and citizens alike.

As Callaghy (2001: 144) concludes in his suggestive study of 'HIPC governance' in Uganda, somewhat parallel to the continents centrality in anti-landmine and blood diamond coalitions:

> Africa has been central to the evolution of the international regime on public debt, although not its primary driving force. New actors and processes have been unleashed in response to Africa's plight that might significantly alter the way the larger development regime functions. In the long run, the most significant changes may well not be HIPC itself, but rather the new processes and transboundary formations that it helped to unleash.

In short, discussions of Uganda as a developmental state are enriched by considerations of actors and issues usually outside the ambit of orthodox analysis. Only by doing so can the full richness of Uganda's governance strategies and structures be understood and can grounded analysis of the country's experiences be appreciated. This is not to say that the state is irrelevant; far from it. But work that brings in 'alternative' perspectives on the notion of a nation in a process/processes of development adds to our understanding of the diverse forms that a developmental state in Africa can take.

4

The Developmental State in Africa: The Case of Botswana

Ian Taylor

The current neo-liberal understanding of economic development is highly problematic, particularly its attack on virtually all state involvement in the economy. Of those countries in Africa that have recorded respectable levels of economic development, it is precisely the developmental states of Botswana and Mauritius that have performed well. Indeed, the examples of these two countries contradict orthodox accounts of how development is best pursued, suggesting that retaining a competent and efficient state structure, rather than dismantle it as Structural Adjustment Programmes (SAPs) demand, is the key to future development—as history has demonstrated (Weiss and Hobson 1995).

For Africa, the various international financial institutions have argued that African states lack the capacity to pursue policies similar to the developmental states of east Asia, whilst being far too susceptible to vested interests in the political realm. Known as the 'impossibility thesis', African states that remained in the business of guiding development threatened to bring disaster and had to be reined in by SAPs. Elites in Africa have frequently taken on board such advice and have come to believe that a minimalist role for the state is required. Whilst recognising the problematic nature of a great deal of African state formations, across the board liberalisation and state rollback has been similarly dubious. It is not so much the level of state involvement per se that matters, but what type and quality. Examples do exist in Africa that contradicts to a large degree the neo-liberal position and which may be used to provide some lessons to the rest of the continent. Botswana is one such case from which, it is argued, the continent can learn from.

Botswana as a developmental state

Botswana is famed for its diamond resources and it is true that the revenues from diamond extraction has powered the country's growth. However, obviously an abundance of mineral wealth on its own explains nothing in looking at Botswana's success—as the case of Sierra Leone demonstrates, natural resources may in fact sabotage nation-building and development. As Clark Leith (2000: 4) has remarked, 'the growth of the Botswana economy is not simply a story of a mineral enclave with an ever growing government, attached to a stagnating traditional economy'.

There is of course a major problem in defining a developmental state simply from its economic performance: not all countries with good growth rates are developmental states. As Thandika Mkandawire (1998: 2) remarks, 'the definition of the 'developmental state' runs the risk of being tautological since evidence that the state is developmental is often drawn deductively from the performance of the economy. This produces a definition of a state as developmental if the economy is developing, and equates economic success to state strength while measuring the latter by the presumed outcomes of its policies'. Referring to Africa specifically, Mkandawire goes on to add:

> In Africa, we have many examples of states whose performance up until the mid-1970s would have qualified them as "developmental states" in the sense conveyed by current definitions, but which now seem anti-developmental because the hard times brought the economic expansion of their countries to a halt. Recognition of episodes and possibilities of failure leads us to a definition of a developmental state as one whose ideological underpinnings are developmental and one that seriously attempts to deploy its administrative and political resources to the task of economic development (ibid).

Following on from this, in Botswana there has been a definite commitment by the state to pursue development. This goes back to the first presidency of Sir Seretse Khama who was conscious of developing what had been hitherto a relative backwater of the British Empire (see Parsons, Henderson and Tlou 1995). A conscious and disciplined leadership has seen as one of its main duties the need to develop professional institutions with competent bureaucrats. Indeed, the very process of nation-building post-independence took on a nature that was inspired by the fundamental task of development at all levels of society and government. This developmental ethos was accepted and advanced by both the political and bureaucratic elites and by the institutions that they built up (Tsie 1996). This echoes Ha-Joon Chang's argument that a developmental state should act as an entrepreneurial agent whilst engaging in institution and capacity building. Certainly, the robustness and levels of capacity of state institutions in other developmental states has been crucial (see Weiss 1998). In 1981 the then Minister of Finance and Development Planning, Peter Mmusi, spoke of the need for a 'purposeful government which acquires the expertise to deal with companies on its own terms...the important word is purposeful—and I believe our government has been able to put together strong negotiating teams, has backed them up with well-worked-out negotiating mandates, and has then overseen the implementation of our major mining agreements with detailed care as well' (quoted in Harvey and Lewis 1990: 119). Attempting to account for how and why a disciplined and competent state apparatus emerged post-independence is what we shall turn to next.

Explaining the 'Miracle'

Explanations and accounts of Botswana's development trajectory are diverse. One school of thought may be called the 'African Miracle' school (originally coined by Penelope Thumberg-Hartland), which is mainly positive and largely economistic in its approach and misses the inherently *political* nature of Botswana's post-independence experience (see Vengroff 1977; Thumberg-Hartland 1978; Picard 1985; Picard 1987; Harvey and Lewis 1990; Danevad 1993; Stedman 1993; Dale 1995). Though of course this 'school' is varied, it does in the main approach Botswana's post-independence from a largely uncritical stance, asking whether Botswana is indeed *A Model for Success* (Picard 1987). Those working more from a political economy perspective have been more critical. Such analysts do of course acknowledge the rapid economic growth and efficient state machinery, as well as the long-running liberal democracy. However, they are more critical of the profound contradictions that have developed alongside Botswana's developmental trajectory (Colclough and McCarthy 1980; Parson 1984; Tsie 1995; Gulbrandsen 1996). These scholars question the scenario where there is *Poverty in the Midst of Plenty*, blaming it on deliberate policy choices made as part of the developmental state project (Gulbrandsen 1996).

The most recent work to emerge, and that attempts to account for why Botswana's developmental record is so radically different from most other African states, is Abdi Samatar's 1999 book *An African Miracle*. Touching on one of the main factors in accounting for Botswana's relative success, Samatar asserts 'a key force that distinguishes successful from failed states is the social chemistry of the dominant class and the discipline of its leadership' (ibid: 6). Like many of the political economists, Samatar is critical of the social polarisation and disparities of income within the country. But, and I think this is where Samatar's approach is superior to the overly negative accounts provided by some, he argues that Botswana's wealth grants the elite a certain space that can be used in order to resolve the more iniquitous inequalities through determined policy choice and implementation.

According to Samatar, Botswana's success as a developmental state is located in a professional bureaucracy that has conducted and implemented policy-making efficiently. This has been made possible by an essential alliance amongst elites. Patrick Molutsi has identified five fractions of the ruling elite in Botswana: elected representatives; traditional rulers; the higher echelons of the bureaucracy; the business elite; and leading cattle-ranchers. Much of these actors can be located in two or more of these ranks (Molutsi 1989a: 105). This elite alliance has privileged policies that have sought to attract private FDI (whether mineral or manufacturing—mostly the former). Receipts from this have been diverted into national development projects (Hill and Mokgethi 1989). Another leg of these policies is to promote, support and protect local businesses, primarily in the urban areas—the Financial Assistance Policy (see below) is a classic example. Such interventions have been possible because a strong state apparatus was built post-1966 that did not deteriorate into private patronage networks as elsewhere in Africa. Rent-seeking activities have thus been minimal (Theobald and Williams 1999; cf. Good 1994).

Crucially, at independence the first president, Seretse Khama, enjoyed a legitimacy, drawn from his position as (former) chief of the dominant Tswana tribe that was unrivalled. This coupled with the legacy of neglect left by the British meant that there was no real opposition to Khama's agenda. 'Unlike in most other African countries, Britain left no army, no strong bureaucracy, and a weak middle class. This situation created a critical technical and political vacuum at independence. The Tswana educated elite [among whom Khama was one of] was so small that it ended up collaborating with the colonial state, the chiefs and European settlers to form the new ruling class at independence' (Molutsi 1989a: 104). This vacuum was a double-edged sword, for whilst it meant a state with emasculated capacity at independence, it also gave Khama and his circle the space to strip chiefs of their political power. Any chiefly threat to the new state's legitimacy then was nipped in the bud (ibid.). The Chieftainship Act of 1965 meant that power was granted to the president to recognise, or not recognise, a traditional ruler, making all chiefs subordinate to the central government. In addition, a House of Chiefs was established, but with no legislative powers (Somolekae and Lekorwe 1998). This at one blow meant that potential opposition to building up a strong state apparatus and organising concerted opposition to the new government was dissolved and the potential site of alternative power removed. Instead, traditional rulers, dependant on the state for official recognition, served as facilitators for the implementation of policy, particularly in the rural areas. In this sense, their role within Botswana was re-invented and chiefs became agents of the government at the grass-roots level.

Furthermore, the post-colonial elite have dominated the National Assembly in such a way that state resources were not diverted to maintain patronage networks but rather were able to be deployed for development. There has been a relative autonomy which has allowed the political and bureaucratic elite to formulate policies that have benefited national development (even whilst benefiting traditional elites e.g. policies vis-à-vis cattle production). Daron Acemoglu *et al* (2001: 44) have put it thus:

> [T]he members of the BDP and the political elite that emerged after 1966 had important interests in the cattle industry, the main productive sector of the economy. This meant that it was in the interests of the elite to build infrastructure and generally develop institutions...which promoted not only national development, but also their own economic interests. This development path was considerably aided by the fact that the constitution and policies adopted by the BDP meant that there were no vested interests in the status quo that could block good policies.

One of the key explanations for Botswana's development trajectory has been the commitment to development and the willingness to articulate a national vision for development by the elite or, as Modibedi Robi puts it, Botswana has established 'a national perspective that will carry the national psyche to a level of providence, with a sense of future, so as to define its ambition or desired level of progress' (Robi 1994: 487). The centrepiece of the state's development efforts since the inception of the first National Development Plan (NDP) from 1968 to 1973 has been to raise the standards of living of the population of Botswana. In line with this, development plans have been guided by the planning objectives of sustainable development, rapid economic growth, economic independence, and social justice (Republic of Botswana 1997a). The NDPs have the added advantage of granting policy implementers a great degree of space between them and the politicians. By this it is meant that a technical document, drafted by experts and then approved by elected representatives, serves as the blueprint for government policy. 'Once the new plan is approved, politicians' proposals not in the plan are turned aside on the grounds that only emergency measures can be adopted until the next plan is formulated' (Molutsi 1989: 112). Botswana then echoes the developmental state of Chalmers Johnson where 'the politicians reign and the state bureaucrats rule' (Johnson 1981: 12).

In addition, and in a conscious imitation of another developmental state's Vision 2020 (i.e. Malaysia), a Presidential Task Group produced a document entitled 'A Framework for a Long Term Vision for Botswana'. The 'Vision 2016' is supposed to be a national manifesto to guide future NDPs as well as broad government policy and is a statement of long term goals with proposals for a set of strategies to meet these (Republic of Botswana 1996, 1997b). According to Thandika Mkandawire, 'it is this ideology-structure nexus that distinguishes developmental states from other forms of states. In terms of ideology, such a state is essentially one whose ideological underpinning is 'developmentalist' in that it conceives its 'mission' as that of ensuring economic development' (Mkandawire 1998: 2).

Vision 2016 and the various NDPs are, I believe, an indication of the developmentalist nature of Botswana as 'by planning within the context of a market economy, government policy has tended to influence the direction of government expenditure during the planning period while providing an environment in which private sector activity can thrive' (Edge 1998: 334). But, the state elite's commitment to development alone does not explain Botswana's experience. As Zibani Maundeni puts it, 'developmental commitment needed to be matched with institutional capacity. Creating a truly developmental state requires that the whole state machinery must be subjected to the leadership of an economic agency of the state' (Maundeni 2001: 18). This economic agency was, as I have pointed out above, the Ministry of Finance and Development Planning, staffed by an able civil service.

Following on from this, economic advice has been sought from technocrats, particularly in the preparation of national development plans and budgets. Indeed, the link between finance and national development is made explicit by existence in Botswana of one Ministry of Finance and Development Planning (MFDP) which is located in the Vice-President's office. In fact, it is pertinent to point out that prior to becoming president after Seretse Khama's death, Quett Masire was Minister of Finance and Development Planning and had been Vice-President for fourteen years. Similarly, prior to assuming the presidency in 1998, current president Festus Mogae had been Masire's Vice-President and Minister of Finance and Development Planning for five years. In addition, Peter Mmusi, who resigned as Vice-President in 1993 under a cloud had also been Minister of Finance and Development Planning. Such a Ministry and its close links to the Executive has secured a balance between development planning and budgeting, as well as strengthening the capacity to implement national goals and demonstrating a commitment to economic development.

Such a commitment came about after a struggle within the Ministry of Finance in the immediate post-independence period. Essentially two factions fought over the new country's future economic policy. On the one hand, the Permanent Secretary Alfred Beeby, insisted on the need to 'balance the books' and 'refused to entertain any ideas about economic development until money's in hand' (Morton and Ramsay 1994: 63). Opposed to this highly conservative stance were a group of young economists such as Pierre Landell-Mills and Quill Hermans who favoured an 'aggressive planning for economic growth, identification of potential projects, and then finally lobbying internationally for potential sources of aid or loans to finance the projects. Moreover, they even promoted the idea of borrowing money to finance development' (ibid). The latter fraction, fortuitously, had the ear of Quett Masire, then vice-president. Beeby had Landell-Mills thrown out of the civil service for 'insubordination', which for a period of six weeks (November–December 1966) caused a rift between Masire and President Khama. The matter was finally resolved after a commission of enquiry that eventually saw the creation of the Ministry of Development Planning with Hermans as permanent secretary and Landell-Mills as senior government economist. It would not be too much of an exaggeration to say that the foundations for the Botswana developmental state were laid during the 'Landell-Mills affair' in the sense that afterwards the key Ministry of Development Planning was developmentally-driven whilst the objectives of the bureaucrats were politically-driven and supported by both Seretse Khama and Quett Masire. Meredith Woo-Cumings has argued that nationalism and a national vision lies at the heart of a developmental state (1999b: 8). The slogan *ditiro tsa ditlhabololo* ('work for development') has underpinned the trajectory post-1966 with a strong sense of nationalism: 'in many respects development has been Botswana's ideology' (Lewis 1993). As Sir Seretse Khama argued:

> When we attained independence in 1966 we had no economic base from which to proceed with the development of our country. Our chances of survival as a viable country were almost nil but we were not discouraged nor could we ever willingly return to the old days of colonial neglect. Having accepted the challenges of independence we had no other alternative but to get don to work to make our independence a meaningful one (Khama 1980: 323).

In his book, which specifically understands Botswana as a developmental state, Samatar argues that the Batswana elite has successfully utilised the receipts from the country's diamonds to expand the state as a facilitator (or 'entrepreneurial agent'). This sea-change in philosophy from Beeby's fiscal conservatism to Landell-Mills et al's more development-oriented policies has been crucial, with the state not shying away from an active involvement in promoting the market. Pilot institutions have been built to stimulate growth in the private sector—the Botswana Development Corporation being a prime example. Botswana Development Corporation Limited (BDC) was established in 1970 as Botswana's main agency for commercial and industrial development. All its ordinary shares are owned by the government of Botswana. The BDC's primary objective is to assist in the establishment and development of commercially viable businesses in Botswana. Its roles include the provision of financial assistance to investors with commercially viable projects, building partnerships with investors capable of creating and growing commercial viable businesses and supporting projects that generate sustainable employment for Botswana. An important aim of the BDC is to encourage citizen participation in business ventures (see Botswana Development 1985; Botswana Development Corporation 1995, 2000).

Similarly, the remit of the Botswana Export Development and Investment Authority, set up by the government in November 1997, is to promote investment into Botswana with special emphasis on export oriented manufacture, identify market outlets for products manufactured in Botswana and construct factory buildings. Reflecting the close links between the public and private sector, the board of directors of BEDIA is made up of private sector representatives as well as representatives from the Ministry of Commerce and Industry and the Ministry of Finance and Development Planning.

I have touched on the role of the bureaucracy in Botswana's developmental state but this needs expanding. The country possesses an effective and competent bureaucracy that has been able to implement policy directives whilst not miring itself and the country in over-expenditure and other pitfalls associated with a large number of bureaucracies, particularly in Africa. Expatriates were retained (as opposed to much of the rest of Africa) in order to help train up a local but competent and educated civil service (symbolically for a number of years the head of the civil service was a white Kenyan). Because of the lack of education afforded to local Batswana under the colonial period, this gradualism was necessary. The local cadre of bureaucrats therefore underwent a period of tutelage and learning that has enabled them to gradually—and smoothly—take over the running of the country (Du Toit 1995: 98-99). Now Botswana's civil service has a 'proven capacity to take pre-emptive policy action and generally pursue policies in the long-term interest of the country' (Charlton 1991: 265). This, combined with well-trained and well-educated Batswana with a low tolerance threshold of corruption means that the bureaucracy in Botswana is a tool rather than an obstacle for development. Furthermore, and relating Botswana's bureaucracy to the developmental state literature on the autonomy of the bureaucracy, I agree with Pierre du Toit (1995: 121) when he asserts that:

> [T]he autonomous bureaucracy, in coalition with the ruling Botswana Democratic Party has succeeded through its technocratic priorities of growth and stability (at the expense of participation and equity), in establishing a solvent enough state which is able to deliver public goods (roads, schools, watering facilities, clinics etc) on a non-tribal, non-regional basis, so as to ensure that the minimum requirements of jointness of supply and non-excludability are met. Ensuring that the state is seen as neutral, not as an ethnic body…contributes to its legitimacy and that of the regime.

According to Zibani Maundeni (no date: 10), 'Botswana has maintained a strong and relatively autonomous and effective bureaucracy by insulating the planning bureaucrats from societal pressure, employing expatriates and by targeting the training of locals'. 'In practice the civil service, not the political leadership, has dominated policymaking' (Somolekae 1993: 116). The autonomy of this bureaucracy was of course socially anchored within the wider milieu of webs and networks that linked the cattle-ranchers, politicians and bureaucrats together. This sort of 'embedded autonomy' (Evans 1995) characteristic of developmental states, created a dynamic interaction between the various (cross-cutting) groups that stimulated policies favourable not only to the elites themselves but also to development. Clearly, developmental states must be involved in a network of ties that secure them to groups or classes that can become allies in the pursuit of societal goals. What has occurred in Botswana is a typical developmental state situation where the bureaucracy and the ruling party mesh. Evidence to confirm this is 'the commonness of the recruitment of senior civil servants directly not just into the ruling party politics but into senior government posts' (Charlton 1991: 283). The classic example being, of course, current president Festus Mogae, who has variously been Planning Officer, Director of Economic Affairs, Alternate Governor for Botswana at the IMF, Governor of the Bank of Botswana, Permanent Secretary to the President, Secretary to the Cabinet, Minister of Finance and Development Planning and finally vice-president in 1992 before taking over the presidential reins in 1998. In short a career technocrat and civil servant!

Some claims have been made that the state has overly favoured an elite fraction of cattle farmers (see e.g. Picard 1980; and Parson 1981). However, this presupposes a high degree of influence over policy by interest groups. But as John Holm has pointed out talking specifically of rural development and the supposed influence of some 'bovine elite', 'the critical debate on a policy takes place within the government, not in parliament or in public discussion...it is dominant ministries which shape policy outcomes' (Holm 1985: 175). Patrick Molutsi (1989b: 126) has gone further to assert that:

> Without denying that important government policies benefit the rich and influential sections of society...the state is not *sui generis* an instrument of local shopkeepers and cattle owners. Instead it is capable because of its relative autonomy from the major classes in society of concurrently advancing accumulation programmes in favour of the propertied classes on the one hand and welfare programmes for the poor masses on the other. The latter especially is important if the state is to establish itself as legitimate for the entire population.

It can be argued that the embedded autonomy of the bureaucracy and diverse ministries have thus served Botswana well, cushioning policy from special-interest lobbying, though perhaps at a cost of the democratic accountability of the bureaucracy (Molomo 1989). The limitations on organised labour in particular (in the name of nation-building) has been highlighted by some observers (Mogalakwe 1997). Having said that, like in other developmental states, social engineering is integral to the project. This has been facilitated (i.e. there has been minimal opposition to the dominant elites' programmes) in Botswana by the fact that civil society has been poorly developed and disorganised and democratic input weak in any case (Molutsi and Holm 1990). The fragmented opposition in particular has meant that the BDP has enjoyed hegemonic—if not wholly unchallenged—status since independence (Mokopakgosi and Molomo 2000; Osei-Hwedie 2001).

Freed from such diverse pressures emanating from below, the bureaucracy has served a crucial role and it is true that 'the government [has] invested heavily in infrastructure, health and education and attempted to foster industrial development. The key to all this was the creation of a meritocratic bureaucracy and extensive state capacity' (Acemoglu et al. 2001: 29). Subsequently, 'public sector development administration is at once broader and more focused than traditional public administration because the state itself serves both as the engine of growth within the economy and as the primary source of social development nationally' (Edge 1998: 336-337).

Following on from this, parastatals have been created in a country that lacks sufficient local capital—the most notable examples being Botswana Power Corporation, the National Development Bank, Botswana Railways, Botswana Development Corporation etc. In order to finance these, the government created a mechanism whereby funds are transferred out of the Consolidated Fund into three special funds, namely the Domestic Development Fund, which is the state's own contribution to capital projects as opposed to donor aid; the Revenue Stabilisation Fund which absorbs short term revenue increases and is used to provide short-term funding to parastatals and local government; and the Public Debt Service Fund which provides long-term funding to parastatals. This mechanism controls excess spending by central government. Derek Hudson (1991: 57) has written that 'the government has had mixed success with these loans, from a credit worthiness point of view. From a development point of view however, they have been a great success'.

The state has been keen to diversify the economy away from its traditional export base and towards manufacturing, particularly as minerals are a finite resource and 'the economy's prospects of continuing rapid growth must lie mainly with the further development of manufactured exports' (Harvey 1991: 337). Indeed, the government noted with alarm the vulnerability of Botswana to an over-reliance on diamonds with the issue of 'conflict diamonds' (*Daily News*, Gaborone, 6 July 2001). To this end Gaborone has followed a conscious policy of promoting the industrial sector as a means of diversifying Botswana's economy. The Financial Assistance Programme (FAP) has been a part of this policy (for a critical discussion of FAP, see Kaplinksy 1991). Established in 1982 and revised in 1989 and 1995, FAP was created to assist businesses which produce or process goods for import substitution or for export. Large-scale mining and the cattle industry are excluded from FAP. Eligible activities for assistance include manufacturing, small and medium scale mining, agriculture other than cattle, selected 'linking' service industries and tourism. Linking service industries are defined as those which provide a marketing or collection function for the productive activities, including associated repair and maintenance facilities. Brewing or distilling operations do not qualify for assistance.

New projects and expanding productive businesses can apply for assistance but only those which raise the national income and have a reasonable chance of becoming financially viable will receive assistance. Businesses which qualify for assistance are classified into three categories:

- *Small Scale Projects* – having fixed capital investment of less than P75,000. FAP assistance in this category is restricted to citizens. Assistance is in the form of grants, with amounts determined by location, woman ownership and number of jobs created.
- *Medium Scale Projects* – having fixed capital investment of between P75,000 and P2 million.
- *Large Scale Projects* – having fixed capital investment in excess of P2 million.

Small and medium scale industrial projects which qualify are administered by the Department of Industrial Affairs in the Ministry of Commerce and Industry. The Ministry of Finance and Development Planning administers the Large Scale Projects. However, such mechanisms have largely failed to diversify the economy: despite the best efforts of the state, Botswana has been unable to emulate the developmental states in Asia such as South Korea or Taiwan in building up a large-scale competitive manufacturing base. This has been a failing of the country's development experience (Mhone 1996).

Concluding remarks

Before concluding, it is important to point out that Botswana is not some sort of utopia in the Kalahari. The country faces serious problems related to equity within society (Good 1993; Hope 1996; Nteta, Hermans and Jeskova 1997; Jefferis and Kelly 1999). It is a moot point that not everyone has benefited meaningfully from raised incomes or higher standards of living, setting aside for one moment the extensive provision of health and education facilities as well as access to potable water and a decent transport infrastructure. As Louis Picard has pointed out, 'the primary beneficiaries of government policy in the areas of economic and rural development have been the organisational elites, bureaucratic, professional and political, who dominate the system' (Picard 1987: 264).

Although Botswana is a 'cattle country', this obscures the fact that almost half of Botswanans own no cattle at all, with less than 10 percent of the population owning about 50 percent of the country's cattle. These cattle barons have benefited from government policy vis-à-vis beef, although the receipts from meat exports of course do also go into state coffers. One might say that the Botswana Meat Commission, that manages the country's beef industry, 'has nurtured the collective interest of the dominant strata while providing services for the many small producers' (Samatar and Oldfield 1995: 661). Four out of five rural households survive on the income of a family member in town or abroad. 'That still leaves a significant number of rural households, usually female-headed, with no source of income known to statisticians' (Parsons 2000). The Executive Secretary of SADC, Prega Ramsamy, has argued that Botswana will have reduced poverty by half by the year 2012 if they continue to sustain their current economic performance (*Daily News*, Gaborone, 19 July 2001). But this calls for determined policy to ensure this occurs. In fact, the creation of a more equitable society and the fairer distribution of resources is now Botswana's greatest developmental challenge and on which will define the success or otherwise of the post-independence project. A less elitist and more egalitarian aspect of Botswana's developmental state is urgently required. Although some of the inequality in the country is due to specific policy choices, it is also true as Balefi Tsie (1998: 15) points out, that 'some of the contradictions of Botswana's development policy are rooted in the capitalist system that the country has followed...Here one has in mind the tendency of capitalist economies to generate severe income inequalities in the early stages of their development'. Now that Botswana has established the fundamentals of a working bureaucracy and excellent infrastructure with a large amount of foreign reserves, a more pro-active stance on inequality should be put in place (see Botswana Institute for Development Policy Analysis 1996).

The commitment to development then by both the political and bureaucratic elites is central, but not enough. Plenty of African states have been developmental on paper, but very few indeed have been successful. What seems to have separated Botswana from other African states is the strategy of putting into place institutions which have helped sustain growth. This has been part of a broader national developmental vision which has sought to co-ordinate investment plans. With the state acting as an entrepreneurial agent, there has been, to varying degrees, a co-ordination between the private and the public sectors—the parastatals being a prime example. According to Wayne Edge:

> In Botswana, the developmental state is based on a foundation of capitalism in which the government, through a wide variety of incentives, actively promotes private investments by national and multinational corporations, while creating profit-based public enterprises and investing directly in private firms (Edge 1998: 334).

All this has been facilitated by an efficient and well-trained bureaucracy that has resisted the descent into corruption that has been the hallmark of much of the civil service in other parts of the continent. Indeed, skills development, not only in the bureaucracy but also in the wider private sphere have been an important aspect of Botswana's success—the National Productivity Centre, which came about after fact-finding missions to Malaysia and Singapore, being a prime example.

Despite the criticism of inequality within the country, it is still true to say that 'state intervention can play a vital role in creating the conditions for sustained trade growth and in ensuring that trade expansion translates into poverty reduction—as the examples of both Botswana and Mauritius in Africa have demonstrated (see Carroll and Carroll 1997). The Botswana developmental state *has* achieved respectable accomplishments and it can be argued Botswana's strategy has shown that 'a disciplined activist African state that governs the market is essential for industrial development and recovery' (Owusu and Samatar 1997: 270). In this sense, the lessons that Peter Evans has asserted states may pick up from the Asian experience, namely the construction of 'local counterparts to the proximate institutional prerequisites of East Asian success—bureaucracies with a capable economic core and government-business relations based on scepticism combined with communication and support in return for performance delivered', might also be applied to Botswana (Evans 1998: 83). I would concur with the assessment that 'Botswana [has] defied the thrust of prevailing development orthodoxy, which claims that African states cannot enhance industrial development through interventionist strategy. Botswana's state-governed industrial strategy supports recent research on the 'East Asian miracle', which underscores the fundamental importance of state intervention in industrial transformation' (Owusu and Samatar 1997: 289). Equally, the 'primacy of politics' in the complex process of development has been fundamental and decisive (Leftwich 2000), inferring that it is not *how much* state intervention should take place, but rather *what kind*.

Obviously, as Christopher Clapham points out, the very different historical and cultural contexts that various development experiences have evolved from make direct comparisons and borrowing of models problematic (Clapham 1996). Developmental states cannot, as Leftwich (2000: 169) points out, 'be had to order'. Nonetheless, it is possible to suggest that there is such a thing as a broad developmental state model that helps account for the relative success not only of Taiwan or Singapore, but also of Botswana and that we should not write the possibility of more developmental states off on the continent (on this, see Stein 2000). As Peter Evans has written, 'in the best of all possible worlds, African and Latin American countries would follow the lessons generated by the East Asian experiences in the same way that East Asian policy-makers followed western models of capitalism: with such originality and inventiveness as to outperform the original. Hopefully the art of leapfrogging is not yet dead' (Evans 1998: 83).

5

Uganda's Institutional Framework for Development Since Colonialism: Challenges of a Developmental State

James Akampumuza

Recovering from colonialism's neglect and the ugly chronic instability experienced between 1971 and 1986, Uganda has had a fast growing economy. Essential commodities which previously were either not available or when they were, had to be rationed by politicians, bureaucrats and chiefs either through lining up or issuance by chits due to scarcity, now litter shops. The phenomenon of 'scarcity' has been replaced with that of 'individual choice' and 'affordability'. Despite this spectacular economic growth, poverty and income inequalities persist as servicing and repayment of debt remains high. That is perhaps attributable to post turbulence policies that strove to introduce a market-based economy, where a few people control the majority of the country's wealth.

Institutions play a vital role in fostering (and impeding) development in a developmental state. Yet, Uganda's institutional frameworks for contract negotiation and fund utilisation are routinely criticised. The presence of such factors that imperil debt repayment possibilities, and by extension development, prompted my analysis of justification for the study of the legal framework. This is embedded in the institutional framework for development and shaped by myriad processes whose efficiency helps determine a developmental state.

The genesis and context of Uganda's institutional framework

In pre-colonial Uganda, informal village institutions transacted business, guided by the culture of trust. Deviants from the basic norms were punishable via sanctions like curses, voluntary restraints and ostracism. Clan leaders and outspoken elders implemented the informal rule. That arrangement is less favoured in today's virtually impersonal dealings between strangers engrossed in protecting individual stakes.

British colonialism found Uganda advantageous to its quest for 'privileged spheres of foreign trade' and 'foreign investment' (Mangat 1969). Far from developing Uganda, the advantage was to guarantee its unobstructed resource exploitation. The institutional framework for realising this policy objective bestowed Uganda a protectorate status, which meant minimal colonial engagement in establishing local development oriented institutions. This was supplemented by a policy that barred foreigners' acquisition of land. Effectively, they were proscribed from establishing permanent residences or investments whose sustenance would add a new cost of infrastructure development to that of colonialism and trade.

Through carefully orchestrated legislation and dubious contracts, schemes with little value to the indigenous societies were institutionalised. Thurston, a Colonial agent bluntly explains how, 'I had a bundle of printed treaties which I was to make as many people sign as possible. This signing is an amiable farce which is supposed to impose on foreign governments and to be equivalent of an occupation' (Murkherjee 1956: 125). Examples suffice here. The only consideration for ceding territory and resources in the 1893 Protectorate agreement was a pittance of beads and mirrors. This consideration was conveniently secured through technical contractual terms written in a language the illiterate indigenous signatories could not comprehend without translation. The signing was possibly under the mistaken belief that it was for acknowledging receipt of the pittances or a gesture of friendship. But as subsequent events show, it lacked mutual consent. When Kabaka Mwanga tried to opt out, he was greeted with a military might that culminated in his banishment. Had there been mutual consent, the excessive force would have been avoided. But the precedent thenceforth institutionalised the legacy of payment of no value for value in Uganda's politics. It also heralded the dreadful preference of violent pursuance of political goals to plausible institutional frameworks that came to characterise Uganda's profile.

Through the 1900 agreement a new institution of chiefs was introduced as a facet to sidestep the authority of the traditional rulers. This dispossessed them of their hitherto government powers. For their collaboration, the agreement bribed them with portions of the land they prior superintended over in trust for the masses, and thereby for the first time turned the masses into squatters. The treaty was marked with undue influence to an infant Kabaka and misrepresentation to his Regents.

Because it was not meant to develop Uganda, the agreement rooted a land tenure system counter to national development. Rather than fostering comprehensive land consolidation, it was retrogressively fragmented to reward collaborators. That way, only institutional arrangements needed to safeguard colonial economic interests were instituted. Infrastructure development, especially railway construction focused on facilitating colonial exploitation. Leaders of both the dominant Labour and Liberal Party stressed that colonial development was 'part of the attack on British unemployment' (Brett 1973:132). The debate conspicuously ignored the colonies underdevelopment.

Development matters were left to fate, while priority was given to lopsided laws meant to protect colonial economic interests. Colonialism practised an intertwined exercise of powers, where the District Commissioner (DC) doubled as the Magistrate, administrative head and legislator of bye-laws (Murindwa 1991; Akampumuza 1992). Not only was this a fusion of the institutional framework but it was also conscious detachment of Africans from activities that would give them professional skills. That way, colonialism arrested the establishment of professional institutions it didn't deem central for controlling semi-barbarians. Consequently, high levels of illiteracy, a low managerial and administrative base and only one University are the attributes inherited at independence in 1962. Post independence regimes preserved colonialisms' modus operandi as a country chief was an administrator, judicial officer and enacted by-laws. Developing local institutional capacity would have unnecessarily meant tampering with such convenience.

Confronted by the colonial policy's blowback, a World Bank Mission acknowledged that 'the creation of a large enough class of successful local entrepreneurs is bound to take a long time' (IBRD 1969: 106). Public bodies set up to rectify this institutional gap such as the National Trading Corporation were reduced to bureaucratic conduits of largesse to reward party loyalists. Funding for these odious aims was secured under the guise of promoting African skills via borrowing on tough repayment terms. The sham development institutions were set up by legislation to champion development. However, no corresponding institutional framework to check their functioning was set up be it legislatively or administratively. This could have been a deliberate omission as the authors of the legislation turned out to be the loopholes' actual beneficiaries.

Meanwhile those privileged were pre-occupied with their 'eating', sections of the society resorted to criminal activity to forcefully get a share. This manifested in *Kondoism* (endemic robbery), speculative practices like *Mafuta Mingi* (economic war), *Magendo* (smuggling) and *Bichupuli* (fake investments). These were symptoms of a failed institutional framework. Instead of tackling the cause, the institutions futilely misdirected their interface to enacting penal legislation and convictions to suppress the symptoms.

The postcolonial state therefore continued the instrumental application of the law to achieve policy objectives. The new global ideology of development planning, championed by donor proxies such as The World Bank, ensured the new administration remained reliant on foreign financing. Imperialism thus slyly established a parallel donor government regime to control Uganda's policy and law making. Consistently, conformingly designed policies are judiciously presented as antidotes to that pattern.

Meanwhile, wealthy tycoons entered into partnerships with top government and the ruling UPC party functionaries to access public funds to run private enterprises. These were informal public private sector relationships operating outside any institutional framework. Such informality involving use of public funds and institutions predictably furthered corruption and bribery that reached alarming levels (Mamdani 1976). Feigning political concern, the executive through Parliament enacted a cosmetic 1970 Anti-corruption Act to assuage public outcry. But given its superficiality, the Act failed dismally as its sponsors consciously instituted no institutional framework to ensure its effectiveness. Obviously, the major culprits of the partnerships were the very Act's sponsors, which explains their desire to keep it ineffectual. Unabatedly, public sector partners enjoyed unlimited access to public funds, which they often disguised in the tycoons business accounts to avoid detection. For example, a prominent Asian's pre-expulsion files catalogued more than 90 percent bureaucrats indebted to him, yet there was no prosecution or investigation of the culprits to establish what business justified such indebtedness. This was perhaps because the very beneficiaries were the custodians of that institutional duty. Even the few corruption cases that went to Court were often dismissed for lack of 'sufficient evidence'.

In 1972, shortly after Amin had expelled the Asians, the realities of the cosmetic institutional framework were laid bare in his declaration of an 'economic war' to check 'saboteurs'. This turned out to be rhetoric sloganeering to justify a policy aimed at widening his political functionaries' economic base. Expropriated businesses were allocated to an incredulous class of henchmen using the criteria of Amin's friend or soldier. No institutional formality was followed as Amin personally 'allocated' them *gratis*. Like the inequitable policies fostered under colonialism, this was a moot private enterprise policy that bore serious repercussions. Besides the inherited cancer of lack of professional skills were added non-skilled management and ownership which inevitably had to fill in the institutional vacuum the policy created. Key government skilled personnel were equally affected and so were vital institutions, the worst hit being the judiciary. With the new style of transacting government business, a Siamese informal parallel black-market called *Magendo* was developed too. This outperformed state— controlled marketing agencies, owing to the unskilled nature and strategic place of some of its key actors in the institutional framework of the very agencies.

Politicians exploited the scarcity engendered by their bad policies to make personal fortunes. Amin and his protégés drew foreign currency from Bank of Uganda (BOU) without any backup local currency. Ministers placed orders overseas for personal ventures and incurred commitments against the national budget, without either the consent or knowledge of the treasury. The resultant high net capital outflow between 1971 and 1977 depleted Uganda's foreign reserves Special

Drawing Rights (SDR) by 51.2 million (Kaberuka 1990). A bankrupt treasury and a whooping debt of US$ 700m greeted the post Amin regime in April 1979. The weak laws, alongside a fallen institutional framework thus had put the poor policies on trial.

To reverse this trend, Uganda has undergone two structural adjustment programmes (SAP), one between 1981 and 1985 (Obote II), and the other between 1987 and the present (Museveni's regime). However, the challenges of the weak institutional framework still abound. Alas, even the architects of the policy reforms are implicated in perpetuating the very vice the policies sought to stamp out. For instance, 'an IMF team once engaged in a dialogue with a team of Ugandan 'negotiators' from the Ministry of Finance, Planning, Education and Bank of Uganda. When the Ugandan team questioned some of the IMF assumptions, its team stormed out of the meeting and drove directly to Obote, who promptly signed the agreement. The Ugandan negotiating team only learnt of the signing from the news media (Hansen and Twaddle 1991: 63). Such patronising attitude is not healthy for development, especially in the light of an already fragile institutional framework. Permitting their institutional mandate to be compromised deflects expectations.

Ultimately, political functionaries irregularly access the funds while international institutions obligated to ensure the project's success passively look on. Invariably the moral basis to escape liability for failed projects is lost, disqualifying their neutrality posturing as 'outside third parties without a stake in the outcome' to monitor the transaction and reduce the risk' (Shirley 2002). That perhaps explains Uganda's unabated privatisation scandals without reprimand of those implicated, despite donors' constructive and physical presence.

All in all, no matter the specific point in time, policies conceived since colonialism were presented as developmental but in tandem exhibited opposite objectives in practice. The shared denominators in their functioning was political rhetoric not backed by any development oriented institutional framework and omnipresent penal legislation to bully dissent. The executive thus through the legislature legislatively shielded inequitable policies to ensure their unimpeded operation.

The Asian property question

It is now apparent that post independence regimes did not inherit any strong institutions or an educated workforce. The eventual transfer of power to unpractised politicians and/ soldiers of limited intellect was thus not accidental, but rather arose out of colonialism's deliberate refusal to impart local skills and develop local institutions. Politicians and civil servants who took over the reins of political power lacked the technical know-how, to formulate and implement government policy. This was a sure blueprint for anarchy, given the inherited alien form of politics that enshrined the tricky rule of law they were to implement.

Their remedy was a scapegoat political solution they found in the trading Asian community. This came to gain prominence in various development policies hence the phrase 'Asian question'. The Asian question is central both in policy and institutional framework that successive Ugandan regimes, right from colonialism to Obote I (1962–1971), Amin (1971–1979), then Obote II, Tito Okello Lutwa (July 1985–January 1986) and Museveni have had to institutionalise policies on its handling. This has intertwined it with Uganda's development process. Often marked with violence, its nature and intensity has been varied by the evolution of the political conditions it has propagated. At certain points, it caused antagonisms between indigenous Ugandans and Asians, which undesirably manifested in violent widespread lawlessness expressed in violent boycotts, kondoism and subsequent guerrilla activity. Such manifestations were a reflection of survival tussles by indigenous Ugandans and a censure to government and the global community's complacency.

Amin's Asian expulsion nurtured a horrendous effect of cumulative economic mismanagement, attributed to deepening social and political tensions within the undeveloped economy. The ensuing property expropriation lacked a parallel legal enforcement institutional framework. The immediate effects of the expropriation are best discernible from a theatrical hypothecation of 'throwing a carcass amidst a den of hungry hyenas, part of them charged with handling it among the rest- thus causing wrangles over it' (Asian property). Decrees were later made to govern the expropriated properties' disposal. A Government Parastatal body, the Departed Asians Property Custodian Board (DAPCB) was supposed to hold the properties in trust, an impossible task given the days' politics. True to Amin's character, expropriated properties were wantonly dished out to cronies and government functionaries as charity. Yet the Decrees lacked an enforcement institutional framework given the impotence of the then Ugandan judiciary already cowed through disappearances and massacres of its senior personnel by extremists from the executive. That in turn eroded the notion of the rule of law.

Insecurity of property continued to inhibit investment as the informal and illegal sector activities grew remarkably, escaping both legal and statistical scrutiny. Private property accumulation by mainly uneducated, inexperienced, opportunistic allocatees followed, creating the speculative class which came to be baptised 'Mafuta Mingi'. This grew to arrogate itself the new speculative economy called *Magendo* in which hoarding, smuggling and over pricing of scarce essential goods were the hallmarks of the 'economic war'. Political patronage in the disbursement of property and positions soared. The DAPCB's held properties were used as facets for favouritism and promotion of personal objectives. Given that jumbled arrangement, the expropriations' purported policy objective of developing the economy through local Ugandan's initiative could never be realised.

The legacy of property allocations outlived Amin while the institutional trustee, DAPCB could at best acquiesce or support the pillage. This was politics of building and dismantling classes, based on politically inspired allocations. Successive regimes made legislation to ease their access to expropriated property. Legislatively, political manipulations conveniently assumed legal form. Simply put, such laws were not development driven, and so couldn't address development priorities. Through its legislation, every new regime deprived allocatees of its predecessor to reward its own protégés. And these were many, given that there have been six governments since Amin. The resultant institutional distortions nurtured conditions for violence from sections that resorted to war to protect lost fortunes. The weak or collapsed institutional framework, engendered self-seeking politics of property allocations that bred internal divisions, graft and a legacy of corrupt practices that to date remain Uganda's biggest challenge to establishment of credible institutions.

The initial passage of the Expropriated Properties Act in 1982 enticed few Asians to return to a country where the security of their life and property was at risk. Donors then set the convalescing of security as a conditionality for disbursement of the restructuring loan. But the institutional framework was not correspondingly synchronised to ensure the policy's success. The law thus skirted the interests of the Ugandan masses. The politicians on their part had a diametrically opposed interest of widening political beneficence through the properties. The Act's intentional loopholes were judiciary legitimised by the then staunch UPC ruling party's appointed Chief Justice Masika in the case of Lutaya, setting a precedent that guided repossession from 1982 until its 1993 overrule in the Sure House case, twelve years after. The overrule was not a reflection of the changed role of the judiciary, but rather, the changed interface between the judiciary and the new political actors in the era of structural adjustment. Given his political leanings, Masika could not apparently conceive of appropriations by the military regime, except those it sanctioned by decree. That interpretation applied wrong principles to achieve political goals. That interface was motivated more by political rather than legal logic as it was deliberate political ploy to except certain categories of properties from repossession, for political rewards and enrichment.

This judgment followed Allen's earlier ruling that the expropriation amounted to outright theft on a big scale and that the expropriation decrees were illegal. Whereas repossession at the time of Allen's ruling was still being done bilaterally without any enabling legislation, save for the politically engineered anti Amin hysteria that shaped the decision. Lutaya however came after the passage of the donor dictated Act which the political class was not keen on enforcing, hence, the Judges deliberate excepting of certain properties. Sure House coincided with increased donor pressure to the government to unconditionally complete repossession and the Supreme Court had to provide a soft landing by overruling its earlier decision, to ensure that it didn't block critical donor funding. This at the general level reflected a policy crisis in the broader economic and political activity in the politics of development planning. Characteristically, the status of the properties was often contested in administrative circles (mostly the Minister) rather than impartial judicial forums.

The Minister of Finance

The constitutional separation of powers in Uganda's politics has been a blotted affair that every regime has abused. As we saw earlier, the emasculation of the judiciary and legislature under Amin was more complete. The Obote II government was equally entrapped in this blotched framework. It administratively empowered the Minister to determine all matters pertaining to repossession, which protracted the trend of intimidation of judicial officers. Detention and brutalisation of advocates became common place, to the extent that a Chief Magistrate was nearly killed by a hand grenade in the courtroom moments before he committed a soldier for murder (Karugire 1988).

Cases decided during this era raise the question of whether the judiciary protects the broad section of the population. The court's refusal in Sure House to extend its interpretation to order for repossession lest it meddles with the Minister's discretion is testimony to shared interests between the executive and the judiciary. Legislatively, beneficiaries in parliament worried by prospects of losing their allocations preceded the case with a private members bill to pre-empt its judicial application.

The National Resistance Movement (NRM) regime bred a further fusion of the executive, legislature and judicial powers in single entities, in its introduction and dual empowerment of Resistance Councils (now [Local Councils] (LCs). Once more, political interference was cited in the administration of justice, as political heavyweights defied court pronouncements to the absurd extent of one Minister irregularly ignoring a court ruling. In *Baluti vs. Victoria Tea Estates* [D.R. Civil suit No 3/1982 (unreported)], a successful applicant for a temporary injunction against repossession of the suit property was blocked by the Minister who in contempt maintained that the plaintiff grabbed the Tea Estate using Mr. Samwiri Mugwisa, Obote's Minister of Agriculture and Forestry. He directed the Special District Administrator to evict the trespassers and return the estate to Mr. Patel. Given the Court ruling, this was manifest interference that explicates the legacy of political interference in judicial matters. The court meanwhile argued that by virtue of inflation, sufficient compensation was difficult.

The minister was legislatively given wide and perpetual power. That was born out of a deliberate policy to protect vested class interests. To that end, the law made a friendly and automatic property acquisition process, but complicated procedures for those legitimately claiming compensation which it subjected to court litigation. The policy consideration behind that one sided provision is explicit in Judge Allen opining that the seizure of business and other property was tantamount to theft on a huge scale and those who became allocatees placed themselves in the same position as knowing receivers of stolen property. That political decision alerted the allocatees to legislatively shield themselves against possible legal actions. This shielding was deemed so vital that the Court of Appeal had to legitimise it when it had not been pleaded before it. In obiter dicta, the Court stated that:

> Although the above matters are unfortunately not issues in the present suit I consider that they are important and relevant background and wished them to be on record. The Military Government's take over of properties and businesses of Non-Ugandans amounted to nationalisation with provision for payment of compensation under the Law (Decree No. 32 of 1972, S.1(2) and Decree No. 12 of 1975, S.15); and therefore there was no violation of Article 13 of the Constitution especially as the non-citizens were no longer eligible for residence in Uganda. As according to the relevant Decrees, the property or business in question vested, first in the Government and then in the Board, which was set up by the Government to manage such property, with powers to allocate some to individual Ugandans or corporations, and as every allocatee was legally bound to pay the Government the assessed value of the property or business received, the analogy to stealing and knowingly receiving stolen property was misplaced in this case.

Needless to say, litigation involves expensive, sophisticated and cumbersome procedures which are not only time consuming but also unaffordable by the majority. Those who acquired the properties through the Ministers' allocation were not the target of this law which in essence gave them a legal cover to simply return dilapidated property shells without renovations. The law was clearly silent about returning the properties in their pre-allocation state or even paying rent arrears to the legitimate owners for the value in use, they derived from them. Not even were there provisions to provide for the post enactment payment of rent till repossession. In short, the Act absolved allocatees from any liability but transferred the mantle to legitimate tenants who genuinely deserved compensation. Not surprisingly, majority compensation court claims were defeated, given the endowment of the new Acquirers in terms of their affordability of legal representation and other niceties it takes to win a court battle. But what does this mean in political and social terms?

What should not be lost to the reader is that the claimants were largely the underprivileged who had through difficulty bought from or entered tenancies with the political allocatees and therefore, in the absence of the protection given to the allocatees and those repossessing, qualified to be *bona fide* occupants who deserved automatic compensation. As we proced to show, this phrasing was carried over to privatisation laws, arbitrarily subjecting existing interests to post privatisation uncertainty similarly couched as 'prompt, adequate compensation'. This left many shareholders, including former workers of privatised companies impoverished, while correspondingly protecting the new acquirers from such liabilities that legitimately existed prior to privatisation. That marked the institutional role of the executive and legislature in designing and passing legislation which the legislature conformingly enforced.

The privatisation institutional framework

Until 2000, the institutional responsibility for privatisation implementation and the use of divestiture proceeds was jumbled up. There was no clearly demarcated institutional responsibility with implementation institutions overlapping authority with those mandated by the Constitution. For example, the Privatisation Unit was enjoined to enter into contracts disposing off public enterprises in which government had an interest, a role constitutionally reserved for the AG. Other enterprises were set up by specific laws or incorporated under the Companies Act, with specific procedures and institutional frameworks (such as the Boards of Directors).

Even the PERD statute made an undesirable overlap of institutional responsibility, by vesting concurrent responsibility to privatise a Public Enterprise in the Line Minister or the Finance Minister. All this jumbling up of institutional responsibility was undesirably the cause of court litigation and multiple administrative conflicts that threatened the privatisation exercise and drained the country's finances through the resultant awards of costs and damages. Meanwhile, donors were biased towards the purchaser's interests. To this end, much of the donor espoused economic literature emphasises establishment of a strong institutional framework for bestowing confidence in those purchasing public enterprises, by giving them assurances that disputes arising out of privatisation shall be resolved in their favour (Shirley 2002: 11). Donors thus ignored the precarious shortage of human, institutional, economic and political capacities to manage privatisation. The stakes of the privatising government, whose development is the policy's supposed aims are conspicuously ignored. Contrary to postulations by the market self regulating ideology, privatisation cannot by itself establish self regulating institutions.

Had the policy been well conceived, supporting laws defining the institutional framework would have preceded its implementation. Ideally, this would have harmonised existing laws such as land laws that restricted foreigner's acquisition of land on which public enterprises stand. Secondly, the Public Enterprises Reform and Divestiture Statute was enacted in October 1993, when some privatisations had been conducted. Thirdly, The Procurement and Disposal of Public Assets Act only came into place in 2003. This should have preceded privatisation which basically entails disposal of public assets. Lastly, to date there are no franchising laws to govern the operations of franchises, yet some privatisations were by franchises. Such lapses were prone to political and institutional corruption; and from the planning perspective reflected a lack of sequencing and timing. A faulty institutional framework aids speculators' unchecked abuse of the process. Unlike a private seller who has no post sale concerns, the privatised products were vital development agents. The failure to properly sequence, time and harmonise governing laws and implementation institutions amidst an alien legal regime, generously ceded them to speculative 'tourists'.

The very existence of human systems presupposes the possibility of human failures and errors. That is why safeguard institutional frameworks were needed. Failing such measures, bungled privatisations like Nile Hotel and Conference Centre are inevitable outcomes. The Minister, confronted by this reality, in defence blamed the failures on 'people, people'. That was a clear admission of the absence or weaknesses in the institutional framework to check the people. That absence engendered a seismic political manipulation that derailed the development process. This, to the extent that the whereabouts of privatisation proceeds has been a contested arena, at times prompting Parliament to suspend privatisation activities (*New Vision* 5 March 1993). Meanwhile, Uganda is still hailed as a privatisation 'success story', yet external debt continues to soar and is now estimated at US $4.32 billion(BOU 2002/2003 Annual Report).

To silence public outcry, donors advanced a loan for short training programmes conducted by the American International Law Institute as part of 'local skill enhancement'. The project covered issues on privatisation but its short duration did not ensure effective transfer of substantial skills to support a strong privatisation institutional framework. A comprehensive institutional reform addressing both the training needs and the implementation framework would suffice. Besides, had there been proper sequencing and timing in designing the policy, this is one of those institutional frameworks that should have preceded privatisation. At the broader level, this was a reflection of pitfalls in government's negotiation framework. The law was but part of the requisite intitutional framework.

Issues affecting the government's negotiation framework

Under the law, Uganda's negotiating framework comprises the line Ministry, Ministry of Finance and Attorney General (AG). This law has however been both the cause and victim of a weak institutional framework. It has been the cause via its failure to sufficiently define the institutional framework and a victim via vagrant breaches by those charged with its implementation. Examples of its breach abound. For instance, Hon. Wandera Kazibwe then Minister of Tourism accused the Finance Minister of bypassing her to sign a controversial Nile Hotel privatisation she had halted (Minutes of the DRIC's 85th meeting of 17 November 1998.) That privatisation soon collapsed, leaving behind huge costs to the government and numerous court wrangles that still rage on.

Cultural and political reforms

Uganda experiences a culture of silence and secrecy among its population. In Uganda's political culture, people rarely criticise government policies directly. They often do it through an informal network of rumour conveniently termed 'radio Katwe'. Views on a particular policy or its implementation shortfalls are thus hard to solicit. That alludes to the absence of a culture of utilising formal institutions. Uganda's political culture is round about in attitudes. Manipulative attacks through rumours are largely employed as the preferred mode of communication of sensitive information. This partly arises from the hierarchical nature of the traditional cultural institutions. For example, it is abominable to openly criticise the Kabaka, the Head of the Ugandan Ganda tribe. The foregoing, coupled with the political repression Ugandans suffered during the turbulent era of military rule and successor anarchic governments if they dared speak out, this culture of manipulative attacks has come to engulf the whole spectrum of Uganda's body politick and negatively impacts on information circulation.

Such an informal rumour network when institutionalised in government dealings plays in the hands of those interested in entrenching secret deals visited with corrupt practices. That retards development prospects. Secret dealings were appropriate when government was a closed entity but with its liberalisation, information flow should follow suit. Political liberalisation reforms Uganda adopted presupposes existence of formal market arrangements, which assume that contracting parties enjoy information symmetry. Valuably, the 1995 Constitution institutionalised the process of liberalising information flow and the Judiciary has been firm in its interpretation, thus operationalising the process. However, a section of politicians, bureaucrats and technocrats remain opposed to that opening up as it runs counter to their cultural experiences. This is so because the culture of secrecy has traditionally supported institutional weaknesses that enabled some sections irregular wealth accumulation.

In 1993, the NRM government institutionalised the policy of decentralisation and devolution of authority to local municipalities and non state actors. Devolving authority to Municipalities from the central government as President Museveni humorously put it 'democratises corruption by decentralising it to widen the spectrum of beneficiaries and this is better than keeping it concentrated in a few hands'. Added to other forms of bureaucratic and economic reform such as downsizing, retrenchment and privatisation, these have diminished the magnitude of the central government. These reforms though were not wholly embraced by political hangers-on, whose traditionally enjoyed political power and patronage they diminished.

Downsizing and public service recruitment freeze though had a serious aftermath on the institutional framework. There was loss of a vital middle level cadreship that followed. This created a generation gap that meant no tier of new bureaucrats acquired skills over a given period and partly accounts for the present lack of middle cadre staff to handle serious institutional responsibility. Because of not instituting a systematic framework to vet non performers for retrenchment, the process phased out a certain skilled and experienced cadre level that has proved impossible to replace. This situation is not helped by the continued loss of bureaucrats to the lucrative private sector.

Bureaucratic and organisational hurdles

In the wake of Uganda's decentralisation and devolution of institutions and power, individual Government departments, both at ministry and municipality, have distinct internal procedures. These define the success or hindrance of the institutional framework. For example, a respondent for this study told of a situation where there is no system of filing government agreements. President Museveni, keen on attracting investors has been weary of such operational drawbacks, which he has condemned as deliberate frustration of investors. But is the problem the bureaucrats or institutional structures, procedures and unfriendly laws?

Uganda's bureaucracy involves an impervious structural and operational work culture. For example, the President directs the execution of a given task but it is not executed. This may arise from failure to interpret the scope and purpose or simply because it is not beneficial to the implementers. It may also be attributable to poor coordination between public sector institutions. Indeed, there is a serious institutional problem of Government inter departmental access to information. This causes inordinate delay or complete unavailability of crucial information for government's planning and subsequent use. Meanwhile, departments struggle to break through institutional huddles, external parties easily access the required information by miraculously reducing delays in moving files or jumping slow moving queues for relevant signatures. Informatively, the former Attorney General (Bart Katureebe) narrates:

> As a State Attorney in 1978, I was told to go with a delegation of Uganda Airlines to purchase a Fokker Friendship aircraft. I asked for the draft contract and I was told, they will give it to you. The first time I saw the draft contract was while we were in a Hotel in Brussels, the night before we signed it. I had never seen a contract of purchase of an aircraft before! If you are buying helicopters and your team goes to look at the helicopters, that is not a legal matter, it is technical. If he comes and says I have seen the helicopters and they are okay, I would put this down in the agreement (quoted in *New Vision*, Kampala, 7 October 1998).

That narration reveals a bureaucratic problem of the line ministries' failure to disclose vital information pertaining to projects being negotiated. Such a practice negatively impacts on negotiation outcomes. This is besides involvement of individuals basing on employment status rather than expertise and experience.

There is also an appointment criteria that sometimes assumes the political correctness ideology dimension rather than proven ability. This occurs amidst a paucity of a public service culture. Public office is regarded by some as an investment for personal aggrandisement rather than offering of service. Such attitudes weaken institutional capacity thereby narrowing possibilities of getting good deals. Meritocratic recruitment guarantees minimal competence and generates an ethical and united work force that works towards institutional goals rather than self-interest. In contrast to bureaucrats enlisted through nepotism or political correctness, those recruited on merit, qualifications and experience first perform to excel while job protection comes last. These latter attributes vitally foster a culture of institutional commitment, a vital element of the institutional framework for development.

An efficient bureaucracy is a vital engine for Uganda's development, as it uniquely fits the private and public sectors. That involves rejuvenating private public business partnerships transactions through the provision of vital information on available investment opportunities. This is especially so since Uganda as a policy actively promotes private investments by privatising public enterprises and investing directly in private firms. As such, Ugandan entrepreneurs' attempts to break into the world trade framework require coordinated efforts to ensure that they are availed information on such issues as laws and standards. An effective bureaucracy would thereby end institutional hurdles in international trade, thus promoting development. As President Museveni has consistently stressed, trade rather than 'aid' is the ultimate panacea for Uganda's poverty and this can only be meaningfully realized through genuine local entrepreneurship rather than those pre-occupied with profit repatriation.

Competent bureaucracies can help individual entrepreneurs overcome coordination problems and instigate new activities. Given that the public sector was accustomed to governmental level dealings, the challenge is to adjust to accommodate work styles outside that setting. That includes a marked departure from the routine classified setting to subtle complex transactions involving a different set of actors. Instituting a culture to shape development oriented work habits and strengthen institutions is imperative. Legal and bureaucratic systems must be functioning predictably, dependably, effectively, efficiently and honestly.

Because of bureaucratic weaknesses, external debt continues to accumulate partly through sheer negligence, fraud, corruption and bribery; amidst a weak institutional framework. As debtors (accused) are financially crippled the creditor (accuser) plays judge, also determines repayment terms and from what source, hence, the near take over of political and legislative power. All this has engendered a negative legacy of 'Bichupuli' (fake deals) which has permeated Uganda's institutions to near institutionalisation of corruption. Consequently, pseudo-investors and speculators purporting to conduct genuine development related activities have hijacked the management of the economy. All this is possible, because of the institutional weaknesses. In a survey conducted in September 2003, respondents said that the process to invest or set up a business is deliberately made unnecessarily long so as to attract bribes. They said that bureaucratic systems and bottlenecks facilitate corruption. It is noteworthy that the police, who are responsible for arrests and prosecution, were singled out as the worst offenders. That weakens ethical and institutional efficiency. Corruption is glorified. An individual, who builds residential or commercial buildings using stolen public funds is praised or seen as successful. Such glorifications alongside complicity by implementation institutions epitomise serious disincentives to institutional development.

From the foregoing discussion, the executive, legislature and judiciary have to interface smoothly in the execution of their roles, without one dominating or setting hurdles for the other for the sake of development. This must rise above cultural and political constraints.

Even more importantly, the interface must refrain from unquestioningly designing policies in conformity with donor demands and obediently propagating them without a supporting institutional framework for enforcement, monitoring and respect for contractual obligations as we proceed to show.

Enforcement institutions

Judiciary

The judiciary is an important institutional framework for interpreting laws thereby setting the benchmarks for those involved in the country's development process. More than ever before, Uganda under the Movement Government boasts of a vibrant judiciary, perhaps one among the best in Africa. There is animated adjudication of civil and criminal cases, interpreting the Constitution, giving effect to its provisions, and providing expertise in interpreting laws. Institutionally, it performs other related duties in promotion of human rights, social justice and morality. Courts freely make pronouncements against the Government and interpret the Constitution which sets out the legislative process, by whom and how powers are to be exercised, even the sovereign power who made it. This represents the independence of the judiciary, a sign of a developmental state. In the case of *Bank of Uganda vs. Banco Arabe Espanol* (SCCA No 1/2001, unreported), the Supreme Court interpreted development policies and demarcated institution responsibilities in the Government institutional framework thus:

> The act amounting to frustration upon which the appellant is relying is that of government's liberalisation policy of coffee trade. By this policy both the appellant and Uganda Government lost control over the proceeds of coffee and foreign currency... it would not have been proper for the appellant to rely on frustration which was self-induced by both the borrower and the appellant's agents. Under the Bank of Uganda Statute, the appellant is supposed

to advise the government of financial and economic policies and that it also acts as government agent in financial matters. It had a duty to advise the government against the policy of liberalisation of coffee trade and more so since the appellant and the government had already committed themselves to paying the respondent out of coffee sales which had to be channelled through the appellant Bank.

The judgment was an indictment of the Bank of Uganda's institutional dereliction to advise government on development policy making and implementation. The major cause here was the panicky liberalisation to beat the donor funding conditionality deadlines. Forsaking existing contractual obligations was reminiscent of the colonial agreements and legislative frameworks carried over to the post colonial regime as vivid in Acts like that on repossession, and equally replicated in donor conditionality. That it returned to haunt the policy makers through recriminations, and inflicted an otherwise avoidable costly litigation should form the basis for proper and cautious advice. Incredibly, the projected benefits went to compensation, a burden absurdly shouldered by the poor taxpayers and not those who dictated an unconditional hurried liberalisation. The tough language in the case is a judicial reminder that in interface with the executive and legislature, deliberate breaches will not be tolerated irrespective of the source and cause. On the positive side however, the case is a reassurance that Ugandan Courts offer viable institutional avenues to remedy any reneging on contractual obligations irrespective of who is at fault. It is a reproach to any attempts to arbitrarily seek or legislate to defeat existing obligations. The interface between the executive, legislature and judiciary brought out in this case is that of promoting foreign direct investment, albeit in separate roles.

But why was this case decided differently from those involving expropriated properties, where an Act equally wantonly trampled on existing contractual obligations but was judiciary upheld? That reflects a new firmer judiciary in its interface with the executive and legislature. Rather than proffering conformist decisions as before, it this time around insisted on the executive's compliance with the Constitution's institutional framework.

Attorney-General

The procedures of Government entering into contracts are comprehensive enough to provide a beneficial institutional framework if strictly observed. The AG must mandatorily give advice on every government contract. This is intended to eliminate abuse of the process and standardise procedures. However, it is open as to the precise point in time the advice should be sought. The AG's legal advice is often sought to fulfil the constitutional 'ritual' of seeking legal advice.

Thus officials negotiate, strike deals, and then approach AG to rubber stamp them. Since these hold public offices, the law should fill the lacuna and prescribe sanctions for such errant behaviour. Such cases are many. Revelations by the AG that, 'the Foods and Beverages Limited sale agreement was signed without reference to our office', indicate a behaviour that undermines efforts to build strong institutions for good governance. The Minister of Finance conceded to the Public Accounts Committee that 'the person who signed a contract was not allowed by the Constitution to sign it' (*New Vision,* Kampala, 9 July 1998). Surprisingly, he only conceded without indicating the punishment meted out to the culprit.

Since it is the AG's opinion that goes to Court, it should be sought at the commencement of project negotiation. The policy consideration behind that institutionalised authority is the need for consistency and harmonisation of sensitive government activities. While stressing this role, the Supreme Court in *Bank of Uganda vs. Banco Arabe Espanol* (Supra) opined:

> The Attorney General is the principal legal adviser to the Government of Uganda. In consequence, nothing could be more authoritative and authentic than the opinion of the Attorney General of Uganda. The opinion of the Attorney General as authenticated by his own hand and signature regarding the Laws of Uganda and their effect or binding nature on any agreement, contract or other legal transaction should be accorded the highest respect by government and public institutions and their agents. Unless there are other agreed conditions, third parties are entitled to believe and act on that opinion without further enquiries or verifications…it is improper and untenable for the Government, the Bank of Uganda or any other public institution or body in which the Government of Uganda has of an interest, to question the correctness or validity of that opinion in so far as it affects the rights and interests of third parties. While it is true that-the Attorney General plays a dual role as Government principal legal adviser on both Political and legal matters, nevertheless, in that latter role the Attorney General is a law officer for the sole purpose of advancing the ends of justice. In this role, the Attorney General has access to all types of advice from fellow ministers who may have negotiated and authorized the signing of contracts. He has a host of qualified and experienced advisers on legal matters.

Remarkably, this judgement stresses the institutional importance of the AG both to Government as well as other parties dealing with Government. It is a censure against the culture of treating the AG as a peripheral participant best suited for proofreading, even with the amount of law involved and the strong presence of the other party's high calibre lawyers. For his part, the AG cannot play safe when deals go bad, pleading that the flaws occurred because he was not consulted.

Inspectorate of Government (IGG) (Ombudsman)

The institution of the IGG is under Article 225 (1) of the Constitution, charged with the duty of: promoting and fostering strict adherence to the rule of law and principles of natural justice in administration; eliminating and fostering the elimination of corruption, abuse of authority and of public office; promoting fair, efficient and good governance in public offices; supervising the enforcement of the Leadership Code of Conduct; investigating any act, omission, advice, decision or recommendation by a public officer or any other authority to which this article applies, taken, made, given or done in exercise of administrative functions.

The jurisdiction of the IGG coincidentally covers officers or leaders whether employed in the public service or not, and also such institutions, organisations or enterprises as Parliament may prescribe by law. The IGG has invoked this jurisdiction to significantly check institutional flaws and abuse of office, such as halting the irregular sale of Sheraton Hotel, when the Solicitor General had advised that the bid continue despite the withdrawal of one of the members in the consortium. The IGG's limitation though remains in the under staffing, overstretched jurisdiction and the over concentration on post-mortem interventions fit for other institutions like Police. As a cautionary note, it must be appreciated that monitoring institutions are also manned by human beings who can fall susceptible to the very vices they are meant to check if they are no counter mechanisms to check their workings.

Opportunely, the Constitutional Court, has held that the special powers that enable the IGG to effectively deal with cases of corruption and abuse of office and authority cannot be construed so widely to include the power to prosecute most of the offences in the Penal Code Act. This decision positively consolidated the IGG's operational scope, after taking cognisance of the dangers posed by overstretched jurisdiction on institutional efficiency and effectiveness of an understaffed and poorly remunerated institution.

Parliament

Throughout Uganda's history, legislative decisions have been politically influenced. In the case of the ruling NRM, the executive has interfaced with Parliament in closed sessions and caucuses for this purpose. Parliament has thus on occasion acted as a rubber stamp as vivid in the Preamble to the Traditional Rulers Restitution of Assets and Properties Statute of 1993:

> WHEREAS the National Resistance Army sitting in Gulu on the 3rd day of April, 1992 after discussing the return of traditional sites to the traditional groups concerned resolved (that) "it has no objection to the relevant national authority entering into discussions with the concerned traditional groups ..., PROVIDED that this does not interfere with the security of the country. "AND WHEREAS on the 30th day of April, 1993, the National Resistance

Council sitting as a political organ under the Chairmanship of His Excellency the President of Uganda, by resolution of the Council directed that certain assets and properties previously confiscated by the State...be returned in accordance with the laws of Uganda.

Three organs viz the National Resistance Army, the National Resistance Council—the Political organ and the National Resistance Council—the legislative organ clearly interfaced in their roles and this has never been questioned by the judiciary, despite court disputes involving the Statute. The legislator's categorical acknowledgement of the NRA's direct involvement in the matter was an open reminder that the military is still alive in Uganda's policy making.

In yet another incident, acting under donor deadline pressures, the Minister of Justice dryly proposed amendment of the Expropriated Properties Act, notwithstanding any other written law, including the Constitution. That reflects the fragrant passage of inconsistent laws that have been routinely nullified by the judiciary, leading to an ugly exchange with the executive and legislature, who interpret this to mean political sabotage.

The authority and functions of Parliament have since been strengthened in Article 159 of the 1995 Constitution. As the legislative and monitoring body it makes laws and oversees government actions. The Constitution empowers Parliament to make laws on any matter for the peace, order, development and good governance of Uganda and to protect the Constitution and promote democratic governance in Uganda. It checks government agreements, inquires and scrutinises government policy. It is possessed with the sanctions of impeachment in case it is the President at fault and censure if it is a cabinet Minister. Invoking that power, Parliament on 18 August 1998, suspended the privatisation process which it maintained was fraught with corruption and served to benefit a select clique of individuals. Minister Matthew Rukikaire's decision to ignore the resolution culminated in a petition to censure him from the executive, and precipitated his untimely resignation.

Parliament has unsparingly executed its mandate. As they preached the gospel of transparency as the bedrock of good governance, international lenders and their sympathisers contradictorily waved confidentiality to conceal their transactions. They argued that their dealings were a preserve of bureaucrats who were parties to the signing of contracts. But Parliament invoked its constitutional mandate to reject inequitable donor projects. In one such instance, The World Bank Country Director succumbed and agreed to engage in open, frank and constructive dialogue. (James W. Adams, World Bank Country Director, Uganda in a letter to the Minister of Finance and the Vice President and Minister of Agriculture and copied to the P/S's of Finance and Agriculture dated August 14, 1997).

That was a principal departure from the usual conditionality dictation. Diplomatically, it was a concession to break the confidentiality cap. For its part, Parliament demonstrated its institutional potential to streamline development projects to accord with people's aspirations. It was an unpalatable reminder to both local negotiators and individual donor agencies' desk officers that their institutional credibility would be tainted by sanctioning dubious deals. Above all, it demonstrated the institutional potential of Parliament to discipline erring donor officials, senior politicians and bureaucrats.

Civil Society

Civil society institutions are accorded a lot of respect and recognition. The state has harnessed the Local Government Councils (LCs) and Non Government Organisations (NGOs) as effective forums for advocacy, public consultation and dissemination of information for developmental purposes. Notwithstanding the fragility that often exists between say NGOs and politicians, there is a reasonable balance achieved between the two institutions and they complement one another on matters of development. The interface with state institutions is via the exchange of vital information collected through the networks of each.

As complimentary partners, LCs, NGOs, journalists, academics, the private sector, (professional bodies like the Alternative Dispute Resolution Forum, Uganda Law Society and Trade Unions), play a vital role in strengthening Uganda's institutional framework for development. This has assumed the form of court challenges, reportage or publication of leaks or analysis that highlight the existence of institutional problems in government functioning. This information is in turn picked up by mandated bodies such as the Director of Public Prosecutions (DPP) Police's Criminal Investigation Department (CID), Parliament, IGG, The Ministry of Ethics and Integrity and so forth to make further inquiry or analysis, leading to further action or debate. The results are evident in the strong public support anti graft Parliamentarians, NGOs and the media have received for exposing the flaws.

Suffice it to say, civil society is still at formative stages and mindful of Uganda's ugly past often treads carefully on contentious issues. Besides, government functionaries do not hesitate to tactfully exploit or manipulate its leadership to achieve selfish goals. This they achieve by denial of licenses, manipulating appointments of their protégés on NGOs Governing boards, intimidation and threats to officials' lives. The important role of NGOs in their interface with state institutions helps to promote Uganda's institutional framework for development. Their vital role surpasses the observed shortfalls, which in any case are not peculiarly exclusive to Uganda.

Conclusions

Uganda's developmental state has emerged from the Movement Government's good post war policies which have exploited Uganda's fortuity of resource endowment. However, the impediment to its full realisation still manifests in the weak institutional framework. This is mirrored in the weak policies that often lack operational safeguards, a virtue exploited by self seekers to undermine development. The implementing bureaucracy remains susceptible to social and political pressures. So, is the problem the law, the weak institutions or lack of developmental initiatives or a combination? The institutional framework appears to have been conditioned by a combination of factors, i.e., deliberate colonial policy, political manipulation and donor complacency. As a result, Uganda's legal profession has remained relatively parochial while its best clients have become increasingly global. That is a serious limitation that needs serious training and exposure. Likewise, the training curriculum should emphasise the area of institutional development, which has hitherto received little coverage.

The disregard of the law, legal institutions and lawyers in policy formulation and implementation is unethical. The processes need harmonising to develop strong institutions as mis-coordination abets squandering of funds in inefficient programmes. Professional incompetence, institutional corruption, collusion and the failure of leadership apparent in some senior officials and politicians need to be seriously addressed. Physical insecurity, bureaucratic inefficiency and corruption are not only inimical to the development of a stable society, but are also serious disincentives to investment. The Government must strengthen the monitoring and enforcement institutions in performance of their roles, increase their participation in initiating, planning and implementing development policies; secure long-term financial resources to undertake sustainable developmental intervention; and set up an effective and efficient mechanism for inter-departmental cooperation. For posterity, an agency to guide, periodically monitor and advise the Government, independently co-ordinate and control policy implementation should be set up by Statute.

Privatising enterprises to investors from and operating within a diversity of jurisdictions presaged a growing number of legal areas demanding rich and cross-border expertise – property rights, taxation, land, the environment, procurement, antitrust, employment law, pensions, International arbitration, and so on. Privatisation entrenched the capitalist system with its associated characteristics. It is thus inconceivable that its vanguards never alongside instituted those laws to check the negative economic effects triggered by privatisation.

The rising phenomenon of same persons acquiring numerous entities points to the emergence of monopolies. Yet, this should have been forestalled by introducing anti trust and competition laws to protect consumer interests and check their negative economic effects. This will help to instil crucial local skills for fresh graduates joining government service.

Finally the AG's office is not and should not be used as an instrument of defence for self-seekers' last minute manoeuvres. The Attorney General must enforce his constitutional mandate by participating in preparation, negotiation, procurement, validating and adjudicating on civil claims. This must be linked with policy formulating organs to ensure harmonisation. Where his advice is not sought or is ignored, transactions so entered should be nullified and perpetrators brought to book. Mere lamentation and endless pronouncements on how the AG's advice is ignored, is a culpable admission of failure to execute a constitutional duty and therefore incompetence that merits automatic resignation.

6

The Institutional Framework of the Developmental State in Botswana

David Sebudubudu

Botswana is the longest surviving multiparty democracy in Africa, and one with developmental aspects. It has achieved remarkable economic growth from 1966 through 1990 (Leftwich 1995; Matsheka and Botlhomilwe 2000). For instance, Botswana's rate of economic growth during the period 1965 to 1980 and 1980 to 1989 was 13.9 percent and 11.3 percent respectively (Matsheka and Botlhomilwe 2000: 41). This rapid economic growth was largely based on minerals, mainly diamonds. Many analysts also attribute this rapid growth to good economic management (Tsie 1996). Wiseman (1995) underscores good policy preferences and a state formation that was not wasteful. It is this good economic performance and an efficient state structure that make analysts classify Botswana as a 'developmental state'. Leftwich defines developmental states as:

> States whose politics have concentrated sufficient power, autonomy and capacity at the centre to shape, pursue and encourage the achievement of explicit developmental objectives, whether by establishing and promoting the conditions and direction of economic growth, or by organising it directly, or a varying combination of both (1995:401).

These are states that are ideologically oriented to use resources to pursue development. Moreover, Leftwich (1995) identifies six main aspects characteristic of a developmental state: a committed elite, relative autonomy, a powerful, competent and insulated bureaucracy, a weak and subordinated civil society, effective management of non-state economic interests; and repression, legitimacy and performance. The Botswana state meets five of these features (Tsie 1998), except the last one. Even then, Tsie (1998: 14) contends that the legitimacy of the Botswana state has never really been seriously questioned. This is the case because since independence, successive free multi-party elections have been held whose results the contestants have generally accepted.

In one way or the other, the Botswana state fits in the category of a developmental state. Although the Botswana state has helped to create an environment that facilitates economic growth, development in Botswana has been state-driven since independence through institutional structures such as the Ministry of Finance and Development Planning (MFDP). Economic development in Botswana was not only 'state-led' but 'state-directed' as well (Charlton 1991 quoted in Leftwich 1995: 412), and 'with the MFDP serving as its economic high command, generating policy' and playing an active role in economic planning (Leftwich 1995: 412). As Leftwich notes 'the political purposes and institutional structures of developmental states have been developmentally-driven, while their developmental objectives have been politically-driven' (1995: 401). In Botswana, not only was there a devotion to develop the country by the political leadership but this 'developmental commitment [was] matched with institutional capacity' (Maundeni 2001: 18). Edge (1998) traces the character of the Botswana state as a leading apparatus in economic development to independence when the first National Development Plan was put into place. The National Development Plan as Edge (1998: 334) put it, 'placed the [Botswana] state at the centre of economic and social planning, primarily because no other sources of development were evident or readily available. By planning within the market economy, government policy has tended to influence the direction of government expenditure during the planning period while providing an environment in which the private sector activity can thrive'. In short, the Botswana state attaches a lot of importance to planning yet it allows the private sector room to function. The 1970–1975 National Development Plan noted that:

> The government wishes to stress its belief in the necessity of planning the social and economic development of the nation. Available resources are limited and the problems so great that only by careful planning can these resources be put to their most effective use. A rationally planned and guided economy is the objective of government policy. However, a balance must be struck where private initiative has ample scope within the general confines laid down by government. It is government's duty to set forth clearly its objectives accordingly, and to assist the private sector in every way consistent with the attainment of these goals (Republic of Botswana 1970: 11).

Such declarations have brought positive benefits in the case of Botswana as they enjoyed the support of a relatively non-corrupt state structure. Wallis (1989) notes two main points that were of critical importance in ensuring that Botswana's planning process was effective: 'first, the Botswana case suggests that political commitment and support for planning makes a substantial difference. The First President (Seretse Khama) and his senior ministers showed greater support for development planning than has often been the case elsewhere. Secondly, planning and budgeting have been closely linked' (Wallis 1989: 52). It is this close connection between planning and budgeting, backed by a committed political state structure, that is missing in most other African countries (Wallis 1989). What is distinctive about Botswana is that the political leadership also realized that planning on its own without proper implementation was not adequate. This was clearly articulated by the country's president when it initially opted for planning. The president categorically stated that 'my government is aware, too, that planning by itself is not enough, that efficient implementation of the Plan is even more important and [the government promised that this responsibility is carried out] ....the energies of the nation must now be devoted to the economic and social development of the country' (Raphaeli et al 1984 quoted in Wallis 1989: 71). This demonstrates that the political leadership was not only committed to planning but it also had the will to direct and ensure that National Development Plans are executed.

The other factor that differentiates developmental states from most states is low levels of corruption. Leftwich contests that 'all developmental states have been led by determined elites, which have been relatively incorruptible, at least by comparison with the pervasive corruption' found in most developing countries especially in Africa (1996: 285). This description fits the Botswana state as it is not only led by a committed elite but has also avoided some of the problems—such as corruption—that other post-colonial African states have suffered from. In Botswana, the importance of the state, the pressure for public resources to be distributed and clientelism have not created corruption that is out of control. We suggest a number of reasons for this. First, Botswana is relatively ethnically homogenous. Its economy grew steadily since independence, and its population is also small compared to most African states (Holm 2000). A small population means the size of the political class is small. As a result, there is less competition amongst elites in accessing resources. Moreover, a small population has meant that the state has had to face relatively less political pressure or demands. For Wallis, Botswana 'is a small country with...relatively simple issues to resolve' (1989: 72). Although the demands on the state have been moderate, mineral revenues have strengthened the ability of the state to respond to demands placed on it (Wiseman 1977). As a result 'there is an absence of overloading on the input side of government which has also contributed to political stability and to the maintenance of the multi-party-system' (ibid. 77). The state was able to satisfy elite demands and to some extent mass demands. Thus 'the government [of Botswana] has managed to spread the benefits of [mineral led] growth widely enough to keep the population reasonably satisfied' (UNDP 1998:48). Riley asserts that Botswana possesses some unique features that are lacking in much of contemporary Africa. These features include amongst others 'political stability, sustained high economic growth rates whose benefits are reasonably spread, a relatively unified elite committed to foreign investment and maintaining public integrity' (2000: 153). Even then, in the absence of a 'conscious and disciplined leadership, no amount of diamond revenues would have been sufficient to make Botswana an African miracle' (Samatar 1999: 188). In this way, it is difficult to appreciate how this miracle was generated without understanding the critical role performed by the leadership (Samatar 1999).

Second, Botswana has ensured a moderate reputation of good political economic management since independence; a characteristic dissimilar to much of Africa. Corruption and patronage politics have not been at the heart of Botswana politics. Good management did not only limit corruption but also limited patronage and clientelism. For example, in most African states the public service is used, as a major source of patronage and this is not the case in Botswana because entrance into the public service is mainly based on qualification and merit. 'As in other developmental states, the bureaucracy in Botswana is recruited, and promoted on the basis of merit' (Tsie 1998: 13). This is not however to say the public service in Botswana is free of patronage, especially with regard to senior appointments and in devising policies that favour the ruling elite.

Third, reasonable levels of corruption in Botswana are attributed to the nature of the ruling elite that assumed power at independence (Holm and Molutsi 1992). They were relatively wealthy even before assuming power because they were engaged in cattle production. And as such 'this class did not necessarily see the state as a source of self-enrichment' (Tsie 1998: 13). Therefore, rising to power was not a means of attaining wealth but to gain influence.

Nevertheless, the developmental challenges that Botswana faced at independence necessitated that the state took deliberate decisions and actions to drive economic development from the start. Thus, it is in this sense that the Botswana state has since independence played an active part in the economy through a number of institutions that were meant to stimulate economic growth and development.

Taking a leading role in economic development by the state from the start was necessary as Botswana was one of the poorest countries in the world with a per capita income of around US$80. It is this active participation in the economy, through these institutions, that partly transformed Botswana from being one of the poorest countries in the world to a middle-income country as per World Bank rankings. This was made possible by the infusion of finance and development planning into one powerful ministry, the Ministry of Finance and Development Planning (MFDP). This linked government revenues with development projects and thus only projects in the national plan were budgeted for. Development planning seeks to accomplish the national objectives of economic independence, social justice, sustainable development and rapid economic growth (Republic of Botswana 1997). Thus, planning by the Botswana state 'is intended to ensure that maximum benefit is derived from the limited financial resources available to Government by prioritising policies, programmes and projects. [It] also allows

Government to set targets against which its performance can be objectively evaluated' (Republic of Botswana 1997: 85). This is what distinguishes Botswana from most other African countries. It is these institutions that were established to facilitate development that I now turn to.

The Ministry of Finance and Development Planning (MFDP)

Developmental states have pilot institutions that direct and plan economic affairs. As Leftwich puts it 'economic co-ordination and development in [developmental states] has been [and continues to be] managed by specific institutions, whose task has been to organise the critical interactions between state and economy. These have been the economic bureaucracies, the core centres of strategic economic direction [in these states]' (1995: 411-412). What distinguishes these institutions from planning institutions found elsewhere in most developing countries 'is their power, authority, technical competence and insulation in shaping the fundamental thrusts of development policy' (ibid. 286). The Ministry of Finance and Development Planning (MFDP) in Botswana is one such agency. The MFDP is a key institution that has played a pivotal role (and continues to do so) in Botswana's developmental process. It is not only 'the institutional brain of the economic brain of the economic policy-making process' (Samatar 1999: 85) but 'the institutional nerve center' of the Botswana state (ibid. 82). It is the institution which plans, coordinates, monitors and ensures that projects that are being implemented are not only in the National Development Plan but have been budgeted for. Not only does it oversee approved plans but it also offers economic advice and information to government departments (Republic of Botswana 1970). In this sense, 'no expenditure can be incurred on a project which has not been included in the plan', and when ministries submit projects for inclusion in the plan, it is often emphasised that ministries should ensure that costs are not only reasonable but be within the government financial constraints (Wallis 1989: 2). This is made possible because the Ministry of Finance and Development Planning is run by professionals who are trained and have the expertise in economic policy making. More importantly, because the country lacked the required expertise at independence, 'considerable emphasis [was] placed upon the recruitment of a highly competent economist cadre for the planning organisation', and to ensure this, 'there [was] a relatively high dependence on expatriates' (Wallis 1989: 52). Similarly, Taylor noted that 'expatriates were retained (as opposed to much of the rest of Africa) in order to help train up a local but competent and educated civil service' (2003: 4). That is, the process of localisation was not rushed at independence. And 'through effective use of expatriate technical assistance (TA) and steady development of local capabilities, the country has achieved a remarkable record of economic planning and management' (Wallis 1989: 52). Interconnected to this, 'was the effort made to ensure that a strong policy-analysis capability was established, together with a planning staff which was continuously involved in budgetary and economic planning' (ibid. 52). Through these efforts, the Botswana state was able to build capacity within key ministries and line ministries, thus, resulting in a bureaucracy that was competent, efficient and largely non-corrupt. In this way, Botswana largely avoided some of the pitfalls (such as lack of capacity) that negatively affected planning in most African countries (Wallis 1989).

To demonstrate the importance the Botswana state attaches to this Ministry, traditionally it has been in the Office of the Vice President (Wallis 1989; Taylor 2003). Taylor states that 'such a Ministry and its close links to the Executive has secured a balance between development planning and budgeting, as well as strengthening the capacity to implement national goals and demonstrating a commitment to economic development' (2003: 4). Moreover, the Ministry's close links with the executive did not only protect the bureaucracy from societal or public pressure but also gave rise to a more or less autonomous, strong and effective bureaucracy (Taylor 2003). Somolekae makes a related point. She observes that 'Botswana's bureaucracy has remained one of the most effective and corruption-free in Africa' and the institution enjoys 'far greater institutional autonomy than its counterparts elsewhere in the region' (1993: 119). This is unheard of in most African countries where bureaucratic institution were 'neutralised' immediately after independence. This institutional autonomy has brought positive results for Botswana. Leftwich argues that in developmental states 'both the developmental determination of the elite and the relative autonomy of the state have helped to shape very powerful, highly competent and insulated bureaucracies with authority to direct and manage the broad shape of economic and social development' (1996: 286). In reference to Japan's developmental state, Chalmers Johnson states that 'the first element of the [developmental] model is the existence of a small, inexpensive, but elite state bureaucracy staffed by the best managerial talent available in the system' (1999: 38).

With respect to Botswana, Holm points out that 'lack of democratic control over the state bureaucracy has been central in Botswana's development' as 'top bureaucrats excluded elected politicians from most key decisions' (1996: 97). This was possible as the bureaucracy was secluded from political intrusion by the country's presidents, Seretse Khama and Quett Masire, and politicians were instructed to deal with senior bureaucrats, who were equally directed by the presidents not to give any political favours (Holm 1996). And as Holm puts it 'the leadership of the Botswana state, namely permanent secretaries and the first two presidents, have taken advantage of the state's autonomy to implement an ambitious development agenda' (ibid. 110). This development agenda has been greatly successful as Botswana's civil service has guided and produced one of the best economic growths in the third world (Holm 1996). Thus, economic development in Botswana was not only steered but also influenced by the bureaucracy. Somolekae argues that the policy making process in Botswana 'reveals the extent to which the bureaucracy is influential in initiating policy and determining its final content' and more often than not 'by the time [it] goes out to be scrutinised by the political leadership and the general public, its major form and content have been thoroughly defined' (1993: 117). This was the case as the political leadership lacked the required expertise needed in policy making and 'the bureaucracy was the only developed organ of the state' (ibid. 117). It is in this context that the bureaucracy was given such an influential role. The Botswana story shows that the MFDP was mainly successful in its role of a 'high command' as it had the expertise and capacity to perform this critical role. Institutional competence in the MFDP was realized through the establishment of planning units which were manned by qualified professionals (Samatar 1999).

In an effort to expand the poor manufacturing base it inherited at independence, the Botswana state introduced a number of measures to encourage or promote industrial development or investment. Such measures entailed the introduction of agencies and policies such the Botswana Development Corporation (BDC), the Financial Assistance Policy (FAP), Citizen Entrepreneurial Development Agency (CEDA) and the Botswana Export Development and Investment Authority (BEDIA). These efforts are examined below.

Botswana Development Corporation (BDC)

The Botswana Development Corporation (BDC) is the principal national organisation that was introduced in 1970 through an Act of parliament to promote industrial development. 'For a developing country [such as Botswana] the creation of an industrial development agency is usually considered to be crucial to economic expansion', as 'industrialisation is usually perceived as a measure of the level of a country's economic development' (Simukonda 1998: 55). The BDC needs to be understood in this context. It was established as 'the country's main financing agency for commercial and industrial development' in which 'the Government of Botswana owns 100 percent of the issued share capital' (Botswana Development Corporation 2002: 2). And its 'primary objectives are to develop infrastructure and create employment by providing capital to fund investment and economic growth' (ibid. 7). Thus, it identifies business enterprises that involve both domestic and foreign investors and 'participates in financing of the projects with some combination of equity and loan funds' (Republic of Botswana 1997: 152). The National Development Plan 8 1997/98–2002/03 states that the functions of the BDC are: 'to create and sustain employment opportunities; to enhance economic diversification; to promote investment; to encourage citizen participation in business ventures; and to develop and enhance management and technical skills of Botswana' (Republic of Botswana 1997: 12). To facilitate these, BDC provides assistance in the form of short and long term loans, investment advice, management services and factory buildings and funds viability studies (Republic of Botswana 1997).

The Financial Assistance Policy (FAP) and Citizen Entrepreneurial Development Agency (CEDA)

In 1982, the Botswana state introduced the Financial Assistance Policy (FAP) as a way of reducing over-dependence on minerals. This was not only aimed at diversifying the economy but also to boost employment prospects (Republic of Botswana 1985). This was possible as the financial situation of government had improved because of an increase in mineral receipts. FAP provided 'direct financial assistance to both existing and new enterprises' (Chipasula and Miti 1989: 77). Projects assisted under FAP fell under three categories: small, medium and large. In supporting both new and expanding projects, FAP had three major aspects to it. Firstly, government money was to go towards projects that demonstrated a realistic prospect of generating benefits that offset the expenses. Secondly, financial support was to be provisional, at most lasting five years. And lastly, government financial help was to go to ventures that were in keeping with its goals of promoting job creation and expanding the economic base (Republic of Botswana 1985).

FAP had some successes. It was able to create 'a large number of new and small enterprises, expanding established ones, increasing unskilled employment substantially, and expanding opportunities for women in these sectors' (Samatar 1999: 187). Notwithstanding their good intentions, these efforts or policies have greatly failed to encourage manufacturing and to diversify the Botswana economy (Edge 1998; Taylor 2003). Most FAP funded projects were not successful because of a number of factors: tough competition, limitations of the market, misuse of funds by beneficiaries, failure of potential beneficiaries to raise their contributions towards the project, lack of raw materials in the rural areas as well as their growing costs and the poor quality of the products (Chipasula and Miti 1989:78/9). Perhaps one other reason why it has largely failed was that it lacked the institutional capacity to administer projects it supported.

Following the National Conference on Citizen Economic Empowerment in 1999 and the fourth evaluation of FAP in 2000, the Citizen Entrepreneurial Development Agency (CEDA) was established in 2001, and it took over the financial responsibilities of FAP as well as projects that were administered under FAP and the Small, Medium and Micro Enterprises (SMMEs). CEDA, which is an autonomous private organisation, is answerable to government through a Board of Directors. Unlike FAP, CEDA provides loans (with subsidised interests) not grants to possible projects. CEDA also aims to expand the economic base (diversify the economy) and to promote employment and citizen entrepreneurship. It also supports businesses that have the reasonable prospect of being viable. Since its establishment 'CEDA had approved 792 applications, amounting to P421.1 million, while disbursements for approved applications stood at P247.7 million' by the end of December 2002 (Republic of Botswana 2003:4). Out of the approved projects, 45 percent are in the service sector, 25 percent in retail, 13 in agriculture, 10 percent in manufacturing and another 7 percent in property development. Once fully functional, these projects are likely to generate more than 7000 jobs. CEDA also engages private sector consultants to help to train, monitor and mentor those who have been assisted. It is thought that this will provide citizens with the required business skills to run businesses (Republic of Botswana 2003). It is too early to make a conclusive assessment of CEDA as it is still in its infancy. But one wonders if CEDA has yet the necessary institutional capacity to carry out its mandate.

Botswana Export Development and Investment Authority (BEDIA)

BEDIA, which is an autonomous entity, is another agency that was established in 1997, but started to function in 1998 to encourage investment flows into the country, especially export-oriented ventures that are necessary to create employment opportunities and to diversify Botswana's economy. It seeks to vigorously promote 'manufacturing activities that can utilise the country's raw materials such as leather, jewellery, glass and beef by-products, as well as service industries, like information technology and tourism' (Republic of Botswana 2002: 18). Moreover, it also plays an active role in promoting Botswana's products (ibid.: 2002). The establishment of such an agency is opportune as investment promotion is highly competitive. In trying to execute its mandate, BEDIA has faced the challenge of 'being an integral part of the country's programme for economic diversification through the development of an efficient export sector' (BEDIA Annual Report 2003: 8). BEDIA has also had a problem concerning 'the quality of local companies and lack of information' which render 'it difficult to embark on an aggressive export promotion strategy as the range of products manufactured locally is [not only] limited' but companies do not have the capacity to deliver quality goods at economical prices as well (Mokhawa 2003: 58). Despite these, the Africa Growth and Opportunities Act which allows products manufactured in Botswana to enter the American market without any duties levied on them offers some ephemeral opening that BEDIA seeks to utilise (BEDIA Annual Report 2003).

The Directorate on Corruption and Economic Crime (DCEC)

One factor that attracts long-term foreign investment into a country is low levels of corruption. In order to reassure foreign investors and to ensure that corruption remains under control, Botswana has established the Directorate on Corruption and Economic Crime (DCEC), a specialised anti-corruption agency.

Corruption in developmental states has not been destructive to development (Leftwich 1995). Leftwich notes that developmental states do not 'manifest the corrupt, corrosive and pervasive patrimonialism of non-developmental states' (1995: 407). This is the case in Botswana. Compared to most African states, Botswana has experienced low levels of corruption since independence, owing to a relatively good record of governance since independence (UNDP 1998).

Although cases of corruption have been reported in recent years, corruption in Botswana does not affect the whole political system, as is the case in most African countries. Tsie (1996) observed that in Botswana the state did not develop into the one and only vehicle for amassing wealth. In an effort to ensure that Botswana remains the least corrupt country in Africa (as per Transparency International rankings) and that it continues to attract foreign investment, DCEC was established in 1994 to nip corruption in the bud. This was as a result of a series of corruption scandals in the early 1990s.

The government created DCEC for the following reasons:

1. To demonstrate that it is keen to reduce corruption because it is a danger to social, political and economic development.
2. Despite Transparency International's Corruption Perception Index which considered Botswana as the least corrupt country in Africa, corruption was a danger to Botswana.
3. Botswana was addressing a legitimacy problem. Following the three Presidential Commissions of Inquiry, the government wanted to address the problem of public perception and apprehension.
4. It wanted to ensure business confidence, including the reassurance of foreign investors and aid donors, that Botswana is a place where investors can invest their money without any fear of it being abused or of them losing it.
5. The existing legislation and resources were inadequate in the face of emerging cases of corruption.

DCEC, which is a replica of the Independent Commission Against Corruption (ICAC) in Hong Kong, fights corruption through a three pronged strategy: investigation, crime prevention and public education. Moreover, in terms of section 6 of the DCEC Act, it was conferred with extensive powers to investigate corruption and economic crime (Republic of Botswana 1994). The creation of DCEC was necessary as corruption is difficult to tackle once it is out of control. However, the Directorate has been faced with a number of problems and criticisms since its inception, that include lack of autonomy, and this casts doubt on its legitimacy and public reputation. Despite this, its establishment has made corruption in Botswana a public issue.

Conclusion

Botswana's relative success story demonstrates the importance of politics in promoting development. Despite its poor manufacturing base at independence, the Botswana state has played a central role in promoting development. One way has been through the establishment of institutions such as those discussed above which requires a state that is ideologically oriented to commit and use resources to pursue development. In an effort to demonstrate the significance of politics in development, Leftwich noted that 'for while no one would deny the importance of institutions and rules, it is political processes which bring them into being and, crucially, which sustain them' (1996: 20). Botswana is in this sense a showcase. The commitment by the state has not only nurtured but also directed key institutions such as the Ministry of Finance and Development Planning to ensure that policies are directed at development. This has put Botswana well ahead of most African countries. Its record exemplifies that the realization of economic development in a country is dependent 'on the autonomy, legitimacy, and discipline of its leaders and institutions' (Samatar 1999: 188). However, the Botswana story is of course not without problems. The Botswana state faces a number of challenges, such as poverty, inequalities, over-dependence on diamonds and unemployment, which are a threat to its developmental achievements. These contradictions need to be addressed without fail.

7

Decentralisation and African Developmental States: Experiences from Uganda and Botswana

Neema Murembe, Gladys Mokhawa & David Sebudubudu

Decentralisation is defined as the transfer of legal, administrative and political authority to plan, make decisions and manage public functions and services from central government to local government units (Nsibambi 1998). At some level, it has been conceived as 'a natural, indispensable counterpart to pluralistic democracy: it extends the work of local democracy and fulfils democratic aspirations' (Reddy 1999). In the post-colonial era, the state in both Botswana and Uganda took on the responsibility of development intervention—local government institutions were transformed from general administrative structures to become development institutions as well (besides roles pertaining to general law and order functions). Their portfolio of responsibilities was thus broadened quite considerably after independence—and the management of this has obviously varied within the two countries. In recent years, decentralisation strategies have been advanced as one way of providing solutions to some of the problems experienced in delivery processes.

Decentralisation therefore is significant in development planning in the sense that it facilitates the formulation and implementation of development plans, securing people's participation so that greater attention can be given to the needs and priorities of the local population. In short, decentralisation is any act through which a central government formally transfers powers to actors and institutions at lower levels in a political administration and territorial hierarchy. This means the local level acts on behalf of the central government; strengthening state capacity in service delivery to the people.

Rondnelli (1984) identifies four distinct forms of decentralisation, depending on the degree of autonomy, amount of power sanctioned and resources and functions delivered to local government to manage their affairs:

a) De-concentration – a transfer of power to local administrative offices of central government (Power at districts).
b) Devolution – a transfer of power to sub national political power entities (power at regional level).
c) Delegation – a transfer of power to statutory or corporate bodies for example councils, boards or commissions.
d) Privatisation – a transfer of power and responsibility to private entities, for example companies, NGOs, and individuals.

Whether marginally or in totality, the above are evident in planning for development, provision and management of public or social services such as education, roads, water and sanitation facilities, construction of health centres and employment distribution. In an attempt to achieve this, Uganda and Botswana have applied several strategies (to differing degrees). Decentralisation has been part of this. The chapter starts with the case of Uganda and it is this that we now turn to.

The case of Uganda

The Constitution of the Republic of Uganda provides for decentralisation as a system of local government. Article 176(1b) of the Local Government Act, 1997, stipulates that decentralisation shall be the principle applying to all levels of local government and in particular from higher to lower government units, to ensure peoples' participation and democratic control in decision-making.

The decentralisation policy currently under implementation was launched in a major presidential policy statement on 2 October 1992 (Tukahebwa 1998). In 1995, a new constitution provided for the sovereignty of the people, the devolution of powers to popularly elected local governments and for basic freedoms and liberties underpinned by the commitment to the rule of law and the protection of human rights.

Accordingly, the long-term aim of the decentralisation programme in Uganda has been to build a more democratic government that is responsive and accountable to the people. It focuses on promoting capacity building at the local level and to introduce local ownership of resources, power, plans and decision-making (Lengseth 1996; Cheema and Rondnelli 1983).

The essence of decentralisation in Uganda is captured in the underlying objectives of the programme namely:

1. To transfer real power to the district and thus reduce the load on the 'remote' and under-resourced central government officials, who are often remote in

terms of geographical distance and frequently unknown to the local people in terms of language, culture, interests and values.
2. To bring political and administrative control of services to the point where they are actually delivered and thus reduce competition for power at the centre and improve accountability and effectiveness in service delivery.
3. To free local managers and administrators from central constraints and thus allow them to develop organisational structures tailored to suit local circumstances.
4. To improve financial accountability by establishing a clear link between payment of taxes and the provision of services they finance, such as infrastructure development.
5. To restructure government machinery in order to make the administration of the country more efficient and effective, thus reducing bureaucratic procedures that sometimes complicate and delay decision making.
6. To create a democracy that will bring about more efficiency and productivity in the state machinery through involvement of the people at all levels (Decentralization Secretariat 1993).

In all, decentralisation is officially aimed at creating a local government system that is democratic, participatory, and development-oriented. This indicates that the system empowers communities 'to take charge of their own destiny through local institutions of self governance and resource mobilization' (Nielson 1996:2).

Historical development of decentralisation in Uganda

Decentralisation is not strange to Uganda; it has its roots in the historical development of the country. Before the arrival of the colonialists, the local area had kingdoms and settlements. Among the kingdoms, there was Buganda which was a highly centralised monarchy but with semi-decentralised structures of '*Ssaza*' (county) '*Gombolola*', (sub-county) '*Muluka*' (parish) and '*Byalo*' (village). This structure was headed by chiefs who were determined by the Kabaka, whom he changed as he so wished.

When the colonialists assumed authority over Uganda in 1894, they used Buganda as a model and replicated its administrative structure to other areas in the country. The whole country was transformed into villages, parishes, sub-counties, counties—all of which formed kingdoms. These units had powers to collect revenue, manage their communities and implement government policies on behalf of the British. This was known as 'indirect rule'. But this was not decentralisation per se as it practised politics of patronage with no empowerment of the local people to make autonomous decisions.

The 1962 independence constitution virtually maintained the system of local government inherited from the colonial period. Buganda enjoyed devolved powers with a federal status and other semi federal kingdoms, such as the Ankore and

Busoga kingdoms, enjoyed decentralised powers only in that these kingdoms maintained a patronage relationship with the central government. For example, these kingdoms had powers to raise revenue through taxes, draw and implement budgets to provide services. Central government funded these kingdoms to provide services, but continued to interfere in matters of the district councils, such as administration and accountability. This situation remained in place until 1966 when the constitution was abrogated and replaced by the 1967 republican constitution that centralised all the powers and halted the decentralisation dream.

Under the infamous Idi Amin regime, the constitution was suspended, parliament abolished and district councils dissolved. Centralisation was the norm, continuing throughout the post-Amin, pre-Museveni period. The NRM government (post-1986) however brought a difference in the system of administration. Local Administrations were called Resistance Councils, a hierarchical structure of councils and committees that stretched from the village up to the District. This was a total break from the past and the hitherto authoritarian tendencies of local chiefs were significantly undermined. It is to these councils that powers, functions and responsibilities of the local government have been decentralised. Resistance councils were later named Local Councils.

In Uganda, decentralisation was cemented by the 1995 constitution that stipulated that Uganda was to be governed in a decentralised form of local government. In the 1997 Act it was provided that administrative units would be based on, in rural areas, the county, parish and village; and in urban areas, on parishes or wards and divisions. A council at each level of the administrative unit was envisioned. At the village level all persons of eighteen years of age or above residing in that village are council members. An executive committee of nine people is elected. The village elects a chairman who then nominates six executive members as vice-chair, general-secretary, secretary for finance, secretary for security, secretary for production and environmental protection, and secretary for information, education and mobilisation.

Each parish elects two councillors one of whom must be a woman elected by all the people in the parish who are above 18 years. The second councillor can either be a man or a woman. Both councillors can be women but not men. The election is done by secret ballot. The District Council is a powerful local government unit. All sub-counties in the district elect councillors. Youths and people with disabilities meet and elect two councillors each. As provided in the Local Government Act, the district is powerful as district councils have powers to make laws not inconsistent with the constitution or any other laws made by the legislature. This strengthens the state capacity to be effective in solving local people's problems.

Financial management of local governments

The 1997 Local Government Act defines the procedures and explains the means of revenue collections, distribution and accountability of expenses. District councils prepare development plans incorporating the plans of lower levels of Local Government for submission to the National Planning Authority. This is supposed to ensure that the needs of the people are planned for right from the national level. The district is the intermediary unit for effective co-ordination of services to the people.

The 1995 constitution gave local government powers to levy and collect tax. Indeed, local government have powers to levy, charge collect and appropriate fees and taxes in accordance with any law enacted by parliament, although no tax shall be imposed except under authority of parliament. I argue that implementation of these articles gives Uganda aspects of a developmental state in the sense that it has in place an effective and competent bureaucracy that is able to monitor and even evaluate the taxation policies and procedures. And these resources are used, albeit unevenly, to promote development within the country. Of course, local government revenue collections are a mere 8 percent of total income: 92 percent comes from the central government as grants. But it should be pointed out that this financial support from the central government to the district is not meant to patronise them, but to give them the required support in order to competently deliver services to the people.

District local revenue is collected at the sub-county level and as earlier mentioned, this is only 8 percent of the total district revenue. This 8 percent is interpreted as 100 percent of locally generated revenue; 65 percent of this revenue is retained at the sub-county and 35 percent is transferred to the district. The remaining 65 percent at the sub-county is made 100 percent and distributed as follows; 5 percent is transferred to the county, 5 percent to the parish and 25 percent to village councils. This means that the sub-county retains 65 percent.

Strengths of decentralisation in Uganda

Decentralisation can be seen as one of the cornerstones of Uganda's governance and demystifies central power by bringing it closer to people at the grassroots (Makara 2000; Oyugi 2000; Fofana 1997: Tukahebwa 1998; Chikulo 2000). This is what Uganda has experienced since 1986 and it can be argued that decentralisation has helped Uganda to overcome its authoritarian and dictatorial legacy (Manor 1999: 85). In Uganda, it is important to note that the exploitation of the appointed local chiefs, which had lingered on since colonialism, was broken by decentralisation through the introduction of elected local councils, which has also provided an opportunity for marginalised groups such as people with disabilities, women and youths to present their views and participate in public affairs. Seats are reserved for these groups in local councils. In regard to this,

Makara (2000: 89) contends that decentralisation has gender sensitive aspects and empowers women, while Manor (1999: 84) points out that decentralisation facilitates fairness to women. In other words, decentralisation is all-inclusive and from this perspective can be seen to be developmental.

Decentralisation has also given opportunities to citizens to access channels of decision-making. These channel includes local councils where citizens can therefore articulate their interests and demands to public officials. The issues of local communities can easily be addressed on the political agenda and considered in the decision-making process. Obviously, the system is not perfect, but such access can be seen to indicators of good governance, a characteristic of development. This is further bolstered by the improved resource mobilisation that decentralisation has brought; most districts have realized sharp increments (as big as 350 percent of original funds) in a very short while. For example, Iganga district's income rocketed from 300 million Uganda shillings in 1994 (out of taxations, signing of agreements, trade permits, tenders licences and court fees etc) to 1 billion shillings in 1995 (Jubilee Plus-Uganda 1999: 7). Because people have seen that their money is put to good use, through provision of education, security, the development of infrastructure and employment opportunities, Ugandans are today more willing to pay taxes than before due to evident returns.

Furthermore, decentralisation has led to improved service delivery, mainly in areas such as road maintenance and infrastructure development. Local leaders are mandated to locate services and the system has effectively integrated isolated communities into regional economies. There is effective monitoring and evaluation in implementing development projects. Narrowing down gaps in accessibility to social amenities and bringing social services nearer to the people is also a feature of decentralisation. It has improved accountability of the public services—for instance, incomes and expenditure at sub-county level are displayed on notice boards for the taxpayers to view and comment. This is one of the key features of a 'developmental state'—having an effective and competent system which is able to deliver services, and even evaluating system that is accountable to the people.

Decentralisation has also improved performance through building local government's capacity to plan, implement, monitor and evaluate their own development projects basing on their respective unique circumstances. Because of decentralisation, citizens participate in planning and management of their own affairs. They are enabled to locate priority areas and design appropriate strategies to implement them. As local needs are channelled to the central government, there is closer contact between government officials and the local population, hence facilitation to the formulation of more realistic and effective plans.

As a development policy, therefore, decentralisation has turned into a blessing in managing development and projects efficiently and effectively from the centre to lower levels in terms of planning and control of development activities. Administrative performance, transparency, accountability and legitimacy have all been arguably realized in Uganda. Locally elected leaders are generally more responsible and accountable to the electorate because it has powers to recall their representative or leaders. Local councils act as 'watch-dogs' over civil servants working in their areas. This minimises abuse of office, corruption and embezzlement of public fund.

This of course is not to overlook problems. There is currently a lack of consciousness and understanding of the roles and responsibilities of executive members at the different levels introduced by decentralisation. Elected local chairpersons are often in dispute with appointed civil servants over roles. At the same time, citizens frequently do not know that it is their role or do not have the capacity to demand and put pressure on their leaders to deliver. Furthermore, local councils have the challenge of preparing their own budget, yet they frequently do not have the skills. The required qualification to be the chairman or on the council is only form four and no academic qualification is asked for at the lower councils, as long as one is a citizen of Uganda, illiterate or not!

Threats to decentralisation

It is clear from experience that with resources, power and prestige there must be struggles and competition. This affects the benefits of decentralisation. In Uganda, decentralisation under the NRM may partly be explained as a check and measure against the demands of federalism. It is however pertinent to add that it has taken a new turn in being used for political campaigns and election purposes, hence the mushrooming of districts like Kanungu, Kyenjojo, Yumbe, Nakapiripirit, Sironko and Kamwenge. The viability of some of these districts is still in doubt but they are there in the name of decentralisation. The people of Ibanda and Kikagati sub-district are pressing for the further 'slicing' of Mbarara district in the name of bringing services nearer to the people. But there is scarcity of resources at the local level. Inadequate physical infrastructure, transport and communication linkages all have hindered development. Some areas are remote and the local authorities may be unable to overcome such problems, making those areas more prone to being under-serviced. Unless the central government intervenes such areas will remain lagging behind.

Furthermore, despite the argument that NRM was to give people power to govern themselves through grass-root participation, the local councils have basically become grounds for rewarding supporters of the government. Mamdani (1992: 112) has characterised decentralisation in Uganda as decentralisation without democratisation whilst Tukahebwa (2000) argues that it has endangered some elements of democracy.

Certainly, recruitment of personnel at the district is based on know-who rather than know-how. The problem of tribalising staff through selective recruitment cuts across all districts. The district service commission reward supporters of district elected officials and their relatives. The district service commission has failed to uphold the merit principle that is vital in the public administration, which threatens to undermine the developmental potential of decentralisation in Uganda. Patronage and clientele politics is more evident at the local level. But, decentralisation, however imperfect, has contributed to Uganda's development and demonstrates the potential rewards that can be achieved if implemented properly.

The case of Botswana

Having discussed the case of Uganda, we now turn to the case of Botswana. It has already been noted elsewhere, the Botswana state actively engages in planning through a number of institutions, with the Ministry of Finance and Development Planning as the key institution that energises the planning process. This section discusses the role of local authorities in Botswana's planning process through decentralisation.

National Development Planning is a deliberate effort by the government to coordinate economic decision making to achieve development objectives (Todaro 1994). The Botswana case of development planning has defied views that National Development Planning has retarded rates of economic growth and discouraged the evolution of institutions and procedures that could lead to more effective decision-making. National Development Planning has occupied centre stage in Botswana's development trajectory and the success of development planning in Botswana has been linked to the decentralised nature of the planning process as well as to the commitment of the country's political leadership.

The existence of local government dates as far back as the colonial period and beyond, where the chiefs were the major players in the administration of the country. It was not until after independence that democratically elected local government institutions came into being. As a unitary state, parliament has powers to legislate for all districts of the country without exception. Local authorities in Botswana such as city councils, town and district councils etc do not derive their existence directly from the constitution but are a creation of an ordinary act of parliament. The implication of this is that local authorities exist at the mercy of parliament, that is, they can be established and dissolved by parliament. Although local government in Botswana covers Tribal Administration, District Administration, District Councils and Land Boards, this chapter focuses on District Councils and District Administration as the two institutions which are of particular importance in district development planning. The two institutions are discussed below.

i) District Administration

There has been some controversy surrounding the issue of whether district administration is a form of decentralisation. District administration has been associated with a 'deconcentrated' form of decentralisation. And this deconcentration has been seen by some as merely a method by central government to increase its powers by more effectively curbing liberties (Mawhood 1983). In fact, the District Commissioner is the senior representative of the President in the district but he/she is administratively responsible to the Ministry of Local Government. This has been seen by some as proving the existence of the central government's hand at the local level.

This particular local authority is headed by a District Commissioner (DC) who is the most senior central government representative at local or district level. He/she coordinates the overall implementation of developmental projects at district level. In doing so, he is assisted by the District Officers (these are trained professionals, an important aspect of development planning). Additionally, the District Commissioner is the chair of the District Development Committee (DDC) and the District Officer (Development) is the executive secretary of the DDC.

ii) District Councils

District Councils represent a form of decentralisation often referred to as devolution. They are semi or wholly autonomous institutions at the district or local level. It should be noted that the term autonomous (referring to these local authorities) has been used loosely. The political cadre of the District Council is comprised of the Council Chairperson as the head and councillors who are democratically elected. At the same time, the administrative cadre is made up of the Council Secretary as the head and permanent staff who are professionals. The Council Secretary jointly manages the District Development Committee with the District Commissioner. The key person in the district planning process is the Council Planning Officer (CPO). The CPO is responsible for all council planning matters and plays a major role in the formulation and implementation of the district development plan. And in so doing, he closely works with the DO(D).

District Councils have the statutory responsibilities of providing basic social amenities in the form of primary education, primary health, potable water, construction and maintenance of ungazetted roads, sanitation and recreational facilities, social and community services, fire services. In addition, they work as an approving body for the district plans.

Development planning and decentralisation in Botswana

i) National Development Planning

As stated in the Eighth National Development Plan, planning in Botswana is done in the context of a free market economy and it is intended to ensure that maximum benefits are derived from the limited financial resources by prioritising policies, programmes and projects. The National Development Plan is the most important aspect of Botswana's development process.

The preparations of national plans involve various government departments, heads and planners. Each ministry is tasked with the responsibility of drawing up a development plan. These plans are then submitted to the Ministry of Finance and Development Planning for consideration and inclusion in the National Development Plan. The Ministry of Finance and Development Planning has an important coordinating role in the development process. The Economic Committee of Cabinet, which comprises ministers, permanent secretaries, heads of defence and police services and the governor of Bank of Botswana, makes the final decision about resource allocation between various ministries and organisations, to settle any outstanding policy issues. This will then result in the Draft National Development Plan. The plan will then be placed before the national assembly for approval.

ii) District Development Planning

Botswana's commitment to decentralised planning is echoed in the District Planning Handbook of Botswana. The district planning handbook suggests that the district planning process must take into cognisance the fact that people are involved in rural development. It further states that district planning process aims at providing a decentralised planning and implementation capacity which is sensitive and responsible to the needs, problems and priorities of local communities (District Planning Handbook, 1999:79). The assumption here is that at the heart of district planning there is people.

The two most important institutions in the district development planning are the district council and district administration. The hub of district planning is the District Development Committee. This committee is responsible for coordinating activities at the district level and it is chaired by the District Commissioner as noted earlier. Since district development planning is a joint endeavour, it brings together contributions from central government ministries, council, non-governmental organisations and community based organisations. This mixed bag of representatives ensures diversity in viewpoints and experiences.

Although the District Commissioner plays a pivotal role in the formulation, implementation and monitoring of the district development plans, approval powers rest with the district council. After the CPO has prepared and presented the district plans before the village development committee, he presents them to the DDC for approval and thereafter they are presented before council for approval. Councillors are supposed to be a crucial ingredient during the approval of the plans as they are the people's representatives. Unfortunately, this is not the case however. The calibre of councillors has been an area of concern for sometime. Most councillors lack even the minimum education making it difficult for them to comprehend issues of planning and development. Botswana hence suffers from similar problems as Uganda on this score.

Following the approval of the district plans by council, they are then compiled into one plan by the DO(D) and submitted to the Ministry of Local Government for presentation to the district plans committee. This committee is made up of officials from the Ministries of Local Government and Finance and Development Planning.

The very idea that the DC is central in the district development planning has led critics to suggest that district planning is the domain of the DC, hence central government. It leaves one to wonder whether the felt needs and aspirations of the grassroots are represented as their participation is minimal if not non-existent. Makgatlhe (1995) in a rebuttal posits that the making of district plans is based on extensive consultation with the district community and hence the overall plan is the reflection of the aspirations of district residents regarding their future needs in their respective district. In essence, the argument is that district planning is characterised by bottom-up planning. This bottom-up planning, it is assumed, is achieved through district and village development bodies like Village Development Committees, village extension teams, district extension teams, farmers association and the *Kgotla* (often times seen as the Tswana democratic institution). However, Noppen (1982) dismisses this claim arguing that the *Kgotla* neither allows young men, women, poor people to influence the decision making process. One possible explanation for this is that the *Kgotla* is a formal institution and this to some extent hinders participation. In addition to Noppen's claim, the *Kgotla* has been used as a forum to legitimise the (BDP) government's policies. It must be said that too much of lip service has been paid to the so-called bottom-up planning approach in Botswana.

The relationship between National Planning and District Development Planning

The district development planning system is supposed to link together all district level agents (blending deconcentration and devolution) and linking them to national planning (Gasper 1990). According to Gasper, this is for the reasons of participation at grassroots (from below district level) and coordination (from district and sub-district level upwards). District development plans should be prepared before the National Development Plan so that the final copy of the

National Development Plan should ideally incorporate input from the District (Hobona 1995). In fact district development plans form the basis for the preparation of the National Development Plan, at least in theory. However, the National Development Plan takes precedence over district planning and this is quite problematic.

It is quite difficult to establish the link between National Development Planning and district development planning. Nevertheless, there are various institutions where the two processes merge. The National Development Plan and the district plan in Botswana relate through the rural development unit in the Ministry of Local Government. District planners can obtain some information on the government policies, projects, proposals, methods and procedures to be followed from this unit. It is often argued that this allows regular contact between the centre and the district. One commentator is of the view that if exercised effectively this could give the districts a chance to prepare development plans consistent with the National Development Plans but in practice the rural development unit has very little contact with the district (Ngwato 1990). Another linkage between the centre and district is the National District Development Conference (NDDC) which has been recognised as the most effective form for information exchange between the centre and the district. Sharma (1999) posits that the NDDC is the avenue where all district level development offices meet with the relevant officers of the central government and serves as an instrument of horizontal and vertical communication. Contrary to the view that there is a relationship between the National Development Planning and district planning, it is contended that maintaining a close relationship between the two is one of the most difficult aspects of DDP preparation and implementation.

Limitations and constraints of District Development Planning

District planning in Botswana is encumbered by a lack of control and financial resources such that at the end of the day district development plans are reduced to mere shopping lists. Makgatlhe (1995) notes this is so because the decentralisation process in Botswana has not been matched with financial control and autonomy. This is evident in projects indicated in the district development plan as they are approved by central government. Funding for development and recurrent funds of local authorities, particularly councils, are mainly derived from the central government, thus making it easy for them to be controlled from the centre. This situation has resulted in some commentators arguing that councils have been reduced to mere appendages of the central government. The District Development Committee in Botswana does not handle funds. In Uganda the situation is more or less the same with the resistance committee which operate like the DCC in Botswana. The resistance committees do not handle their own funds as they are controlled from the centre by the central resistance committee.

Planners in Gaborone particularly in the macro planning unit and with the sectoral responsibilities in the Ministry of Finance and Development Planning, who are tasked with preparing the National Plan possess very little knowledge about rural areas and their problems. In addition, Ellison (1990) argues that many planners have never read a DDP and some admit to not even knowing what they are. He further asserts that some officers have bluntly reported that even if they did have district plans, in the end they proceed without reference to district plans. It therefore, leaves one to wonder whether the DDPs are incorporated in the National Development Plan.

There is also a problem of lack of information from the centre to the district. The central officials do not always avail the required planning information with regard to available resources to districts such that districts plan without adequate information. Ngwato (1990) stresses that as a consequence of this lack of information, the central government often regards district plans as ambitious.

Despite such problems experienced during the district development planning, district development planning *has* managed to bring some services closer to the people. This has been attributed to the commitment of the political leadership to rural development, an imperative intrinsic in developmental states, particularly ones locate in Africa. The onuses are upon the central government to ensure that its official's treat the district development plans with the importance that they deserve during the making of the National Development Plan.

Conclusion

The cases of Uganda and Botswana demonstrate that local authorities through decentralisation are a key part of the development process in both countries, however uneven. This has been possible because the state in both countries is committed to development (though to different degrees). In Uganda, despite the threats to the system of decentralisation, and unlike in other developing countries like Nigeria, which have failed to reap fruits from decentralisation, Uganda's experience has brought benefits to the ordinary person. It has arguably led to participatory and collective responsibility in the development of the country, particularly in the rural areas.

Decentralisation in Uganda has gained momentum making the recovery process from massive degeneration of public service provision and the loss of political accountability quicker. The benefits from the process are surely visible. Though by no means perfect, local government allows the marginalised to air their views through their representatives, right up to the central government. The involvement of women and the disabled is institutionalised. Even in the developed world, it is rare to find such institutionalised empowerment. Resource mobilisation has equally increased and this is now matching the area covered in service provision and quality of service given (service coverage). Staff motivation has been given consideration thus enhancing commitment, crucial if Uganda is to have any pretensions to being developmental, and planning capacity for those who have under gone training has greatly improved. However, there is room for improvement and inclusion for a truly democratic process, particularly creating conflict-free zones at different local levels. The challenge is to make decentralisation work more and more in the service of development.

In Botswana too, although local authorities are allowed to make an input in the development process through district development plans, the final decision as to what goes into the National Development Plan rests with the central government. Nevertheless, local authorities play an important role in Botswana's developmental process and have aided the development trajectory of the country. They have not only brought services such as basic education, roads, health facilities etc closer to the electorate but have also played a key role in their provision. However, as noted above, a lack of resources is one of the major hurdles local authorities face, as they are overly dependent on central government for resources (both financial and human).

In both cases, decentralisation has been used as a tool by the government to improve service delivery and also, and this is contentious, to open up democratic space for input into both policy planning and implementation. In doing so, decentralisation can be said to help legitimise the regimes in both countries, visibly demonstrating to the populace that 'their' governments are delivering. As delivery is key to any notion of a developmental state, this can be said to be of high importance. Of course, as the chapter has shown, problems beset decentralisation in both countries; this is arguably normal and expected as ideal type models do not exist in the real world. But what cannot be denied is that decentralisation within the broader governance structures of both Botswana and Uganda demonstrates commitment to development and this commitment has been proven by demonstrable results.

8

Gender and Developmental States: Botswana and Uganda

Pamela Mbabazi, Godisang Mookodi & Jane Parpart

This chapter asks the crucial question: are the benefits of developmental states gendered? Is there more gender equality, are women more able to access political and economic opportunities and institutions, are relations between the sexes more tolerant and flexible in developmental states? These are the questions that this chapter seeks to address. Each case (Botswana and Uganda) is interesting in its own right. However, a comparison is equally important, as it offers a means of thinking about the different ways that economic development may play out in regard to gender. The comparison reminds us of the importance of contextualising our analysis, and of restraining tendencies to anticipate general patterns without paying sufficient attention to the impact of history, culture and other factors that impinge on attitudes and practices regarding gender.

Both Uganda and Botswana joined many other African states at the end of the first United Nations Decade for Women (1975–1985), when they formally declared the importance of seeking avenues for the full integration of women in the development process. The establishment of state-sponsored women's ministries, the promulgation of laws addressing gender equality, and the rise of civil society activism in pursuit of gender equality, occurred in both Uganda and Botswana. The differences and similarities between these two cases raise important questions about how to understand existing gender practices, with all their limitations, as well as how advocates for gender equality can best effect meaningful change. First, we turn to the case of Botswana.

Botswana

The key economic activities among pre-capitalist Batswana included hunting and gathering, arable agriculture and animal husbandry. Historical and anthropological accounts (Schapera and Comaroff 1991; Tlou and Campbell 1984; Shillington 1985) indicate that pre-colonial social organisation was characterised by the complementarity of women's and men's roles assigned through gender divisions of labour. However, patriarchal beliefs and practices maintained gender stratification; much of the gender inequality revolved around access to and control of resources and political power.

Certainly the institution of chieftainship was male-centred, with succession being passed down to male descendants within the leadership lineage of each group. Matrilineal succession (the claiming of chieftainship through chief's sisters or daughters) was practised only among a few non-Tswana groups such as the Mbukushu (Schapera 1994). The accounts of Isaac Schapera (1955, 1994) and Shillington (1984) note that political office and debates were primarily male domains. Men made overall decisions pertaining to the social and economic welfare of their communities, and oversaw the administration of customary law.

With the coming of British colonial rule in 1889 and new developments in social, political and economic organisation, pre-colonial and Western patriarchal gender-systems merged to produce new gender relations. Women's subordination was effectively institutionalised through their dependence on male cash income earners, discriminatory legal practices and their exclusion from political office.

From the 1870s men from the Southern regions of present-day Botswana were recruited to work in the South African mines in Kimberley, and later the Witwatersrand. This ever-increasing male out-migration had marked implications for the gender division of labour and subsistence agricultural production as women, children and the elderly were left with the responsibilities that had been assumed by men.

As Western influences increased, many traditional practices such as initiation and polygamy were abolished. Consensual relations outside marriage began to lead to the emergence of the single mother family form that is prominent in contemporary Botswana society. At the same time, married women with limited subsistence opportunities relied on remittances from migrant husbands. Isaac Schapera described the situation of women in early to mid-20th century Botswana as follows:

> In tribal law women are treated as perpetual minors, being subject for life to the authority of male guardians; they are also excluded from political assemblies, and although a few have [recently] acted as regents during the minority of a chief, all political offices are normally confined to men (Schapera 1955: 37).

Some customary practices, such as among the Kgatla, permitted women to be allocated and inherit arable land in their own right, however, the productivity of such land was determined by the availability of capital and labour both of which women had limited access to. Among the Ngwaketse, women held temporary regency for their minor male children, however their occupation had no impact on the overall participation of women in political life (Schapera 1955).

But it has to be said that more women benefited from missionary education. By 1946, records showed that a total of 20.5 percent of all females in the Bechuanaland Protectorate could either read or write the vernacular compared to 19.9 percent of all men. The corresponding figures for English were 10.1 percent of females compared to 8.1 percent of men (Schapera 1955: 18). These gender differences were largely attributed to the fact that girls had more access to village-based missionary schools in the villages while boys were required to be resident at the cattle posts for long periods of time.

Since attaining independence in 1966, the state has made great investments in social welfare services, particularly in the provision of education and health. While female access to education and health services has improved, their access to employment lags behind that of men. Botswana has made steady gains on increasing literacy rates, largely due to the goal of universal primary education, which stood at 92 percent in 2000 (Ministry of Finance 2003: 22). The following table indicates enrolment at Primary and Secondary levels from 1981 to 1995.

Enrolment at Primary and Secondary Levels 1981–1995

	1981	1991	1995
Primary			
Total	86.0	93.7	96.7
M	80.0	92.7	97.7
F	92.0	96.5	97.7
Junior Certificate			
Total	11.9	35.3	45.3
M	10.1	29.1	39.2
F	13.3	41.1	51.1
Senior Secondary			
Total	4.2	13.8	19.9
M	4.8	15.1	19.6
F	3.7	12.7	20.2

Source: Government of Botswana and UNDP (2000: 89-90).

While the goal of universal primary education has nearly been achieved, the provision of universal secondary school education lags behind. The above table points to the predominance of female enrolment at primary and junior secondary school levels. The proportion of females at senior secondary school level has increased exponentially due to measures taken by the Ministry of Education to enhance gender equality, such as challenging gender stereotyping in school curricula, and admitting teenage mothers re-entry to senior schools.

There are indications that women are making inroads into university education. It must be noted, however, that most of the females enrolled at university level tend to be in the education and humanities areas, while males dominate the science and technology fields. This has implications for women's employment opportunities within an increasingly technology-driven world.

The Botswana household income and expenditure survey of 1993/94 indicated that 50 percent of all female-headed households were either poor or very poor compared to 44 percent of male-headed households. Limited access to cash income (particularly unemployment) and higher income dependency ratios has been identified as a key cause of poverty – particularly among female-headed households (BIDPA 1997). Poverty among all households is increasingly being exacerbated by the deaths of breadwinners from AIDS.

While many gains have been made in the health sector, new challenges threaten progress, mostly due to the HIV and AIDS pandemic. The infant and under-five mortality increased between 1996 and 2000 from 38 to 57 per 1,000 and 48 to 75 per hundred. The overall life expectancy was reduced from 65.3 years in 1991 to 55.7 years in 2001. The national HIV and AIDS sentinel surveillance report of 2003 indicated the overall prevalence in the country was 37.4 percent. The highest age prevalence was among those aged 25–29 years and the HIV prevalence was higher among women—37.4 percent compared to 23.9 percent among men (National AIDS Coordinating Agency 2003: 62-63). Much of the literature on gender and HIV/AIDS in Botswana (e.g. Ditshwanelo and Datta, Khan and Alexander 1998; Preece 2001; Tlou, Rantona and Phaladze 2001) identify women's subordinate economic and cultural positions as mitigating against their ability to negotiate safe sex. This is further compounded by increases in incidents of sexual violence, particularly rape and incest (Department of Women's Affairs 1999; Maundeni 2001).

Women nurture Botswana's democracy as voters, but few make it into the corridors of power (Datta, Khan and Alexander 1998). Motsei Madisa (1991) attributed this situation to the lack of political education that identifies the structures of their subordination, and empowers them to challenge male dominance through political activity. From independence (1966) to the sixth election in 1989, Dr. Gaositwe Chiepe was the only female elected Member of Parliament, who also held several cabinet positions over the years. The number of women MPs has steadily increased over the years. At the eve of the ninth general election (2004), the number of women MPs was 7 out of 44 (two were specially-elected). Of these, four held full cabinet positions, while one was an Assistant Minister. During the 2004 general elections, the number of women MPs was 6 out of 57 (two were specially elected). Of these, four held full cabinet positions, while one was an Assistant Minister. Only 74 women made up the 490 councillors (Botswana Press Agency, 2004). The proportion of women members of parliament (10 percent) falls far short of the SADC Declaration on Gender and Development of 1997 recommended that women occupy at least 30 percent of the positions in political and 1997 recommended that women occupy at least 30 percent of the positions in political and decision-making structures by the year 2005 (SARDC 1999)

State and civil society in Botswana

The establishment of the Women's Affairs Unit in 1981 was regarded by local women's rights activists and in the international arena as a sign of the political will by the government of Botswana towards the achievement of gender equality. Influences in the policy arena have progressed at a snail's pace as illustrated by the development and ultimate adoption of the Policy on Women and Development. While vast resources have been expended in promoting gender sensitisation, the political will on the part of the State could be best described as questionable. This comes at a time when civil society mobilisation is increasingly facing challenges of financial sustainability and internal transformation.

At its establishment, the Women's Affairs Unit had the broad mandate of integrating women in development. Broadly following the WID approach, the key means to achieving change in development policies and programmes lay in assessing the status of women through research, and sensitising the public and government ministries to the subordinate status of women in Botswana. This was facilitated through the Women's Development Planning and Advisory Committee (WODPLAC) which drew membership from all ministries, as well as representation from women's organisations. In its early years, the Women's Affairs Unit focused on the subordinate economic status of women, particularly with respect to their concentration in economic activities (such as subsistence agriculture and small businesses) that brought low financial returns. Other key areas that were addressed included women's subordinate status under the law, their limited access to education and health facilities. Much of the input in the initial seven years of the existence of the Women's Affairs Unit was at programme level until the drafting of the Policy on Women in Development in 1988. The overall objective of this policy was:

> To address [the] identified women in development issues in a comprehensive and holistic manner and in line with the planning principles of rapid economic

growth, economic independence, sustained development and social justice...
(Ministry of Labour and Home Affairs 1995: 3)

The policy spells out principles necessary to facilitate improvements in the status of Batswana women namely, that all policies of the government should recognise that women and men are guaranteed equality before the law, and that all policies of government should recognise women and men as equally important human resources for economic, social and political development. In addition the policy aims at the promotion of women's health, education and the elimination of poverty among women, particularly female-headed households (Ministry of Labour and Home Affairs 1995). Since the initial draft in 1988, the policy was returned for numerous amendments until its final approval by cabinet in July 1996. The government of Botswana and the UNDP also drew up the National Gender Programme in 1997, which aimed to shift focus from the 'women and development' to the 'gender and development' approach. This was to be achieved through institutional strengthening of the Department of Women's Affairs, as well as expediting gender mainstreaming across all government ministries and NGOs.

However, efforts at gender mainstreaming have had limited effect in Botswana. This is clearly illustrated in the national development planning process. National Development Plan No. 9 (2003/4–2008/09) displays little evidence of gender-sensitivity. Most sectoral chapters neither contain gender disaggregated data nor gendered analysis of development challenges and plans. The only direct mention of gender and development for the planning period appears on one page, containing a brief update of the international conventions that have been signed by the government of Botswana. Rather than providing some insight into progress (or challenges) with respect to gender mainstreaming, the section serves as an outline of plans and activities of the Department of Women's Affairs Section.[1]

While some achievements have been made towards the empowerment of women, much remains to be done. The experiences of the women's machinery point to the rhetorical stance of the state and political leadership towards the promotion and achievement of gender equality in Botswana. Gender activists and researchers (Datta, Alexander and Khan 1998) pointed to the delays in the adoption and implementation of the Policy on Women in Development as illustrating a lack of political will on the part of the government officials and politicians.

Having said that, one can discern a relatively close relationship between the state and civil society organisations with respect to gender issues. While much emphasis has been placed on the importance of women's organisations as partners in the achievement of development goals (Ministry of Labour and Home Affairs 1988; 1997), the close relationship between the two however often leads to over-reliance on state support, which may in turn limit the ability of NGOs to operate from positions of autonomy. While women's organisations have played a major role in criticising government policies and programmes, the consistency of their advocacy has been hampered by limited access to resources and over-reliance on state resources, as well as organisational impediments.

The Botswana Council of Women (BCW) and the Young Women's Christian Association (YWCA) are two of the oldest women's organisations in Botswana. Both are nationally-based organisations that were formed before independence. Much of the earlier work of these organisations revolved around facilitating education and training around women's domestic responsibilities as mothers, wives and other stereotypical roles. Mannathoko (1992: 74) has noted that the BCW serves 'as the forum through which the ruling party obtained political support from women' and the leadership of this organisation was comprised of the wives of ministers and prominent politicians.

During the late 1980s and early 1990s the area of women's legal rights gained a lot of prominence. This owed to the emergence of issues that gave rise to civil society groups such as Emang Basadi[2] and the Women in Law Southern Africa Research Project (WLSA).[3] Both of these organisations were instrumental in laying the foundation for the landmark amendment of the Citizenship Act of 1984. The judgement (1995) of the well-publicised test case *Attorney General vs. Unity Dow* afforded married female citizens of Botswana the opportunity to pass on their citizenship to their children just like their male counterparts.

Women's organisations such as Emang Basadi, WLSA, Women Against Rape and Metlhaetsile Women's Information Centre successfully lobbied for the amendment rape laws, broadening the definition of rape and increasing sentences. Despite this, the number of reported rape cases continues to rise. Women and girls do not get sufficient assistance and relief from the police and courts. In addition, the hidden nature of rape and other forms of violence in domestic settings hampers efforts to address this problem.

Most of the women's organisations have relied on funding from donor agencies to implement their activities (Government of Botswana and UNDP 1997). While Botswana's good democratic governance record provided the basis for financial support from international agencies in the past, many donor agencies ceased to provide funding citing Botswana's privileged status as a middle-income country as the basis of their actions. The dwindling of funding sources has had a negative impact on many organisations' ability to conduct programmes that include education and training, research, legal advocacy, political education and refuge for victims of domestic violence. Most organisations have had to scale down their activities substantially due to their inability to meet their running costs.

Re-conceptualising gender in Botswana

A number of challenges still exist in Botswana's quest to address gender issues. Gender issues continue to be viewed as 'women's issues' in Botswana. Currently, both government and civil organisations target their interventions at women, largely leaving men out of the equation. While there are ongoing debates internationally, that focus on the missing male in gender and development discourses, (Cornwall and White 2000; Chant 2000; Greig, Kimmel and Lang 2000; Morrell 2001), these are relatively new within the context of Botswana. Two areas that are prime examples of this marginalisation of men are in the fields of HIV/AIDS programmes and gender-based violence. Certainly, increasing rates of gender-based violence and the spread of HIV/AIDS are hampering development efforts. The rapid spread of HIV/AIDS in Botswana has generated a lot of research on sexual practices and behavioural change, but while much of this research rightly tries to take gender into consideration, the focus has tended to be on women as it is recognised that culturally-entrenched patriarchal practices prevent women from negotiating safe sexual practices. Yet, men, male sexuality and male gender identities have not been adequately addressed. Only a limited number of pilot studies have targeted men like the 'The Men, Sex and AIDS Pilot Study' (see Ministry of Health 1998).

Police statistics and research conducted by women's organisations point to an increase in the rate of male violence against women (Botswana Police Service 1999; Department of Women's Affairs 1999). Much of this violence can be attributed to cultural beliefs of domination, particularly with respect to sexual relationships. Violence is also a manifestation of uncertainty in gender roles and relations as rapid changes in educational status and profile of women are regarded as challenges to men's authority (Mookodi 2004).

Uganda

The National Resistance Movement (NRM) triumph in 1986 was a watershed for women in Uganda. Supportive government policies, a gender-sensitive constitution and encouragement for the women's movement have raised the status of women in the country and increased efforts towards attaining gender balance. For example, the level of women representation in Parliament has increased from 18.8 percent in 1996–2000 to 26 percent in 2001–2005. The ratio of primary school enrolment for girls/boys has gone up from 94.5:100 in 1992 to 99.3:100 in 2000. The Gender Empowerment Measure (GEM) has gone up to 0.598 for parliamentary representation, 0.428 for legislators and senior managers, 0.827 for professional and technical workers and 0.627 for economic participation. The GEM of 0.417 for 2001 has improved compared to GEM of 0.390 in 1996 (Uganda Human Development Report 2002, p.3). As in the above section on Botswana however, it is necessary to look at the context within which such achievements occurred.

Women and gender in pre-NRM Uganda

Women in Uganda before and during the colonial period were principally valued for their roles as mothers and producers within the household. A high fertility rate of 7.3 live births (Tripp and Kwesiga 2002), early marriage and multiple wives (seen as a marker of status for powerful men), reflected this attitude. This is not to say that the centrality of women's economic activity went unrecognised, only that this role was taken for granted and undervalued.

During the colonial period, men controlled most of the cash-based economy. Women who earned cash often handed it over to their husbands, and whereas men were generally paid in cash, women were usually paid in kind with items like salt, food or soap (World Bank 1993: 29). Women's exclusion from the cash economy had far-reaching repercussions as the value of both men and women to society tends to be measured in relation to their contribution to the monetised economy. The difference between women's and men's access to money, thus reinforced gender inequalities. A man who earned cash was highly regarded even if he could not buy food for his family, whereas a woman who was merely a subsistence producer was undervalued, even if she fed her family.

Furthermore, during the colonial and even post-colonial period, most women were regarded as having no place in politics. Those who managed to get involved were often the daughters of indigenous rulers. In Buganda for instance, the Queen *(Nabagereka)* and the Princess *(Omumbejja)* had considerable influence, but largely as relatives of powerful men (Tripp 2000).

Even after independence, customary law and practice reinforced discrimination against women, who were essentially regarded as minors, without adult legal status. Customary law defined women's and men's rights in matters such as divorce, inheritance, property rights, and the definition and compensation for adultery. Moreover, since women were not their husbands' automatic heirs, they did not have custody of their children. Uganda's divorce laws during the post-independence era for example, stipulated that if a woman committed adultery this was enough ground for divorce, whereas for the men, the law was silent. When a man died, customary laws about inheritance gave first priority to the children with little regard for the wife of the deceased. Clearly women were greatly disadvantaged.

Limited access to education and negative attitudes towards women's employment funnelled the few professional women into jobs in primary school teaching, nursing and secretarial work in the post-independence period (ACFODE 1988). Ugandan women were also not very active as far as fighting for their rights before and after independence. From the time of independence in 1962, women's organisations such as the Uganda Council of Women (UCW) and later the Uganda Association of Women's Organisation (UAWO) came under pressure from the ruling Uganda People's Congress (UPC) president, Milton Obote. While the Obote government did little to address women's concerns, women were nevertheless expected to demonstrate their allegiance to the UPC government. After 1966, when Uganda became a one-party state, women's organisations operated within the context of political instability, suppression of party activities and banning of large meetings, which made it difficult to press for their demands. For the most part, members of women's organisations were reduced to the role of social hostesses at UPC functions.

The problems of an already weak Uganda women's movement were further compounded when Idi Amin came to power in 1971. He set about banning miniskirts, wigs, perfumes and deodorants and embarked on clearing the streets of unmarried women, all of whom he regarded as 'prostitutes'. The army attacked women and violated women's rights on the pretext of maintaining law and order; rape was a frequent terror tactic. Amin suppressed all independent women's organisations and set up the National Council of Women (NCW).

The early constitutions paid no attention to women's emancipation and women's issues. This is not surprising as no women attended the London meeting that set up the first constitution in 1962. Later constitutions in 1966 and 1967 also ignored women's concerns. The latter was debated in parliament, but there was no woman parliamentarian at the time. At independence, the ratio of female to male members of parliament was 2:88 but by 1967 there were no women members of parliament. By 1980 there was still only one female member of parliament out of 143 members (Tripp 2000). Neither Obote nor Amin considered women central to the development process and education and employment opportunities focused on men, not women. In addition most Ugandans continued to see girls as sources of dowry, so their education received lower priority than boys as girls were married off at the first opportunity. Those few lucky enough to get a small bit of education were pushed to become teachers or nurses. The very few women in university were encouraged to study Arts. As such, the economic, political and legal conditions of women stagnated in the post-independence period.

Women and gender under the NRM

The coming to power of the NRM ushered in a new era for women in Uganda; the government believed in gender equality and women's emancipation. Women's concerns were high on the government's development agenda and a number of steps were taken to ensure gender mainstreaming in Uganda's socio-political fabric. Women had played a key role in the insurrection leading to the establishment of the NRM government, and managed, unlike in most post-liberation societies in Africa, to establish a women's movement in Uganda that has remained relatively autonomous from the government. Moreover, it has generally cut across religious and ethnic lines as well as political affiliations.

The NRM government encouraged women to mobilise and women's organisations flourished, including Action for Development (ACFODE), Forum for Women in Democracy (FOWODE), Uganda Women's Network (UWONET), Uganda Women's Efforts to Save Orphans (UWESO), The National Council of Women (NCW), to mention but a few. Strong networking created a movement that has been able to cross class, regional and ethnic lines, bringing grassroots and elite women together in a powerful lobby. Carefully nurtured alliances abroad, as well as a commitment to local autonomy from the Ugandan state, enabled the women's movement in Uganda to expand its agenda. It soon became a political force in the country that challenged the status quo by lobbying and agitating for inclusion of women in political and economic matters.

The relative freedom of association accorded to NGOs in Uganda after the NRM came to power, including women's associations (in spite of pressures for co-optation), created a conducive environment for debating women's concerns in public and private fora. Women's groups seized on the NRM's rhetorical encouragement of women's mobilisation to justify their local battles over their right to participate in public affairs and used their numerical strength to lobby for women's interests, successfully pressuring many government policies to be more responsive to women's needs. Women's groups lobbied government and other bodies on delicate issues such as women's access to land and property, rape and defilement as well as female circumcision. A case in point is the involvement of various women's groups in the discussions that eventually led to the promulgation of the 1995 constitution. The involvement of women's groups in debates over the recently approved Land Bill is also noteworthy. Women's groups also successfully lobbied government to increase budget allocations for the 'Early Nutrition and Childhood Development Project' which has had improved the health of women and children in different parts of the country. Improving women's participation in the leadership of NGOs across the country has been an issue of great concern as well, and some progress has been made (Gariyo Zie 1994).

Donor funding from major development agencies, especially plentiful in the late 1980s and early nineties also strengthened the women's movement in Uganda. As in Botswana, the reduction in funds since the mid-1990s has undermined some of these advances. Most donor money remained in the capital, funding authentic as well as more questionable 'briefcase' NGOs. However, grassroots organisations have continued to thrive, as they rely mostly on local dues from members and income generating schemes.

Women's political representation and decision-making

One of the key elements contributing to the advancement of women in Uganda since 1986 has been their inclusion in politics, representation and decision making. While NRM leaders supported women's advancement, pressure from the women's movement made a difference as well. Soon after taking power, a group of women from the NCW paid a courtesy call on the President, Yoweri Museveni, and handed him a memo requesting that women be represented in the government leadership. This marked the turning point for women's involvement in politics in Uganda (Tripp 2000). Indeed, several women scholars and activists in Uganda (Kwesiga 2000, Matembe 2000, and Tamale 1999) have argued that NRM government's openness both for encouraging the growth of women's movements and for bringing women into the political development process has played a key role in women's advancement since 1986.

The NRM developed a number of strategies to increase women's political participation. Seats for women in parliament were reserved to encourage women to enter political life and make them politically visible so that the electorate eventually would become accustomed to voting for women as leaders. In the 1989 elections for instance, women claimed 41 of all parliamentary seats (17 percent) and by 1996, 52 women (19 percent) held parliamentary seats with 39 of these being reserved seats. Gradually, the mandatory position for women representatives at all levels of governance encouraged women's political participation.

The success of this move to involve women in politics is reflected in the growth of women's decision-making roles at all levels of government. In 2001, they constituted 39 percent of the decision makers at both national and district level, with participation in the political arena reaching 44 percent. At local government level, women occupied 45 percent of the decision-making positions. In non-political service, the participation or involvement of women was highest in the judicial service. Although still lagging behind men, women's participation in decision-making reflects a dramatic improvement over the early 1980s and before.

It should be mentioned, however, that initially many women hesitated to enter politics despite the clear openings, because among other things, not many women were educated. Women also lacked the necessary resources to compete in mainstream constituencies and had to face widespread hostility in the general population towards women's participation in politics. The lack of exposure and techniques in public speaking also inhibited many women, especially rural women. Eventually, with government and non-governmental organisations' support for women's education, sensitisation and conscientisation, more and more women began to enter politics. Looking specifically at the cabinet level statistics, eight out of the seventy-five ministers in Museveni's earlier government (late 1986 to 1990) were women. Notable among these were Gertrude Njuba, Deputy Minister of Industry, Victoria Sekitoliko, Minister of Agriculture, and Betty Bigombe, Deputy Minister in the Prime Minister's Office. By 1995, women constituted 17 percent of all ministers, 21 percent of all permanent secretaries, 35 percent of all under secretaries and 16 percent of all district administrators (Tripp 2000)[4].

Evidently there has been some marked improvement in women's participation in the higher levels of decision-making.

Despite this progress however, women's involvement in Ugandan politics is still low compared to men, and in some cases it seems to be declining. For instance, whereas in 1999 there was a woman Vice President by 2003 both the President and Vice-President were male. The percentage of women in the cabinet has dropped precipitously, from 29 percent in 1999 to 18 percent in 2003. While the percentage in the legislature has increased, access to key positions of power has declined. By 2004, women constituted 8 percent of all ministers and 15 percent of all permanent secretaries (*The New Vision*, 8 March 2004). The resignation of Dr. Specioza Kazibwe, Uganda's first woman Vice-President, was viewed by many as an end of the era for women's political advancement in Uganda. The subsequent reshuffling of the cabinet and the removal of Miria Matembe, one of Uganda's most vocal women activists from the Ministry of Ethics and Integrity, allegedly because of differences of opinion with the President regarding Uganda's political reforms, is regarded as an ominous sign. This has dashed the hopes for high office of many elite women, and raises important questions about women and political power. These concerns are reinforced by the continuing tendency for women to gain representation through reserved seats rather than direct election. Men continue to dominate the legislature (81 percent in 1999 and 75 percent in 2003), with women more often gaining admission through reserved seats. In 2003, women constituted 25 percent of parliamentary representatives with 53 of these being reserved seats.

Many women have shifted their focus to local government, an area where their representation and participation rate is much higher. In 2000, at the district level, almost 45 percent of the nearly 14,000 councillors at various local government levels were women. This is over one-third of local council seats, making Uganda a leader worldwide in female representation at local level government (Tripp 2002).

In terms of the Judiciary, women are also playing an important role, although still not proportional to women's numbers in the population. The Supreme Court has 14 percent female judges and women hold 25 percent of all positions in the court of appeal, 26 percent in the High Court and represent 30 percent of Chief Magistrates.

Thus, many advances have been made in the political arena, but it should be mentioned that the policy of reserving seats for women has of late been a contentious issue. Many women and men argue that although it was necessary initially, a lot of advances have been made and the system should now be scrapped so that women compete directly with men. If this happens, the percentage of women in politics would perhaps decline, at least in the short run.

The Ministry of Women in Development

In order to consolidate government efforts to emancipate women and address gender inequalities, the NRM established a Ministry of Women in Development in 1988. The ministry was charged with the responsibility of ensuring that women's issues were integrated into all government policies and the development planning process. The ministry was later renamed the Ministry of Gender, Labour and Social Welfare in 2001, and given the responsibility of increasing awareness, knowledge and sensitivity among the population and government institutions nationwide about the need to redress prevailing gender inequalities and imbalances.

The Ministry has achieved a number of policy goals, most notably the National Gender Policy and the National Action Plan for the Advancement of Women. The National Gender Policy recognises gender relations as a development concept and regards gender equity as a development issue. The National Action Plan identifies four critical areas for women and girls: poverty, income generation and economic empowerment, reproductive health rights, legal instruments and decision-making and the girl child's education and the problem of violence against women and girls.

However as Aili Mari Trip (2000) argues in her book *Women and Politics in Uganda* 'the greatest hurdle to improving women's lives in Uganda is neither policy and laws nor the constitution – [important as they were/are]…it was, and still is the need to overcome patriarchal assumptions and practices'. This challenge has been a central pre-occupation of the Uganda Women's Movement.

Educational and economic opportunities

The NRM inherited a deeply skewed educational system that favoured boys and males. The government quickly set about addressing this problem as a means of promoting women's advancement. Universal Primary Education (UPE) increased the enrolment of girls in primary schools nationwide. Through affirmative action, admission points for women entering higher institutions of learning were lowered and set at 1.5 points below that of men. As a result, the percentage of females enrolled at Makerere University and other government institutions of higher learning throughout the country rose dramatically (Kwesiga 2000). In 1998 for instance the female enrolment at Makerere was 48 percent compare to a miserable 19 percent in 1987.

As women have attained more education, many have been able to move into good waged jobs. However, most women in Uganda work in agriculture and much of that work is unpaid family labour. Ugandan women entrepreneurs, market traders and cross-border traders are few and face a lot of challenges. Hostility to businesswomen, poor access to credit and increased competition due to neo-liberal policies have combined to limit women's opportunities in this sector. However, the government and NGOs have combined efforts to promote women's entrepreneurship in Uganda. The National Women's Council (NCW), for example, is working with government to implement credit schemes and improve household incomes throughout the country (The *New Vision Daily*, 8 March 2004). Other NGOs, most notably the Uganda Women Entrepreneurs Association, are assisting aspiring businesswomen with skills training and information.

All in all therefore, favourable government policies together with a vibrant women's movement in the country have contributed towards the improvement of women's status and addressing of gender issues in Uganda, although a lot more still needs to be done. We now turn to look critically at the challenges still being faced.

A critical review of women's emancipation in Uganda

Despite the advances towards their empowerment, women still face many problems in Uganda. Elite women in Uganda have benefited the most and although the situation in the rural areas has improved, the majority of rural women are largely illiterate, isolated, and submissive, with their endeavours hardly recognised. According to UNDP's Human Development Report 1999, 70–80 percent of Ugandan women are engaged in agricultural work, but only 7 percent own the land they cultivate. Only 51 percent of them can read and write compared to 74 percent of the men. The same report notes that rural women not only perform most domestic work, they also grow, harvest and store most of the food. Many are becoming heads of households. All of these tasks depend largely on female unpaid labour and yet women are rarely included in major decisions, especially regarding disposal of the products of their labour and/or property that their labour has improved.

The 1995 constitution did go a long way in removing the discriminatory tendencies enshrined in Uganda's 1967 constitution. Yet, while the constitution states that all persons are equal under the law, some patriarchal bias continues to exist. For example, the government has not redressed the 1967 laws stating that a person born outside Uganda could only became Ugandan if his or her father was a Ugandan citizen, with no mention of the mother whatsoever. Also a foreign woman married to a Ugandan man can register as a Ugandan where as a foreign man married to a Ugandan woman cannot. The bill of rights of women in the constitution is largely unoperationalised. The domestic relations bill, the family land rights proposal about co-ownership of land by spouses and the law against gender-based violence, have been largely ignored by the executive. Indeed, the biggest roadblocks to having these laws in place and fully functional have been erected by the highest offices and at times parliament itself. Demands by women organisations to have these laws enacted have been greeted with cynicism and despite the limited gains for women, men are increasingly arguing that the women have had enough. This negative backlash against women is making matters worse.

Indeed, some women have given in rather than face male hostility—such as the Bagisu women who have reluctantly returned to female circumcision because those who refused the practice have been having difficulties finding a husband (*New Vision Daily*, 6 March 2003).

Moreover, the bureaucratic institutions that were meant to liberate Ugandan women have suffered from many of the problems experienced by similar institutions around the continent. The state is still largely a male-dominated affair. Thus it is not surprising that the Ministry of Gender, Labour and Social Development's share of the total Government of Uganda Budget was 0.2 percent in 1998/1999, 0.4 percent in 1999/2000 and 0.5 percent in 2000/2001 (*New Vision*, 11 June 2003). This impoverishment has hampered the bureaucracies and programmes designed to improve the condition of Ugandan women, and undermined lobbying efforts. The National Gender Policy and National Action Plan for Women exist mainly on paper. The gap between policy and practice is particularly disturbing because there has been some backlash against women, who are seen as having received more than their share of help from the government.

Furthermore, as we have seen, the percentage of women in the executive is gradually falling. While in 1999 appointments in the executive almost touched the 30 percent line – the number required in an institution to make a difference – the 2003 reshuffle sharply reduced the percentage of women in the executive and the cabinet.[5] Those few women who are in the cabinet occupy relatively lower status ministerial positions. Thus, even at this level, women are making very little progress and the women's movement in Uganda stands to lose some of the gains made over the years unless the tempo of empowering women increases.

Few Ugandan women, who are wage earners (professionals included), agricultural producers, or petty commodity producers, either live a life of joy and happiness or speak about the injustices that they face. They still tend to be enslaved to the male-construct of a 'woman's place' and the 'man is a boss' despite their education and employment. Those women who speak out about injustices against women are labelled as rebellious and unwomanly, frequently attached to Ugandan feminists like Miria Matembe, current Member of Parliament for Mbarara women and Former Minister of Ethics and Integrity, as well as Winnie Byanyima, Former the Member of Parliament for Mbarara Municipality. Matembe seems to have been mistrusted by men because she is 'too vocal' and does not conform to the female norm.

Thus, it seems that women in Uganda have been inserted into the development process without addressing the underlying issues that bedevil attempts to improve their lives and encourage gender equality. Many women, particularly poor rural women, continue to face severe difficulties like accessing education, adequate health facilities, credit, adequate incomes and political representation and participation. Two major issues reveal the extent of on-going problems facing women, and these problems cross class and ethnic lines; violence against women and the threat of HIV/AIDS. Violence is often a domestic matter[6], involving arguments over male expectations such as food preparation, care of children and the house. However, quarrels and violence frequently arise over male 'rights' especially over obedience from women and sexual access. Women are targets for violence and this is partly due to their physical vulnerability (in relation to men), economic dependence and their responsibility that arises out of their roles as mothers.

Sexual relations are, of course, an increasingly contentious issue as many women decide celibacy is the best way to protect themselves from AIDS. This decision makes sense when one realizes that women in Uganda are considerably more susceptible to AIDS than men; the male to female ratio of AIDS cases in the 15 to 19 year age group is 1:5 (*New Vision Daily*, 8 March 2004). Also, women constitute over half of the 1.2 million HIV infected individuals in Uganda and a majority are infected through heterosexual transmission. Women have been the most hit by the HIV/AIDS epidemic because in most cases they have no say in the factors leading them to catch the disease. They for instance do not have the power to negotiate and insist on safe and responsible sex. It is also hard for a woman to demand fidelity from her partner or insist on condom use or even refuse sex if she knows that her partner is promiscuous. According to the Human Rights Watch report of 2001 entitled *Just Die Quietly: Domestic Violence and Women's Vulnerability to HIV in Uganda*, many women expressed a fear of violent repercussions, which impeded their access to HIV/AIDS information, HIV testing, and HIV/AIDS treatment and counselling. In addition, cultural practices like widow inheritance, genital mutilation, polygamy, wife sharing and wife replacement expose women and girls to HIV/AIDS. Sexual violence, domestic violence, abuse and exploitation in homes and areas of conflict like in Internally Displaced Peoples camps (IDPs), further increase women's vulnerability.

Conclusion

What do these two cases tell us about the conditions and opportunities of women and the possibilities for gender equality in 'developmental states' in Africa? At the level of policy, both Botswana and Uganda have demonstrated a varying commitment to improving the lives of women. Both have established women's ministries and bureaucracies to improve women's lives. Both have passed laws and policies supporting improvements in women's lives. Social services, especially education and basic health provision, have improved for women. Both countries have also been influenced by the demands of local women's associations though an important difference emerges here, as the women's groups in Botswana are more closely tied to the government than is the case in Uganda. Thus, women's groups in Botswana have not been as free to criticise and pressure the government as similar groups in Uganda. This may explain women's lower political participation rates in Botswana as well as the state's open refusal to enforce decisions such as the Unity Dow case and its foot dragging over establishing gender policies and programmes, let alone enforcing them. The greater autonomy of Ugandan women's organisations, and the powerful elite women's lobby, has pushed the Ugandan government further both at the level of policy and action on the ground.

However, a number of issues continue to undermine efforts to improve women's lives and encourage gender equality in both Botswana and Uganda. Patriarchal assumptions and practices continue to hold sway in many arenas. While this is particularly true in the poorer regions of both countries, even educated men (and some women) are critical of the women's movement and the notion of gender equality. The issues of domestic violence and HIV/AIDs are also very crucial. A backlash against women is growing in both countries, inhibiting efforts to reduce violence against women, to address women's concerns about sexuality and AIDS and to improve women's access to education, employment, physical and emotional security. Both cases remind us that economic development is not in and of itself a panacea for women's problems, either in the South or the North. Both cases remind us that long-standing traditions of patriarchy and paternalism are difficult to change. Both cases raise questions about the central role of culture, notions of masculinity and assumptions about gender roles and relations in establishing and maintaining gender inequality. Clearly, a focus on economic development alone is not sufficient. A more truly gendered approach to policy and practice—one that takes history, culture and long-held attitudes about appropriate male and female behaviour seriously—will be required, before even the most successful developmental states in Africa can be truly developmental for both women and men.

9

The Privatisation Experience in Uganda: Prospects and Challenges in its Implementation*

Muriisa Roberts

The profound disillusionment in the North with the record of state involvement in economic and social life has led to a simplistic and rather naïve belief in the magic of the market as the most efficient economic regulator. Globalisation has also fuelled the already growing privatisation drive, bringing a mobile economy in which new direct foreign investments (DFI) have transcended nation-state boundaries and integrated markets. National firms are giving way to multinationals, which produce goods and services in several countries, transforming the 'national' economy. With the breaking of investment barriers, private capital seeks new markets in what had once been the special preserve of state investment: energy, communications, and infrastructure. And governments, anxious to reduce deficits and shift spending to social needs, increasingly welcome this investment.

Privatisation is also part of the new policy agenda, a global export to the South, in part aimed at making the Southern countries become able to pay the debts owed to the Northern donors. Other components of the agenda are liberalisation and democratisation. The assumptions of this ideology are that by cutting their expenditure and allowing private initiatives, the governments would be able to pay back its debts and efficient performance would be enhanced (Hulme and Edwards 1997).

In Uganda, privatisation was largely fuelled by the continued poor performance of the public enterprises (PEs). Like elsewhere, public enterprises at the time of independence were widely seen as the wave of the future (Hood 1994). While these enterprises were created in the early 1960s with a view that they would lead

---

* The privatisation exercice has been ongoing. Data presented in the chapter is for the period up to late 2003.

to growth and development whose benefits would be distributed equally to all Ugandans, by the 1980s they had rather become like punched holes, draining away resources in the form of subsidies from the government budget. Privatising these enterprises under Museveni's regime since the early 1990s has thus become a central feature of the general reform programme of Uganda's economy. Putting government enterprises on the market for sale (privatising these enterprises) has become one of the main strategies for promoting a fundamental change in Uganda.

In the context of development debates, privatisation is seen as one form of governance (a minimal state) where government's major public spending is reduced. If we are to understand Uganda as a potential nascent developmental state, the country has embarked on a reform agenda in which privatisation forms a key component. Privatisation is seen as a means through which government resources can interplay with private resources to bring efficiency and effectiveness, especially in the industrial sector.

The role of a developmental state in promoting industrial growth

In developmental states, the state is seen as a vanguard of economic prosperity through state-supported private industrial investments. The state provides financial support for capital investments and fosters long-term entrepreneurial perspectives among private elites by increasing incentives to engage in investments. In postwar Japan for example, the state acted as the source of missing capital for industrial investment. The role of government structures was central to the Japanese industrial growth. Evans (1995) notes that 'the willingness of state financial institutions to back industrial debt/equity ratios at levels unheard of in the West was a critical ingredient in the expansion of new industries'. Japan's Ministry of International Trade and Industry (MITI), had the role of approving investment loans from Japan's development bank. MITI's authority over foreign currency allocations for industrial purposes and licences to import foreign technology, its ability to provide tax breaks, and its capacity to articulate administrative guidance cartels that would regulate competition in an industry, put it in a perfect position to maximise induced decision-making.

Another role of the state is the provision of a powerful and competent bureaucracy in implementing and negotiating investment decisions. Both Japan's and Korea's industrial growth owe much of their success to the bureaucracy, recruited from the best institutions and universities; recruited on merit and whose professionalism made it possible to implement investment decisions without delay.

In Uganda, the creation of the Uganda Investment Authority (UIA) was a step forward in the creation of a body that would handle all investment matters, by providing advice and at the same time regulating the flow of investments to follow the national investment plans. Although the state has played a minimal role in the provision of financial capital for industrial growth, it has been instrumental in providing investment incentives and concessions, which are important for attracting foreign investments. At the same time, the state has been instrumental in negotiating with international financial institutions like the World Bank and IMF so as to provide financial support to prospective investors. Where the state has provided *direct* financial support to industrial investment, performance has been inefficient.

Although several government parastatals/enterprises had completely been run down before privatisation, a good number that have gradually been privatised are now functioning well. Cases in point include Uganda Telecom, Nile Hotel, Uganda Electricity Distribution Company Ltd, Sheraton Hotel (Formerly Apollo Hotel under Uganda Hotels Ltd) etc. All these examples are evidence enough to show that Uganda should surely leave the economy to the private sector and provide only a steering and regulatory role to allow a conducive environment for the business sector to thrive.

Based on these guidelines, it is important to note that the state as an originator of all public policies is central to the success of their implementation. Taken broadly, implementation of any policy is concerned with transforming the policy into action. According to Van Meter and Van Horn (1975: 447), policy implementation encompasses those actions by public and private individuals or groups that are directed at the achievement of objectives set forth in prior policy decisions. This includes both one-time efforts to transform decisions into operational terms as well as continuing efforts to achieve the large and small changes mandated by policy decisions. Implementation of policy determines the nature and success of the policy initiative.

To understand the need for privatisation policy in the Ugandan context and what the experiences have been, one needs to understand the way public enterprises were created in the past and why.

The growth of public enterprises in Africa

Public Enterprises (PEs) are essentially state-controlled enterprises. The government has either full i.e. 100 percent ownership, or a majority of shares (normally above 50 percent). Various theories explain the growth of public enterprises. According to Hood (1994), it can be explained as a functional response to market failure, a product of nationalism and the development of the modern sovereign state, and a product of domestic politics. It is assumed that private markets as allocation mechanisms created unequal distributions of economic benefits in society and as such public enterprises appeared in response to this market failure.

As a product of nationalism, public enterprises were created to ward off foreign competition and create state sovereignty. It was a way forward to creating economic independence. Many public enterprises in African countries were a response to this consideration. The nationalisation policy was seen as an extension of nationalism in the economic sector. Having got political independence, it was imperative that economic independence also be gained. Therefore, the nationalisation of existing private enterprises and creation of new public enterprises was the answer. African leaders also recognised that there were shortages in the supply of the factors of production necessary for broad-based private sector development. Technical skills, both industrial and entrepreneur, were seen to be in short supply whilst the scale of investment necessary for modern technology exceeded the ability of the indigenous private sector. Domestic private investors lacked the required capital and had no international borrowing power, given their economic position during the colonial days. As such, public enterprises were seen as the only feasible way forward.

The establishment of PEs in Uganda followed the trend that was sweeping the African continent in the 1960s. After independence, countries undertook extensive public investment to ostensibly augment their economic growth (Katz 1992). It was hoped that the nationalised enterprises would lead to equitable distribution of incomes, increased employment and the consolidation of economic independence. The choice of the policy was conditioned by their previous colonial status, resentment of multinational influence, observed market failures and income inequalities within developing countries. Thus the concern was to create an egalitarian style of development. By 1986, there were around 3000 PEs across Africa. In Uganda alone there were about 130 public enterprises (Katz et al 1992:3).

Throughout the ensuing years, however PEs proved to be poor performers. These enterprises were marred by corruption and staffed by bureaucrats who were incapable of taking decisions that required quick responses to commercial opportunities. In addition, decisions are always affected by political concerns whereas the decisions ought to be grounded and driven by commercial factors (Ratnakar and Kamalesh 2000). Additionally, PEs were found to be economically inefficient; they had incurred heavy losses and were heavily indebted to international lending agencies. By the late 1970s and early 1980s, PEs accounted for nearly one-third of all international borrowing by developing countries. Consequently, the World Bank and the IMF decided that privatisation was the most viable option as a policy instrument to reduce the drain of the PE sector on the fiscal budget. In the late 1980s therefore, privatisation became part of the World Bank's lending conditionality.

Privatisation in Uganda

Privatisation implies a move towards divestment of total ownership from the government (the public) to the private sector. It is defined as the transfer of a function, activity, or organisation from the public to the private sector (Cowan 1990: 6). Gayle and Goodrich (1990) define privatisation as the process of reducing the role of the government while increasing that of the private sector, in activities or asset ownership. It may include divestiture, the replacement of budgeted public activity by private market mechanisms, consumer co-operatives, co-production, state management contracts and user charges, just to mention but a few. In broader terms, privatisation refers to the introduction of the market mechanisms into the economy.

From the beginning, privatisation in Uganda was part of Museveni's development agenda. For this reason, the state became highly committed to the privatisation drive. The successes registered in the privatisation exercise in Uganda are attributed to this strong political commitment, especially by the presidency. When the NRM took over power in 1986, Museveni announced that there was going to be a 'fundamental change' (Mugerwa 1998). Privatisation became part of the economic recovery programme that was launched to bring this change. The programme got support from the World Bank and the IMF. In 1989, the government was credited by the Bank for its efforts to rehabilitate the economy. A pre-appraisal mission had undertaken a review of the economy in preparation for this credit. Five issues were raised, namely: incentives and regulatory structures; civil service and related institutional matters; revenue generation; public expenditure; and the coffee sector.

Groups comprising of the World Bank and government officials discussed these issues. Although privatisation was not rejected outright, it was considered to be necessary only in the case of poorly performing and non-strategic sectors. The belief then was that PEs making money or others of strategic interest like the Uganda Electricity Board (UEB) and Uganda Airlines would not be privatised. The World Bank argued that it was necessary to put some 'cash cows' on the market to interested buyers and to signal policy change (Mugerwa 1998: 19).

By putting up such enterprises for sale, it would be proof of the government's commitment to the policy of privatisation. As Obbo (1995) argued in the early years of the privatisation process in Uganda, in reference to the imminent sale of Uganda Commercial Bank (UCB), 'putting on the market the UCB which is one institution from which the political class has fattened, the government will demonstrate that it is willing to cut its own pocket'. If the government had backed away from the sale of UCB, the privatisation programme would have stalled and the credibility of the past sales of PEs would have suffered. UCB was eventually sold off to Stanbic, a South African company.

In general, privatisation in Uganda has been difficult to implement despite the many successes witnessed. Initially the government was only willing to sell off loss-making enterprises, not those which interested the private sector the most. The politicians were opposed to privatisation because political leaders considered public enterprises as important vehicles of state patronage. Privatisation posed a threat to the patronage opportunities of those in power whose capacity to consolidate their position would be undermined. 'Over the years, politicians had been using public enterprises as centres of patronage to reward or appease relatives, friends, political supporters or as sources of profit in one way or another' (Tangri 1999).

Although privatisation was seen as a necessity for Uganda's economic recovery in 1989, it was not until 1993 that a law to guide privatisation was put into place. The 1993 government statute number 9 (Public Enterprises Reform and Divestiture statute), divided parastatal companies into four groups (a) those in which the government would have 100 percent ownership (b) those in which the state would require majority shareholding (c) those to be fully divested (d) those to be liquidated.

Together with the need to sell off PEs came the need to open up the economy to private local and foreign investment. To speed up the process, a clearing agency and one–stop information centre (the Uganda Investment Authority) was created. Its role in the privatisation and investment process was to issue permits, incentives and other regulations, including tax rebates and tax relief and tax holidays, to investors. By 1996 about 2000 investment licences had been issued to domestic and foreign firms. To attract foreign investors, Uganda adopted a generous tax holiday regime: up to 6 years for investments of at least US$ 50,000. This offer however, attracted criticisms because tax holidays were not related to the potential value-added or employment to be generated by the firms. It merely considered the size of the investment. Tax holidays also tended to favour companies with short lead-time, as opposed to long-term investments such as mining.

Some enterprises which were considered to be strategic and therefore to be preserved under the control of the government have now also been put on the market and privatised. These include the Uganda Electricity Board (UPTC). (UEB), Uganda Commercial Bank (UCB) as well as Uganda Posts and Telecommunications. UEB was divided into two companies, one responsible for distribution of electricity in the country and the other for its generation. In addition talks have been opened up to allow a joint venture between the Madhvani group and a Canadian group to build a dam further down the Nile. It is hoped that the dam will be able to generate about 350 MW of energy. This will ease the power problems which the country is currently facing. Uganda Posts and Telecommunications, was partially privatised in 1998, with the government retaining the postal system under a new name Uganda Posts Limited, while allowing telecommunications to be operated privately as Uganda Telecom Limited (UTL). In addition, the sector was opened up for other telecommunication companies to operate. There are two companies, Celtel and Mobile Telephone Network (MTN), offering private communication services. To compete with the mobile networks a new mobile network, UTL-Telcel (MANGO), was introduced by Uganda Telecom. This has eased communication problems in the country since customers are no longer tied up to one telephone service provider. All in all, by December 1997, 78 percent of the total 102 PE companies targeted for privatisation by the PERD statute had been privatised, 20 enterprises had been struck off the company register, while 12, were retained by the government, including Uganda Railways Corporation (URC).

Challenges to privatisation in Uganda

In spite of the marked speed in which the privatisation policy was being implemented, the policy met a lot of challenges. In the first place there was little regard made to involve the people that would be affected—in particular the business community and the elite. Successful policy implementation requires an interactive environment in which government and the private sector keeps on interacting and co-operating with one another. However, this has been lacking in the case of Uganda. There were no consultations with the representatives of the private sector when introducing certain aspects of the policy. This dialogue and consultation gap led to government-private sector conflicts. The problems associated with the introduction of the Value Added Tax (VAT) for example, represent one such instance. The business community was ignored and no efforts were made initially to first educate them about the merits of the tax and the details of its implementation. Although the Ministry of Finance invited a few business associates to a 'briefing session' on VAT, the policy itself had already been determined by the Ministry and the IMF (Tangri 1999: 93). Considering the fact that taxes affect investment decisions, it was important that the business community should have been involved from the on-set. This was not taken positively hence the massive resistance from the business community initially, until modifications were made and more sensitisation carried out.

Dialogue between the political leaders and local businessmen, on the other hand, is limited partly because so many government economic decisions are actually determined by the international financial institutions. They constitute important parts of the policy conditionality of the international donors and therefore, not considered subject for local discussions (Tangri 1999). It should be noted however, that although, the dialogue gap existed, the president recognised the urgent need to include the business and private sector in public discourse. To him, government and private enterprises are partners in economic development and their roles are complementary. Thus in 1995, the Private Sector Foundation (PSF) was created with the support of the World Bank. This is an umbrella organisation bringing together private sector organisations. It is supposed to act as a voice for the private sector. Since its inception, the organisation has presented to the government issues concerning fiscal and tax measures, business licensing, tariff protection, and access to industrial land with recommendations from the private sector. The creation of such organisations has eased the tension between government and the private sector while increasing chances for dialogue and open communication, which are important for successful policy implementation (Van Meter and Van Horn 1975).

To ease the conflicts, private sector organisations have been allowed to evolve. The most influential is the Uganda Manufacturers' Association (UMA). This organisation has members from all regions of the country and is a representative of the manufacturers' interests. On several occasions, the organisation has demanded changes in the tax policy and other decisions. Another influential organisation is the National Chamber of Commerce. This is concerned with trade and business relations both at home and abroad.

The two organisations have had both negative and positive influence on the privatisation policy in Uganda. Althrough the organisations have been influential in voicing the interests of the groups they represent, the two have exhibited conflicts of interests and have presented an investment dilemma. For example, while UMA advocates for tax increases especially on imports, so as to protect their industries, the National Chamber of Commerce advocates for tax reductions on imports. This has led to conflicts of objectives and the government has at times been divided. On the one hand, it has to satisfy the Chamber of Commerce since it is a body that provides a forum for private businessmen who contribute a lot to the tax base. On the other UMA also has to be satisfied since the government is interested in promoting the local manufacturing sector.

Despite the move to bridge the dialogue gap between the business sector and the government, there still exists a large dialogue gap between the government and civil society, particularly about the overall benefits of the whole privatisation exercise to the Ugandan community at large. The major concern for civil society is that the government did not create avenues in which the public would be educated about the whole exercise and the processes involved. As a result, the public still considers that the whole exercise was meant to enrich the president's family, relatives and political favourites. However, on several occasions, the government has put out radio and newspaper programmes to educate the public about the benefits of privatisation.

Another challenge to the privatisation process in Uganda was the opposition from the bureaucrats. The enterprises as already noted were considered to be cash cows; privatising them meant loss of resources for the bureaucrats. Therefore, despite the fact that privatisation was seen as a necessary step for Uganda's economic recovery in 1989, it was not until 1993 that the law was put into place to make privatisation possible. It thus took long to change the minds of and compel the bureaucrats to act.

Political interference has also limited the implementation of the policy. In 1998, the *New Vision* (Uganda's National Newspaper) presented a report of the parliamentary select committee on privatisation. The report argued that political interference has undermined the privatisation process. The newspaper highlighted the following anomalies. Although the law requires that the privatisation unit keeps the payments from sales of public enterprises on interest bearing accounts pending the conclusion of the sale agreement, this was not generally done. The law stipulates that successful bidders should pay not less than 50 percent of the full purchase price on settlement, and the balance must be payable within 12 months, but again, this has not been done.

There has also been a lot of political peddling affecting the quick privatisation of some companies, for example, Uganda Air Cargo, the Coffee Marketing Board, Uganda Airlines and Sheraton Kampala to mention but a few. The sale of Sheraton Kampala hotel is worth highlighting, as the deal failed to conclude because of political interference. Facts of the case indicate that, initially, 80 percent of the shares were awarded to Mr. Karim Hirji, a Kampala hotel tycoon, whose bid for US$ 21 million beat three other bidders. However, MIDROC, an Asian Ethiopian-based company that had bid US$ 19 million (second to Karim) complained that the whole deal involved foul play. After an investigation by the Inspector General of Government (IGG), the decision to sell to Karim was reversed and the tender awarded to MIDROC. The investigations revealed three Ministers having talked to Karim before the bids were opened. Karim conceded to the reversal but allegedly insisted in private that the trio pay him back the bribe amounting to $2 million, which he had paid to them so as to influence the award. This incident however, did not end the controversies surrounding the sale of the Sheraton Kampala Hotel.

In May 1998, MIDROC made a down payment of US$ 2 million as commitment fee but in August 1998 the sale contract was terminated after MIDROC failed to honour up to four extensions granted to pay the remaining US$ 17 million. MIDROC revealed that three ministers and one top army official failed them because of the continued insistence that they be paid US$ 2.5 million before the deal was concluded. The four wanted to pay back Karim's initial US$ 2 million bribe and make a profit of U$ 0.5 million. In 1999, a parliamentary probe team named the three ministers as Mr. Mayanja Nkangi (Minister of Justice and Former Minister of Finance), Mr. Matthew Rukikaire (Minister of State for Privatisation and a close member of the President's family) and Sam Kutesa (Minister of State for Investment and Planning and also married to a sister of Janet, the wife of the President). The army officer named in the deal was revealed to be Salim Saleh (a brother to the president) (*The Monitor Independent Newspaper*, 3 November 1999). Amidst this revelation, MIDROC was allowed to pay the remaining US$ 17 million. However, parliament insisted that MIDROC should first declare publicly the names of those demanding the bribe. MIDROC opted to pull out of the deal instead. To date the hotel has not been privatised. This case is a clear manifestation of the kinds of controversies involved in Uganda's privatisation process. One important point to note however is that despite this revelation of gross corruption by top government officials, they went unpunished, as if nothing wrong has happened.

The other major controversy surrounding Uganda's privatisation policy concerns the money received from the sale of the privatised assets. Members of Parliament (Legislators) felt that they have had little influence on the privatisation process. They also felt that there had been little transparency in the activities of the Privatisation Unit. Thus in 1999, despite the president's insistence that PEs be sold instead of keeping them in the hands of thieving bureaucrats, the parliament directed to suspend the sale. Although the process was resumed in 2000, this evidently shows how different interests can hinder implementation of a policy. One of the most controversial issues was the valuation of assets to be privatised. With considerable expenditure by government on the rehabilitation of these enterprises before they were ready for privatisation, one would imagine the value should have been higher than was being paid. There was considerable public outcry therefore, when it was discovered that the PEs had been sold at give-away prices.

Another problem was the fact that the system of competitive bidding, which was used to sale the enterprises, could not be met by Ugandan businessmen who lacked enough capital base. Many Ugandans were confined to small businesses, service sectors and hotels, while big enterprises like manufacturing were the exclusive domain of Ugandan-Asians. Consequently it was mainly Asians and foreigners (those having connections with state officials) that ended up successfully bidding for and owning the privatised enterprises. This caused further resentment from the already disgruntled (elite) Ugandans. To many Ugandans, this new form of ownership of privatised enterprises was a new form of 'foreignisation' (Mamdani 1993, speaking at a seminar, cited by Mugerwa 1996: 26). It further created a situation in which the president's relatives and political favourites came to run key businesses due to the flawed privatisation exercise. For example, the sale of UCB involved not only shoddy deals with Salim Saleh, but allegations also pointed to the president's son Captain Muhozi Kainerugaba and Ms. Jovia Akandwanaho (the president's brother's wife), as having been involved.

In spite of the weaknesses and challenges cited above, the privatisation policy gained popular support from the elite. Right from the beginning, many urban people had expressed their resentment to state owned enterprises, being clanged on by politicians for political and personal reasons. The urban public expressed their view that state enterprises were inefficient and their divestiture was seen as necessary and beneficial to the economy (*The Market Place*, December 1995: 1).

It should be noted too that there was little resistance from the trade unions and the workers towards the privatisation process in Uganda. This was arguably because workers were getting low pay from state companies put forward to be privatised. The move to create a strong private sector looked promising with more pay, if production could be boosted.

The challenges mentioned above in the privatisation process in Uganda indicate that the policy has only been relatively successful. Privatisation has brought about few economic benefits to the country, like considerable improvements in both increased output and employment generation. Hima cement industry, for example, which, was privatised in 1994, has increased production to about 600 metric tones per day, an increase of about 500 percent since its privatisation. Employment has also more than doubled to about 800 employees (Mugerwa 1996). Today, the policy is almost near completion, with over 80 percent of the PEs already divested. With continued exposure by the press, the corruption tendencies are slowly giving way to transparent divestiture as evidenced by the eventual sale of UCB to Stanbic.

Conclusion

The main argument in this chapter is that Uganda has had marked success in the implementation of the privatisation process. The chapter has tried to show that in spite of the challenges of implementing the privatisation policy, privatisation has brought marked contributions to the development of the country. There has been considerable improvement in employment sector. The chapter has also shown that there was a strong political commitment to privatise, especially the strong commitment of the president to let go of public enterprises. There was strong commitment (at least initially) on the part of the government to remove the enterprises from the hands of 'thieving bureaucrats' so as to avoid plunging the economy further down the road to retrogression.

The chapter has shown that there were steps made to bridge the dialogue gap between state and society through the creation of institutions representing different stakeholders. With the formation of Uganda Manufacturers Association (UMA) and Uganda Chamber of Commerce (UCC), the dialogue between the government and the business community was restored. The establishment of the Uganda Investment Authority, the enactment of the Investment Code and the putting into place of the PERD statute all made investing in Uganda an attractive venture. It is the creation of this institutional framework that largely explains the success of Uganda's privatisation programme.

Finally, it is important to note that in spite of the challenges depicted above, the economic benefits that have accrued to Uganda from its privatisation initiative provide Uganda as one example from which lessons can be drawn to understand the role of the state in industrial development. Although a state can be handicapped by its lack of finance to facilitate industrial development, it can play other roles to facilitate industrial growth as presented for example in the negotiations for financial capital from abroad and the creation of suitable institutional structures to stimulate investment. I would say that these offer tentative lessons for other African countries.

10

The Developmental State and Manufacturing in Botswana and Uganda

Pamela Mbabazi & Gladys Mokhawa

The debate regarding developmental activism has assumed centre stage. As have been argued in the previous chapters, the role of the state in Botswana has been likened in some ways to the development stories of East Asia countries where government policies went beyond the limits set by pure neo-classical policy directions. The Botswana state has been strategically interventionist and as such been able to formulate a series of policies aimed directly at infrastructural development and economic growth within the country. However, Botswana has been unable to stimulate a large-scale, internally-generated, competitive manufacturing sector like its counterparts in Asia (Edge 1998). Conversely, Uganda has often been described in derogatory terms as a parasitic or predatory state. But in this paper, we argue that Uganda is in many ways trying to be a developmental state and struggling to industrialise. That it faces numerous challenges is undeniable, but attempts at such policies are evident. We attempt to demonstrate that the textile industry, given opportunities under the Africa Growth and Opportunity Act (AGOA), could contribute to the industrial development of these two states. We suggest that the state is an important player in this whole equation and cannot be sidelined.

Development of the textile industry in Uganda: A background

Uganda's industrial sector played an important role in supporting the strong economic performance of the country in the initial years following independence. Between 1962 and 1970, the industrial sector, though small, helped to sustain a Gross Domestic Product (GDP) growth rate of 5.8 percent per annum (UNIDO 1999). This was made possible by supplying the economy with a wide range of basic inputs and consumer goods and the increased contribution from foreign exchange earnings brought in by textiles and copper.

Before Idi Amin's accession to power in 1971, Uganda had one of the most prosperous economies in Africa. Appropriate macro-economic policies together with a stable agricultural base enabled the economy to expand at an impressive annual growth rate of 6 percent between 1962 and 1971. There was a substantial degree of price stability and Uganda made significant strides in developing her industrial base. It should be mentioned, however, that during much of this period, it was the Asians that dominated the private sector and most business transactions. Very few Ugandans were involved in the private sector, and in some sectors like processing and manufacturing, indigenous entrepreneurs were almost non-existent. The country's steady economic prospects were, however, decisively shattered with Idi Amin's rise to power. The political chaos that followed, together with the absence of coherent economic policies led to terrible economic regression. The economy was enmeshed in a web of government controls on imports, access to foreign exchange, prices of goods, interest rates and on bank credit. This plethora of controls made it very difficult for the private sector to do business.

Perhaps most damaging for Uganda's economy during Amin's reign was the misguided/miscalculated decision to expropriate assets of foreign companies and expelling the Asian community, who represented the heart of the commercial and industrial sectors in the country. The industrial sector was the worst hit and its average annual growth rate went as low as 1 percent. Between 1973 and 1980, both growth fixed capital formation and exports fell by just under 10 percent annually. This reflected a number of macro economic imbalances, not least an average annual inflation rate of 45.4 percent (Bigsten and Kayizzi 2001).

Virtually all aspects of Uganda life and particularly the industrial sector suffered dramatically during the period 1971–1985. Mass expropriation of foreign assets deterred potential investors whilst infrastructure deteriorated. Protectionist policies, coupled with greater (but highly inefficient) involvement of the public sector in economic activity meant that economic and financial discipline suffered. By the end of the 1970's and mid 1980's the manufacturing sector was operating at less than 10 percent of its capacity (UNIDO 1999).

Following President Milton Obote's return to power in 1980, the government embarked on an IMF stabilisation programme. The government however was short-lived and did not get time to continue other important adjustment processes. The fairly sound macro-economic management programmes implemented however led to a considerable revival of financial assistance and culminated in debt rescheduling agreements with the Paris Club.

Nonetheless, the intensification of civil conflict from mid-1983 onwards undermined all stabilisation efforts and ultimately the Obote II government was forced to abandon them altogether. By the late 1985, the economy had virtually collapsed. Inflation had reached unprecedented levels (triple digits) and the relatively impressive start initiated by Milton Obote in 1980 was completely eroded.

In effect therefore, after registering steady growth of the industrial sector in the first decade of independence, the second decade was that of economic regression. This acute economic deterioration was manifested in political chaos, misrule, policy inadequacies as well as adverse external economic conditions.

However, all this, was to change with the accession to power of the NRM government in 1986. Today, Uganda has proved to the world that state support for industry is essential. This has been confirmed by the fairly successful story of exporting textiles through the AGOA in the past few years, through the factory at the centre of this: Tri-Star Apparels Factory in Bugolobi. Though this factory has been riddled with problems of late, this does not discount the progress made and in particular the employment opportunities created and the fact that Uganda is able to export its textile products and apparel to the United States.

When the NRM took over power in 1986, Uganda's economy was in total ruins. In the previous 15 years (between 1971 and 1986) per capita output had fallen by 42 percent. In other words, the income per head was little more than half of what it had been at the start of the 1970s. Not only had the economy shrunk dramatically, its composition had also changed markedly with the virtual collapse of much of the industrial sector and other formal sectors of the economy.

But perhaps the most critical indicator that shows the extent of economic devastation in Uganda was the fact that by 1986, industry accounted for less than 3 percent of GDP (Bigsten & Kayizzi 2001). Faced with very few options, the NRM government launched a comprehensive economic recovery programme in 1987, designed explicitly to redress the acute macro-economic disequilibria. With the support of the entire donor community, the NRM government was able to formulate and implement strategies aimed at revitalising the industrial and manufacturing sectors.

Institutional framework for industrial development under the NRM

Upon taking power, the NRM government looked at ways to restructure and rehabilitate the institutional framework of the country. The introduction of the Economic Recovery Programme (ERP) in 1987 was critical to reviving industrial development in Uganda. High on the priority list of this plan was the revival of the manufacturing sector, in particular, the rehabilitation of the country's critical infrastructure and the encouragement of foreign investment, specifically by seeking to resolve the issue of dispossessed Asian properties (EIU 1995). The government tore down many of the organisational structures, and psychological barriers, that were serving to inhibit the private sector's progress in manufacturing. Uganda's numerous marketing boards for instance, were steadily phased out. The Produce Marketing Board (PMB), which had exclusive export control over five food crops, had its monopolies removed in 1989. The coffee and cotton marketing boards were equally fully liberalised in 1991 and 1994 respectively (Brett 1995).

Within the government structure itself, a fully-fledged Ministry of Trade and Industry was introduced. This became a key organ for industrial policy and development. Headed by a minister, with the full support of a permanent secretary, and composed of three directorates (foreign trade, industry and technology and co-operatives and marketing), the Ministry of Trade and Industry was seen as a pillar for industrial development (World Bank 1993).

At the same time, new institutional structures to promote industrial development emerged on the scene in the private sector. These came into effect with the formulation and establishment of the Uganda Manufacturer's Association (UMA) set up in 1988. UMA acts as the umbrella organisation representing the country's over 300 manufacturing firms (Lamout 1994). Indeed, UMA has become a serious partner in the policy arena representing private sector interests. The strength of the private sector in industrial development was further inspired by the formulation of the National Chamber of Commerce and Industries, and the Uganda Exporters and Importers Association.

In effect therefore, a combination of institutional strategic changes and an organized private sector worked to revive the industrial sector in Uganda. Indeed, between 1986/87 (when the economic restructuring began) and 1994/95, the share of the manufacturing output in relation to total GDP rose from 4.8 percent to 7.2 percent (Bigsten and Kayizzi 2001). An IMF study conducted in 1996 revealed that this leap forward in manufacturing activities was supported by the reduction in macro-economic distortions, the liberalisation of investment and trade licensing requirements, as well as increased access to foreign exchange and improvements in tax and tariff administration (Sharer et al 1996). We now take a look, specifically, at the development of the textile industry in Uganda.

The textile industry in Uganda

The textile industry in Uganda has its roots way back in 1903 when Borup came up with a spinning mill. By 1906 different ginneries had started developing and at this time Ugandans were producing cotton for British textile companies. By 1970 there were a number of textile industries in Uganda e.g. Nyanza, Pamba, and African Textile Mills. But in 1974 the government came up with a so-called National Textile Board to 'manage' the textile industry in Uganda. The period that followed was characterised by an irregular supply of spare parts for the industries, no working capital, expulsion of technicians and Indians in general from Uganda. By the mid-1980s the machines and equipment in most textile industries were in a sorry state due to inadequate maintenance and obsolescence. As a result of these constraints, there was a sharp decline in the textile industry, falling from 18.6 million square metres in 1982 to 2.6 million square metres in 1985 (UNIDO 1997:72). This resulted in Ugandans importing fabric from different countries such as India, Malaysia, and Dubai etc. At the same time the importation of second hand clothes also started.

It was the 1986 economic reforms followed by the restructuring of the 1990s that led to the rejuvenation of the textile industry in Uganda. The government opted to instead privatise the textile industries so as to revitalise their operation. As a result, textile-manufacturing output in Uganda has steadily increased, from less than 2 percent in 1986 to 17 percent by 2000 (Bigsten and Kayiizi 2001). Today there are several textile industries that have been revived and these include: Sigma, Nytil, Phoenix, Tri-Star, Eladam, Kyosimba Textiles and Johnnie Spinning Industry.

Some of the constraints, which impede the growth, development and competitiveness of the textile industry in Uganda, include a limited availability of primary raw materials especially cotton due to the collapse of the marketing structures and ginneries over the years of economic decay. Unreliability and the high cost of power supply and other utilities, plus the limited access to finance and credit to further investments and operations have taken their toll too. Importation of second hand clothes (commonly called *mivumba*) in Uganda has also been a big blow to the development of the textile industry. Other challenges faced by the textile industry include the over-valued exchange rate and relatively weak institutions. At the same time the infrastructure and other support systems have crumbled. This has led to low productivity, low quality goods leading to marketing problems, especially faced with the competition for better quality second hand cloths.

The case of Tri-State Apparels Factory in Uganda

To give the world's poorest countries greater access to the US markets, the Clinton Administration earmarked a total of 58 nations from Africa and Latin America as beneficiaries under Africa Growth and Opportunity Act and the Caribbean Basin Parity Act, signed into law by President Clinton in May 2000. President Clinton said the programme 'will help promote economic development, alleviate global poverty and create new opportunities for America business and workers' (African Agenda 2000).

In Uganda, AGOA has been received with mixed feelings. Whereas some sections of the population envisage the factory as a saviour in as far as economic empowerment of the country is concerned, others have big reservations. To the government however, AGOA is the best thing that the West has done for Africa since independence. AGOA reduced and eliminated tariffs and quotas on more than 1,800 items and has helped develop a number of textile factories across Africa, as foreign investors, (mostly from Asia) seize upon its incentives to export garments to the US. We think AGOA is aimed at giving the underdeveloped countries a chance.

In Uganda, the Tri-star factory, based in Bugolobi-Kampala a few kilometres from the heart of Uganda's capital city, is headed by a Sri Lankan businessman Veluppilai Kananathan. Over 1,400 girls were recruited and trained on the job in various areas of specialisation like hemming skirts, stitching pockets or attaching buttons. President Museveni once commented that every time the girls stitch a pocket, attach a button or hem a skirt, they perform acts of patriotism that will help transform Uganda's economy (*New Vision Daily*, Kampala, 6 July 2003).

Labels like 'Made in Uganda' (or from any other African country) attached to the clothings on display in different US department stores today like Target, Sears & JC Penny, is not a mean achievement. Although these tags represent tiny percentage of apparel imports to the United States, they give tremendous pride to countries that have been at the margins of global trading systems. To this effect, Uganda has seen its exports to the United States increase from a minuscule US$ 32,000 in 2002 to US $909,000 in the first nine months of the Tri-star Factory's commencement.

The contribution of the Tri-Star industry to Uganda's employment sector cannot be underestimated either. Like her sister countries of Kenya, Lesotho, Malawi, Mozambique and Botswana among others, the largest employer in Uganda is no longer the government but the private enterprise. Tri-Star has opened up chances for over 1,500 people (including casual and technical staff); Kenya has projected 50,000 AGOA-related jobs will be created; while Lesotho estimates a total of 10,000 jobs.

However, challenges remain if AGOA is going to have any lasting effect in Uganda. The Tri-Star Apparels Factory has been enmeshed in a lot of controversies and uncertainty lately, and one wonders whether it will survive[7]. In effect, to get into the market, Uganda heavily subsidised Tri-Star, giving it an abandoned factory, waiving taxes and paying for six months of training of the workers to introduce them to sewing machines. However, it is not all free gifts as the government gets social security tax on the worker's modest salaries and utility fees on the company's water and electricity.

In facilitating Tri-Star's operations, the Ugandan state at least tried to do something to promote industrialisation and the country seemingly appears to have so far benefited from AGOA (despite the uncertainties of the Tri-Star factory). Obviously, a lot more needs to be done—the trade law in itself is set to expire in 2008, which is a short time away for investors (although there is a move to extend it for seven more years). Also, even if AGOA remains, a prime benefit that the trade provides will be undermined in 2005 when World Trade Organisation quotas on clothing and textiles expire. The elimination of the quotas will take away one of the most powerful incentives that foreign businesses now have to invest in Africa.

Challenges to industrialisation in Uganda

Looking at the institutional framework for industrialisation in Uganda today, there are several institutions that can lead the process of development. There is the state and bureaucracy, coordinating agencies, the ministries, banking institutions, insurance houses and the capital market to mention but a few. However what is currently lacking is a strong vibrant institution linking the state intermediate institutions and integrating the state with private organisations. The exiting institutions like UMA are not strong and vibrant enough. There must be a nature of cohesion between the state and other related institutions.

The bureaucracy must also be competent, organized and competently recruited. But this is one of the biggest setbacks in Uganda's industrial development. It is important to develop a strong indigenous entrepreneurial class, which is still lacking in today's Uganda.[8] The country lacks the right kind of human resources to propel industrialisation and hence the heavy reliance on foreign investors. The trend the world over is attracting human capital that you do not have but these have to be the right kind.

The other important question is how does Uganda acquire the technological know-how? It must industrialise by learning and strategically socialise with the international community in order to be able to build its own capacity. If Uganda wants to industrialise, it should at least develop its human resources first, then its institutions. Britain was the first country to industrialise and the French learnt by working in the British industries as messengers. The same was the case for the South East Asians learning from the Americans.

Uganda as a developmental state: Which way forward?

While the dominant ideology today is economic liberalism, one alternative to this is the notion of a 'developmental state'. A developmental state was not God-given to countries in East Asia nor to Botswana; it was instead politically-driven. In Uganda, this political agenda must define the country's long-term priorities and transform the national economy from primary commodity production to industrial production. Although the Ugandan state has in some ways adopted elements of developmental state activism, by creating the necessary institutions, most of these are currently weak. Modernisation of the economy will not come about this way—what is needed is the adoption of proper developmental activism. Institutions matter and need further developing and strengthening.

Late industrialisation calls for state intervention in guiding the economy. There is no country, early or late, that has ever industrialised without the state. Chalmers Johnson (1990) argues that the dominant ideology should be 'economic nationalism' and not [plain] 'economic liberalism'. The state has to guide the market using a pilot agency playing an entrepreneurship role, as has occurred in Botswana. A developmental state has to consult with the stakeholders before announcing policies so that affected stakeholders are part of their formulation and development. In developmental states, politicians reign but the bureaucrats remain and have to be permanent so that the process of policy formulation is consistent. In Botswana they recruited only high quality bureaucrats and this is exactly what economic nationalism is all about. In Uganda however, this is probably the biggest challenge for our progress as most of our policies and decisions are politically-driven.

Industrial development in Botswana

At the time of independence Botswana possessed very little industrial development. The economy was dominated by subsistence arable agriculture and cattle production. Beef processing was the only major manufacturing. The post-independence period however ushered in the exploitation of minerals (particularly diamonds) which, later became the engine of growth. However, dependence on diamonds is quite problematic in that the prices of primary commodities tend to be volatile and diamonds have been exposed to the potential risk of consumer discontent over the so-called conflict diamonds. The other problem with diamond dependence is that, dependence has meant that there has been a continuous transfer of resources to the mining sector at the expense of other sectors. As such the government is aware of the un-sustainability of a mineral-led growth (Mokhawa and Osei-Hwedie 2003). The government has thus identified manufacturing industry as a potential area for diversification.

The manufacturing sector in Botswana is relatively small, accounting for an estimated 4.5 percent of Botswana's GDP, yet it employs more labour than the mining sector and it is considered a potential growth sector. Several reasons have been put forward for the slow growth of manufacturing. These include the small size of the domestic market and the limited resource base of the country. It is therefore imperative to showcase the role played by the state in the development of manufacturing sector with specific reference to the textile industry.

From independence (1966) through to the 1970s, the government neglected some sectors of manufacturing and this included textiles. Manufacturing then consisted principally of processing beef for export. The textile industry was characterised by basically uniform making. Botswana school uniform producers then had 40 to 70 per cent of the school uniform market but protective clothing and institutional uniforms (Botswana Defence Force, Police, Mines and Hospitals) were completely controlled by South African suppliers.

It was not until the 1980s that textiles started to perform well. In the 1980s, textile surpassed meat industry in both total capital investment and number of jobs created. Tsie (1989) notes that its vigorous growth then, unlike the meat industry, owed little support to the state. The development of textiles during this period was largely due to Zimbabwean investments. A study undertaken by the government argued that the textile industry in Botswana has been developed primarily to service the Zimbabwean market: a large portion of the industry appeared to be controlled from Zimbabwe (GoB 1984). Many Zimbabwean companies decided to relocate their companies to Botswana to avoid the uncertain situation in Zimbabwe, and Botswana provided advantages such as access to the South African market, the availability of foreign exchange, and a liberal foreign exchange regime. Surprisingly, the current political turmoil in Zimbabwe has however not resulted in further relocations of industries to Botswana.

But, the relocation of the 1980s stimulated the government to accelerate its attempt to attract foreign investment. Thus, the government created the Financial Assistance Policy (FAP) in 1982. The FAP attracted textile investments but mostly managed to attract fly-by-night investors who abandoned their workers and disappeared. Cowan (1997) had supported FAP arguing that it involved a rigorous cost benefit analysis intended to demonstrate that the proposed project could generate an economic rate of return of over six percent over a ten year period. But Kaplinsky (1991) argued that Botswana's FAP provides a good example of how getting prices right helped the wrong people.

In addition to the FAP, the government established Selebi Phikwe Regional Development Programme (SPRDP). It was set up to diversify the economy of Selebi Phikwe away from mining. Although the overall package offered to foreign investors seems very similar to those available in export processing zone (EPZ) found in other developing countries, the SPDRP was not really a zone because firms in Selebi Phikwe were not special enclaves because they did not have privileges in being able to import goods duty free for processing and re-exporting as in most EPZs; and though facilities were good at Selebi Phikwe, they were not superior to those found in major urban areas of the country. In addition, firms in Selebi Phikwe had to deal with government bureaucratic procedures, unlike under many EPZs arrangement for example, in order to obtain manufacturing license or work permits Cowan (1997).

There have been some mixed results so far with the development of the textile industry. The Bank of Botswana reported that manufacturing was adversely affected by the poor performance of textile. Jeffries, quoted in the Bank of Botswana Report (2001), however, feels that the government is trying to level the playing field by extending 15 percent tax concessions to the manufacturing sector including textiles. BIDPA (2001) reports a growth in the textile exports. The growth is thought to have started in the 1990s and reached a peak in 1998 at P303 million in exports revenues. A decline of 18 percent and 5 percent was recorded in 1999 and 2000, respectively. The decline was thought to be due to the closure of textile companies that had taken advantage of government incentives. An improvement was witnessed when manufacturers started taking advantage of market opportunities offered by AGOA and the EU, as well as in South Africa.

The nature of state assistance

It is believed that currency transferability and convertibility, political stability and macroeconomic stability are key factors affecting a business decision to invest in a country. Additionally, supportive infrastructures, conducive institutional frameworks and a competitive business environment are things that matter to investors. In responding to the above, the country has designed some incentives for investment in manufacturing. There exists a favourable macroeconomic environment, and institutional, regulatory and policy frameworks in Botswana are fairly conducive. These incentives comprise of the FAP, corporate tax of 15 percent, regulatory frameworks concerning repatriation of investment with no restrictions on foreign exchange transactions and repatriation of capital, profits, dividends and expatriate salaries (BEDIA 1999) and institutional support.

The wage rates, averaging US$80 per month are set by the government to guide foreign investors (BEDIA 1998). The normal working week for factory workers varies between 45 and 48 hours. The wage rate for unskilled labour is set at P2.75 per hour. Wages in Botswana are said to be high compared to productivity and whilst industrial relations were said to be good, they were, as Taylor (2003) puts it 'severely constrained' until threats of strike action by various groups of workers in the late 2002.

The FAP was specifically created for labour-intensive production. It contained wage subsidies for the company for five years, training subsidy of 50 percent of training cost of any Botswana citizen, and a capital subsidy of 40 percent to 55 percent on investments based on jobs created for Botswana citizens averaging $215 per job. The training component was introduced as an incentive for improving skills and productivity levels in manufacturing. The majority of manufacturing industries would not have been set up in Botswana without the existence of FAP support, for instance, Northern Textile Company (one of the leading textile manufactures) benefited from the subsidised training. In fact, manufacturers' reasons for investing in Botswana are the inducements offered through FAP.

However, there were some elements of fraud and abuse, in addition to inadequate administration and management of projects. In fact, there is a widely held perception that FAP attracted companies (especially in the garment industry), which only wished to benefit from the grants and which closed down after the expiry of the grants and/or re-emerged as different companies to benefit from new grants (BIDPA 2000). Actually, BEDIA has noted this:

Doubts are raised especially based on the negative experience of previous investors who came to the country and then sneaked away quietly after having benefited from the FAP of the government. Some even came with equipment fit for a museum. Obviously their equity in projects was very low, if any investment was made at all (quoted in www.cleanclothes.org/publications/01-11-botswana.htm)

The experience with FAP led the government to come up with a new scheme, the Citizen Entrepreneurial Development Agency (CEDA). It has been established in response to the concerns on the adequacy and effectiveness of the existing citizen empowerment schemes. Therefore, revision of existing and the creation of new empowerment schemes was found to be necessary. CEDA is meant to redirect, energise, and invigorate existing schemes with respect to citizen business development with the objective of enabling Batswana to participate meaningfully in every aspect of the economy. It is believed that CEDA will benefit the textile industry. Nevertheless, a breakdown of CEDA lending by sector shows that manufacturing has not had enough lending as compared to sectors like service:

Total Lending by Sector

Sector	Value (Pm)
Agriculture	38
Services	160
Manufacturing	40
Retailing	60
Property Development	40

Source: Annual Economic Report (2003)

It is however expected that CEDA will encourage enterprises in establishing sectors like manufacturing to take advantage of lower tariff and non-tariff barriers that have resulted from Botswana's trade agreements such as AGOA, Cotonou Agreement, SACU and SADC (GOB 2003).

Institutional support has been in the form of institutions like Industrial Affairs, BEDIA, BDC, and the Botswana Bureau of Standards. The Department of Industrial Affairs is an arm of the Ministry of Trade and Industry and promotes entrepreneurs, helping them to get established in the sector. It issued licenses and permits to companies (a duty undertaken by BEDIA now), and served as an administrator of FAP. Currently, Industrial Affairs is entrusted with the responsibility of drawing up an export policy.

As a result of their promotional efforts, BEDIA has been able to attract twelve manufacturing companies while fifteen of its projects are at an advanced stage of implementation (GoB 2002). The companies are already operational and have created 1600 additional jobs in the manufacturing sector. Five of these are textile companies including Band M Garments, Rising Sun (Pty) Ltd, Benrose Ltd, Star Apparel (Botswana) Pty Ltd (BEDIA 2001), and Dinesh Textiles.

The Authority helps existing manufacturing enterprises to sort out any administrative problems that they may be confronted with. However, critics are saying that BEDIA is more interested in attracting companies to Botswana than maintaining them, which is counter to their motto 'BEDIA takes good care of you'. Additionally, BEDIA have been central in the AGOA negotiations for the reclassification of Botswana from a middle-income country to a less developed country under AGOA II to allow Botswana to develop a thriving export-based textile industry

The Botswana Bureau of Standards is essential in that exporters are assisted to meet quality standards for export markets. The establishment of the Bureau of Standards is an important step towards this objective. It provides testing and standardisation services, makes available international quality standards organisation (ISO), trading standards and provides certification under ISO 9000 and ISO 14000. The acceptance of Botswana products in foreign markets will be made much easier if they carry the appropriate standards approval.

What is missing in Botswana's strategy?

Despite the levels of state assistance, questions have been raised as to why the textile industry had failed to attract enough investment to the country. A number of explanations have been proffered. The textile industry globally is highly competitive and Botswana does not have the raw materials and primary processes to cater for the garment industry. Most raw materials are imported from SADC neighbours, with South Africa as the dominant source and then the Far East. The other issue is that entrepreneurs are 'doing it small', that is, most companies are doing little to equip themselves with modern technology. Some commentators, on a different note, argue that textile holds potential for diversification but the problem with the industry is that it is not integrated. It is worth mentioning the superficial way in which existing productions are integrated into the Botswana economy. The textile industry in Botswana is of the Cut-make-trim (C-M-T) type, that is, the textile industry is engaged in the last stage of production rather than in all processes of production from beginning to end—this affects employment creation.

There is a generally accepted view that it is difficult to run a textile company in Botswana because of a number of challenges. These challenges include the high cost of utilities, for example electricity and water—a problem highlighted by Hughes and colleagues (Hughes et al 2003). They are of the view that investors are guided by hard facts and reputations. Furthermore, they assert, that while Asia has developed a reputation for quality workmanship and low costs, Africa has developed a reputation for corruption, war and high cost. Other challenges identified were exorbitant transport costs since Botswana is landlocked and 'third class' industrial workers who are not productive. Actually unproductive workers have been found to be a predicament.

Specific problems that face the textile industry in Botswana include the fact that raw materials as a percentage of sales is extremely high, unit labour cost is also high, measured in terms of value added per production (a clear manifestation of low labour productivity), high interest rates on loans, lack of training institutes (currently Botswana has no university-level training in textiles) and an absence of linkages.

However, there is adequate state support in the textile industry. The government has done and is continuing to do much for the textile industry in Botswana. The government has identified the textile industry as one of the growth sectors and so it has been sensitive to new opportunities. The state has tried to play an entrepreneurial role through the activities undertaken by BEDIA such as identifying markets for locally produced products and by introducing CEDA which has components for helping Batswana develop habits of entrepreneurship. One may view this as suggesting that the state has played its part. Sentsho (2002) argues that for the state to realize economic diversification there must be a willingness by the state to have the private sector play a dominant role in economic development while at the same time the state should be willing to fill gaps in areas where the private sector is non-existent or is not forthcoming. The state also has to be willing to privatise as soon as it becomes profitable for the private sector to run state-created institutions. These recommendations fit in with the East Asian experiences and Botswana state surely has done the above by establishing institutions like BDC and BEDIA to take advantage of emerging opportunities. BEDIA has been established to identify markets for the companies and assist in the marketing of those companies. It has also been central in educating the companies about AGOA

Botswana's experience with AGOA

As in Uganda, AGOA presents opportunities to increase Botswana's exports to the most lucrative market in the world, that is, the American market. Countries like Mauritius, Kenya, Swaziland, Madagascar and Lesotho have received tangible benefits from scrapping of US tariffs on a range of products such that these countries have recorded double-digits growth in textile exports to the US. Benefits have already accrued from AGOA exports to Botswana. For instance, the total volume of textiles and apparel exports under AGOA from 2001 was US$2,206,910; in 2002 it increased to US$ 5,144, 511. In 2003 it was US$4,657,844. Today, about nine companies have registered to export under AGOA, but only six of these are actually exporting textiles and apparels to the US, with outstanding performances by a company named Caratex.

However, Botswana has not received as much benefit under AGOA as Lesotho. This has often been associated with the fact that Botswana was initially classified under the middle-income economies, hence could not actually enjoy benefits offered under AGOA I. AGOA I provided for the growth of apparel imports made from fabric and yarn produced in a beneficiary African country, from 1.5 per cent of overall US apparel imports to 3.5 per cent over the eight year period (AGOA Report 2002). It was not until the country negotiated for the consideration of the country as a less developed country that tangible results surfaced. But this is just about to end in October 2004 since clothing from African countries will only receive preferences if the fabric is regionally produced or bought from the U.S.

Conclusion

The relative successes of late developing countries like Botswana and Uganda has been due to state intervention. In both countries, the state has consistently intervened in the development of the textile industry. In Botswana's case however, some argue that the Botswana government has not seriously engaged in textiles development in the same way as the NICs in East Asia. This could be the result of a dependence on ready revenue pools such as diamonds, European Union beef quotas, and receipts from the Southern African Customs Union (SACU). The problem may perhaps be the nature of producers who take advantage of government schemes such as FAP but who are footloose and exploitative, something seen also in Uganda. It may as well be the fact that producers are small and cannot compete against larger producers in the region especially those from South Africa or Kenya. Local producers face barriers to regional exports because of other competitors in stronger countries; Botswana in particular faces South African industrial hegemony.

For sustainable development of this industry the government of Botswana should take Sentsho's (2002) criticisms seriously. But this seems unlikely, especially given global neo-liberal pressures for limiting state involvement in industry or the economy. Thus, it seems that while textiles may be a good basis or form a platform for national development, it is more likely, that development of this sector will be haphazard, reactive, and overly dependent on the willingness of foreign producers to 'find' Botswana on the world production map.

As for Uganda, there is no country in the world that has been able to industrialise in the context of free markets and Uganda is not going to be the first. Developmental activism is not optional but vital. In the Asian Tigers, the state practiced developmental state activism and economic nationalism (but not economic liberalism), enabling them to produce goods that had a potential to penetrate the global markets. In both Botswana and Uganda however, the scenario today is rather different and of course the world has moved on. But emphasis on high-level bureaucratic competency and a conducive institutional framework are vital in both countries under review; Botswana has achieved a lot of success, though Uganda needs to do much more. Both countries need to recognise the potentiality that the textile industry offers for national development and both need to stay the course in using the offices of the state to promote and nurture this nascent industry.

Conclusion

Developmental States and Africa in the Twenty-first Century

Pamela Mbabazi and Ian Taylor

The ability or otherwise of both Botswana and Uganda—as well as the rest of the continent—to pursue policies outlined in this book are of course both contingent and, to a large degree, influenced by the global milieu. Since the early 1980s a philosophical approach to economics and development, one that is broadly in alignment with the neo-liberal mantra of liberalisation, privatisation and the 'free market' has become hegemonic, and this invariably informs the debate on what constitutes 'development'. We use the term hegemonic in the Gramscian sense whereby the ideological, moral and cultural values of neo-liberalism have become broadly accepted as 'common sense' and largely unquestionable. Whilst we cannot overlook the coercive disciplinary aspect of this hegemony, in general the values and norms associated with neo-liberalism have become largely accepted as the consensus.

It is against this 'standard' that all are judged and 'development' itself must square with the familiar neo-liberal package if it is to receive the stamp of approval from the important powers-that-be within the global economy. The idea of a 'developmental state' obviously tends to jar against such prescriptions. Of major importance is the scenario whereby 'mono-economics', i.e. the belief that there exists a universal set of economic laws that apply across the board has emerged as a means of informing and shaping development practice. This is however highly dubious if not dangerous if we are to advance a developmental agenda, not least if Africa is to advance *democratic* developmental states.

State administrations in the developing world are held hostage to a Janus-faced dilemma with regard to the pursuit of development. On the one hand they are now supposedly beholden to their (increasingly dissatisfied) domestic constituencies whilst on the other, and probably much more so, they are accountable to unelected external creditors and donors. This has resulted in the creation of highly fragile 'democracies', which remain unable to satisfy the demands and aspirations of the poor majority whilst socio-economic improvements and development plays second fiddle to the requirements of the IFIs and donors. In the light of shifting definitions of what constitutes development we can say that this very powerful term is evidently a historically contingent form of knowledge, closely tied to dominant structures and global power relations. It is not some sort of ahistorical set of universally applicable goals. The type of neo-liberal precepts that underpin the contemporary development discourse associated with good governance and particular notions of democracy helps contribute to a continuation of a profoundly undemocratic world order, despite the claims made by its promoters. Navigating this precarious situation is something which state administrations throughout the developing world have to perform—some better than others.

Yet at the same time globalisation brings opportunities and agency. Improved technologies and greater interaction between peoples can be empowering and uplifting. Virtual solidarity across the internet cannot be waved away as irrelevant and lessons from other parts of the developing world on strategies to cope with—and perhaps transform—impulses associated with globalisation can be disseminated at a speed previously unthinkable. Whilst the neo-liberal aspects of globalisation are profoundly questionable, especially the reification of the 'free market', other elements associated with globalisation such as intensified communication, human interaction and improved access to such technologies as the mobile phone can have positive developmental spin-offs. The question is, how is globalisation managed and how can its positive aspects be directed towards development so as to maximise its benefits. In essence, whilst globalisation is mostly about the reconfiguration of power on a global scale, it is also about epoch-making changes regarding economic *as well as* social, gender, and cultural relations. These changes provide opportunities for developmental thinking as well as problems and barriers. In this sense the notion and potentiality of 'development' should not be seen as closed off under the conditions of globalisation, but rather demands a rethinking of what exactly it constitutes in the modern era. Much of the pessimistic readings regarding globalisation may after all, be simply failures in the imagination. Thus in the context of this volume, how and in what ways states plot a course in constructing a 'developmental state' within the globalising confines of the contemporary period is absolutely vital and is perhaps one of the foremost tasks before Africa's leadership. Yet there is the danger that if left unchecked the state in Africa (or what is left of it) may become a 'transmission belt' for economic globalisation, rather than a mediating influence seeking to craft beneficial partnerships that promote development.

In essence, the dominant line on how development might be 'factored in' to globalisation, but which neglects major structural issues in the global economy, is likely to be counter-productive. It is simply not good enough to predicate such calls around 'growth' and hope that development will somehow occur. In this light, the current debate between the North and the South is likely to fail to address developmental aspirations as it fails to advance any concrete agenda regarding the asymmetric power relations between the two, and in many ways undermines the potency of constructing developmental states. It is this inequality that is a significant cause of maldevelopment and a huge hurdle for any developmental project to get off the ground.

So where does all this leave countries such as Botswana and Uganda? It is surely axiomatic that economies at different levels of development have different requirements when it comes to regulation and social values. After all, there are qualitative differences between Northern Europe's social corporatism and Thatcherism; between Asia's diverse communitarianism and hyper-liberalism; and between South Europe's co-operative ventures and the ruthless 'free market'. Any economic historian would admit that policies that spurred development in the North were not based on neo-liberal ideas which fetishised the market beyond all—quite the opposite. In fact, all late industrialisers, as well as earlier ones, deployed various forms of economic nationalism and protected themselves—the total opposite of what the one-world neo-liberal globalists assure is the way forward to growth and development. Surely, it not unreasonable for states in Africa to be afforded the same kind of space?

A developmental project on the continent might be expected to allow countries to maintain national differences in areas where it was felt that the intrusion of international competitors would erode or destroy local activities that have broad backing. A more nuanced acceptance and understanding that if practices run counter to the developmental or social aspirations of the populace then caution and restraint should be exercised and part of any developmental project.

This book has been critical of the inequality within both countries under review and is certainly not enamoured by the two states, for varying reasons. But, the context of these problems must be understood and despite all the problems, the states in both countries have achieved respectable accomplishments in various fields. Botswana's strategy in particular has shown that 'a disciplined activist African state that governs the market is essential for industrial development and recovery' (Owusu and Samatar 1997: 270). Indeed, we might concur with the assessment that 'Botswana [has] defied the thrust of prevailing development orthodoxy, which claims that African states cannot enhance industrial development through interventionist strategy. Botswana's state-governed industrial strategy supports aspects of recent research on the 'East Asian miracle', which underscores the fundamental importance of state intervention in industrial transformation' (ibid.: 289). Equally, the 'primacy of politics' in the complex process of development has been fundamental and decisive, inferring that it is not *how much* state intervention should take place, but rather *what kind and why* (Leftwich 2000).

Contra the neo-liberals, as Crawford Young wrote, 'there is no conceivable alternative to the state as prime organiser of change. Escape from poverty is impossible without collective societal intervention through the state' (1982: 19). This is not to be naïve and ignore the fact that the elites in both countries seek to run a comprehensive and basically authoritarian (i.e. statist) conception of development and that this has taken place in a climate where opposition was muted and/or impotent, even if there was a formal competitive framework, as in Botswana. But the reproduction of the ruling elites domination is not simply based on force but is grounded in varying ways on the success of the economic project to 'develop' Botswana and 'rehabilitate' Uganda. In both cases this is cast as being through the construction of a developmental state.

As we mentioned at the beginning of this book, there is a problem in defining a developmental state simply from its economic performance—clearly not all countries with good growth rates are developmental states. Indeed, up until the mid-1970s many African states would have qualified as 'developmental'. In our definition, a developmental state is one whose ideological underpinnings are developmental and one that *earnestly seeks to* deploy its resources to the *job* of economic development. As Leftwich (1995: 401) notes, 'Developmental states may be defined as states whose politics have concentrated sufficient power, autonomy and capacity at the centre to shape, pursue and encourage the achievement of explicit developmental objectives, whether by establishing and promoting the conditions and direction of economic growth, or by organising it directly, or a varying combination of both'.

Clearly, there are degrees of success and if one was going to 'measure' Botswana and Uganda then different results would be produced, obviously. But, we would assert that a state that is purposefully-driven to promote development and that utilises the offices of the state in order to facilitate improvement, alongside other actors such as the private sector and civil society can, in the particular circumstances the content finds itself, be regarded as 'developmental'. Certainly, the growth record of independent Botswana has been impressive and despite its problems, its developmental trajectory has been relatively impressive. Uganda has similarly made great strides in recent years and may well be seen as an emerging economy. Though controversial, Uganda is largely seen by the international community at least to be doing the right things vis-à-vis tax collection, the struggle against AIDS, women's empowerment etc.

We would argue that the book has shown that the differences between 'successful' states and the experiences of others, is seen as the effective construction of a 'developmental state', as opposed to the development of a predatory state which holds back development.

But overall, the fundamental conclusion that we would draw with regards to developmental states in Africa is that the orthodox approach to the role of the state is misplaced and has seen the construction of minimalist states which lack any real prospective to promote or guide development, leaving it all to the 'market'. We believe this to be a mistake if taken to its extreme. Both Botswana and Uganda demonstrate that there is a role for the state in advancing development and in ensuring a balanced approach to the relationship between the public and private sector. They may not always get it right, but the attempt to promoted development and ideologies this has guided the institutions and organisations that existed within both countries to encourage growth.

The challenges are immense and there can be no willy-nilly of the 'lessons' of Botswana and Uganda to the rest of the continent. But there are things that we feel others can reflect upon. First and foremost of these would be the need for a disciplined leadership that is not rapacious nor overly predatory. Perhaps the historical circumstances in both Botswana and Uganda are unique—but we do not believe so. There are many countries that have had to start from Ground Zero and seek to reconstruct an economy. Uganda is but one. What the country built was not necessarily a strong state, but rather a capable one that has been able to varying degrees to chart a path forwards. Yet whilst the commitment to development by both the political and bureaucratic elites has been central, this has been put into practice in Uganda, as well as in Botswana, by the stratagem of putting into place institutions which have helped sustain long-term growth as part of a broader national developmental vision.

In both countries, the state has sought to act as an entrepreneurial agent in varying ways and has sought to co-ordinate private and the public sectors cooperation. The developmental state project in both states is thus based on a foundation of capitalism but in which the government, through a wide variety of incentives, energetically promotes investment. This is assisted by a bureaucracy that has in the main withstood the plunge into predation that has been the fate of other parts of the continent. Capable state intervention *can* play a vital role in creating conditions for sustained trade growth and that this can be channelled into a variety of development strategies that can produce results. But for a developmental state to 'succeed' or even exist, the importance—if not the primacy—of politics in the multifaceted course of development is essential and key. In other words, it is not how much state intervention should take place, but rather what kind. Finding the right mix and maintaining the balance in any country will remain one of the greatest challenges for Africa. Whilst the way in which this is achieved and how it is upheld will be contingent and different in each country, this is not to say it is impossible nor that it should be attempted. If what Botswana and Uganda at least offer up is an alternative to the Afro-pessimism that many observers seem to have these days regarding the continent's future.

Notes

1 The Department of Women's Affairs is advised by the Botswana National Council of Women (BNCW). This Council draws its membership from civil society

organisations and government. While being touted as the 'highest advisory board to the Government on all matters relating to women and development' (Ministry of Labour and Home Affairs 1995: 37), the Council's work remains at the level of awareness-raising (among Politicians and Traditional Leaders)—efforts that have brought little success.

2   Emang Basadi was established by a group of female academics and activists. The organisation originally mobilised around amending the Citizenship Act of 1984 – later activities include political mobilisation as well as sensitisation with respect to violence against women.

3   The Women and Law in Southern Africa Research Project is a regional network based in Harare, Zimbabwe. The member groups of Botswana, Lesotho, Swaziland, Malawi, Mocambique, Zambia and Zimbabwe have conducted research on Maintenance Laws and Practices, Family Forms, Inheritance Practices and Violence Against Women since 1992.

4   Despite the small numbers overall, never before in Uganda's history had there been these many women involved in politics and higher levels of decision-making.

5   Electoral Commission Report 2001 and Parliamentary Archives.

6   Wife beating is one of the most common forms of domestic violence in Uganda. It is often due to burning food, arguing with husband, going out without informing husband, neglecting children and refusing sexual relations with the husband. For detailed information see: Uganda's Demographic and Health Survey: 2000–2001, UBOS, Entebbe.

7   A recent parliamentary enquiry into the operations and status of the factory revealed that government heavily subsidised the factory. The government had granted loans worth more than Shs 10 billion to Apparels Tri-Star Factory. This was on top of the Shs 5.8 billion that government made available in cash and subsidies to the firm and this raised a lot of eyebrows amongst the legislators. (*The Monitor*, 3rd November 2003).

8   The trend instead seems to emphasise recruiting people based on 'technical know-who' rather than 'technical know-how'.

References

Abraham, K., 1995, *The Missing Millions: Why and How Africa is Underdeveloped*, Trenton, New Jersey: Africa World Press.

Abrahamsen, R., 2001, *Disciplining Democracy: Development Discourse and Good Governance in Africa* London: Zed Books.

Acemoglu, D., Johnson, S. and Robinson, J., 2001, 'How Botswana Did It: Comparative Development in Sub-Saharan Africa', unpublished paper.

ACFODE, 1988, *Women Breaking Through*, Kampala: Action for Development.

Adhikari, R. and Kamalesh, A., 2000, *Privatisation: Expectation and Reality*, Kathmandu: Pro-Public.

Adler, G. and Steinberg, J., eds., 2000, *From Comrades to Citizens: The South African Civics Movement and the Transition to Democracy*, London: Macmillan for Albert Einstein Institution.

African Development Bank, 1991, *African Development Report 1991*, African Development Bank.

Africa Development Bank, 2003, *Selected Statistics on African Countries*, African Development Bank: Tunis.

AGOA Report, 2002, *2002 Comprehensive Report on U.S Trade and Investment Policy Towards Sub-Saharan Africa and Implementation of the African Growth and Opportunity Act, The Second of the Eight Annual Reports, May 2002*, www.agoa.gov/About AGOA/annual2.pdf

Ajulu, R., 2001, 'Uganda's Flawed Presidential Election Bodes Ill for the Future', *Global Dialogue* 6 (2), July: 20-22.

Akampumuza J., 1992, *The Conditions of Labour in the Brickmaking Industry in Kabale*, Makerere University LL.M Dissertation.

Akampumuza J., 1996, *The Return of Asians In Uganda, an Analysis of its Legal and Political Aspects*, Makerere University LL.M Dissertation, unpublished.

Amsden, A., 1994, 'Why Isn't the Whole World Experimenting with the East Asian Model to Develop? Review of *The East Asian Miracle*', *World Development*, 22 (4).

Amin, S., 1996, 'On the Origins of Economic Catastrophe in Africa' in Chew, S.C. and Denemark, R.A. *The Underdevelopment of Development*. California: Sage Publications Inc. pp. 200-216.

Amin, S., 1997, 'Reflections on the International System', in P. Golding & P. Harris (eds), *Beyond Cultural Imperialism: Globalization, Communication & the New International Order,* Sage: London. pp. 10-24.

Anderson, E. J., 1975, *Public Policy Making,* New York: Praeger.

Anena, C., 2001, 'Participation of Civil Society in Policy-related Advocacy for Poverty Reduction in Uganda: An Experience from the Uganda Debt Network', unpublished paper.

Anheier, H., Glasius, M. and Kaldor, M., 2001, 'Introducing Global Civil Society' in *Global Civil Society 2001,* Oxford: OUP.

Ankrah, M., 1996, 'Conflict; The Experience of Ugandan Women in Revolution and Reconstruction', unpublished paper.

Aryeetey, E., 2002, 'A Case for Enhanced Resource Flow to Facilitate Development and Reduce Poverty', *Journal of African Economies,* 11, (2).

Asea, Patrick K. and Darlison Kaija, 2000, *Impact of the Flower Industry in Uganda,* Geneva: ILO Sectoral Activities Programme, Working Paper no. 148, January.

Ayittey, G., 1999, *Africa in Chaos,* New York: St Martins.

Ayittey, G., 1992, *Africa Betrayed,* New York: St Martins.

Baier, V., 1994, *Implementation and Ambiguity,* London: SAGE.

Baker, W., 2001, *Uganda: The Marginalization of Minorities* London: Minority Rights Group International.

Bank of Botswana, 2001, *Annual Report,* Gaborone: Bank of Botswana.

Bank of Uganda, (various years), *Annual Reports,* Kampala: Bank of Uganda.

Bank of Uganda, (various years), *Monthly Economic Reports,* Kampala: Bank of Uganda.

Bank of Uganda, (various years), *Quarterly Bulletin of Statistics,* Kampala: Bank of Uganda.

Barnett, T. and Whiteside, A., 2002, *AIDS in the Twenty-first Century: Disease and Globalization* London: Palgrave.

Barratt Brown, M., 1995, *Africa's Choices: After Thirty Years of the World Bank* Penguin Books: London.

Bayart, J.-F., Ellis, S., & Hibou, B.1999. *The Criminalization of the State in Africa,* Oxford: James Currey.

Bendell, J., ed., 2000, *Terms for Endearment: Business, NGOs and Sustainable Development,* Sheffield: Greenleaf for New Academy of Business.

Bibangambah, J., 2001, *Africa's Quest for Economic Development: Uganda's Experience,* Kampala: Fountain.

Bigsten, A., 1999, 'Looking for African Tigers' in S. Kayizzi-Mugerwa (ed.) *The African Economy: Policy Institutions and the Future,* London and New York: Routledge.

Bigsten, A. and Kayizzi-Mugerwa, S., 2001, Is Uganda an Emerging Economy? A Report of the OECD Project 'Emerging Africa' Uppsala: Nordiska Afrikainstitutet.

Botswana Development Corporation, 1985, Botswana Development Corporation: The First Fifteen Years Gaborone: BDC.

Botswana Development Corporation, 1995, *Twenty Fifth Anniversary,* Gaborone: BDC.

Botswana Development Corporation, 1998, *Annual Report,* Gaborone: BDC.
Botswana Development Corporation, 1999, *Annual Repor,t* Gaborone: BDC.
Botswana Development Corporation, 2000, *Annual Report 2001: Maintaining the Momentum,* Gaborone: BDC.
Botswana Development Corporation, 2002, *Annual Report,* Gaborone: BDC.
Botswana Export Development and Investment Promotion, 1998, *Annual Report,* Gaborone: BEDIA.
Botswana Export Development and Investment Promotion, 1999, *Annual Report,* Gaborone: BEDIA.
Botswana Export Development and Investment Promotion, 2000, *Annual Report,* Gaborone: BEDIA.
Botswana Export Development and Investment Authority, 2003, *Annual Report,* Gaborone: BEDIA.
Botswana Institute for Development Policy Analysis, 1996, *Study of Poverty and Poverty Alleviation in Botswana,* Gaborone: BIDPA/Ministry of Finance and Development Planning.
Botswana Institute of Development Policy Analysis (BIDPA), 2000, *Briefing* Gaborone, BIDPA.
Botswana Institute of Development Policy Analysis (BIDPA), 2001, *BIDPA Review.* Gaborone: BIDPA.
Botswana National Productivity Centre 'BNPC—Functions', www.bnpc.bw/
Botswana Police Service, 1999, *Report of A Study on Rape in Botswana.* Gaborone: Government Printer.
Botswana Press Agency, 2004, *Women Empowerment Drive Suppers Major Setback. Botswana Daily News,* 3rd November.
Botswana Review of Commerce and Industry, 2000, Gaborone: B and T Industries.
Boyd R., 1989, 'Empowerment of Women in Contemporary Uganda, Real or Symbolic?' *Labour Capital and Society* 22.
Bratton, M. and Lambright, G., 2001, 'Uganda's Referendum 2000: The Silent Boycott', *African Affairs* 100(400), July.
Brautigam, Deborah, 1994, 'What Can Africa Learn From Taiwan? Political Economy, Industrial Policy, and Adjustment', *Journal of Modern African Studies,* 32 (1).
Brett, E., 1995, *Structural Adjustment in Uganda, 1987-94,* unpublished paper.
Brett, E., Langseth, P., Katorobo, J., Munene., J., eds., 1997, *Uganda: Landmarks in Rebuilding a Nation,* 2nd ed., Kampala: Fountain Publishers.
Broad, R., ed., 2002, *Global Backlash: Citizen Initiatives for a Just World Economy,* Lanham: Rowman and Littlefield.
Callaghy, T., 2002, 'Networks and Governance in Africa: Innovation in the Debt Regime' in T. Callaghy, R. Kassimir and R. Latham (eds) *Intervention and Transnationalism in Africa: Global-local Networks of Power,* New York: CUP.
Campbell, H., 1975, *The Political Struggles of Africans to Enter the Market Place in Uganda,* Makerere University, MA Dissertation Unpublished.

Carroll, B.W. and Carroll, T., 1997, 'State and Ethnicity in Botswana and Mauritius: A Democratic Route to Development?', *Journal of Developing Areas*, 33 4.

Chambers, R., 1993, *Challenging the Professions: Frontiers for Rural Development*, London, IT Publications.

Chang, H-J., 1999, 'The Economic Theory of the Developmental State' in M. Woo-Cumings (ed.) *The Developmental State*, New York: Cornell University Press.

Chant, S., 2000, 'From 'Woman-Blind' to 'Man-Kind': Should Men Have More Space in Gender and Development?', *IDS Bulletin* 31 (2).

Charlton, R., 1991, 'Bureaucrats and Politicians in Botswana's Policy-making Process: A Reinterpretation', *Journal of Commonwealth and Comparative Politics*, 29 3.

Cheema, G.S, and Rondinelli, D., 1983, *Decentralisation and Development: Policy Implementation in Developing Countries*, Sage: London.

Chipasula, J.C. and Miti, M., 1989, *Botswana in Southern Africa: What Lies Ahead*, Delhi: Ajanta Publications.

Clapham, C., 1996, 'The Developmental State: Governance, Comparison and Culture in the 'Third World'' in L. Imbeau and R. McKinlay (eds) *Comparing Government Activity*, Basingstoke: Macmillan.

Clark, J., 2002, 'NGOs and the State', in V. Desai and R. Potter (eds) *The Companion to Development Studies* London: Arnold.

Cline, W., 1982, 'Can the East Asia Model of Development Be Generalised?', *World Development*, 10, 2.

Colclough, C., and McCarthy, S., 1980, *The Political Economy of Botswana: A Study of Growth and Distribution*, Oxford: Oxford University Press.

Collier, P., 1996, 'A Commentary on the Ugandan Economy: March 1996', mimeo, CSAE, Oxford University.

Collier, P., 1997, 'Ugandan Trade Policy: Liberalisation in an Environment of Limited Credibility', Mimeo, CSAE, Oxford University.

Commonwealth Foundation, 1999, *Citizens and Governance: Civil Society in the New Millennium*, London: Commonwealth Foundation.

Commonwealth Human Rights Initiative, 2001, *Human Rights and Poverty Eradication: A Talisman for the Commonwealth*, New Delhi: CHRI.

Cook, P. and Kirkpatrick, C., 1988, ' Privatisation in Less Developed Countries: An Overview' in P. Cook and C. Kirkpatrick (eds) *Privatisation in Less Developed Countries*, New York.

Cornwall, A., 2000, 'Missing Men? Reflections on Men, Masculinities and Gender in GAD', *IDS Bulletin* 31 (2): 18-24.

Cornwall, A. and White, S., 2000, 'Men, Masculinities and Development: Politics, Policies and Practice', *IDS Bulletin* 31 (2): 1-6.

Costello, M., 1994, 'Market and State: Evaluating Tanzania's Program of State-Led Industrialisation', *World Development*, 22 10.

Cowan, D., 1997, 'The Selebi-Phikwe Regional Development Project: A Case-study of the Costs and Benefits of Foreign Direct Investment' in J. S. Salkin (ed.) *Aspects of the Botswana Economy: Selected papers*, Oxford and Gaborone: James Currey.
Cox, R., 1992, 'Global Perestroika' in R. Miliband and L. Panitch (eds) *The Socialist Register*, London: Merlin Press.
Cox, R., 1994, 'Global Restructuring: Making Sense of the Changing International Political Economy' in R. Stubbs and G. Underhill (eds) *Political Economy and the Changing Global Order*, Basingstoke: Macmillan.
Cox, R., 1999, 'Civil Society at the Turn of the Millennium: Prospects for an Alternative World Order' *Review of International Studies* 25(1), January: 3-28
Crawford, D., 2000, 'Chinese Capitalism: Cultures, the Southeast Asian Region and Economic Globalisation', *Third World Quarterly* 21(1).
Culpeper, R., 2001/2, 'Introduction: Building a Fairer World' in *Canadian Development Report, 2001/2* Ottawa: North-South Institute.
Dabee, R. and Greenaway, D., eds., *The Mauritian Economy: A Reader*, London: Palgrave.
Dale, R., 1995, *Botswana's Search for Autonomy in Southern Africa*, Westport: Greenwood Press.
Danevad, A., 1993, *Development Planning and the Importance of Democratic Institutions in Botswana*, Bergen: Christian Michelsen Institute.
Datta, K, Alexander, E. and Khan, B., 1998, *Beyond Inequalities: Women in Botswana*, Harare: Women in Development Southern African Awareness.
Ddumba, S., 2000, *The Impact of Privatization on Social Services*, Kampala: SAPRI Uganda.
Deininger, K. and Okidi, J., 2002, Growth and Poverty Reduction in Uganda: 1992 – 2000: Panel Data Evidence, mimeo.
Department of Women's Affairs, 1999, *Report on the Study On the Socio-Economic Implications of Violence Against Women in Botswana*, Gaborone: Government Printer.
Desai, V., 2002, 'Role of NGOs' in V. Desai and R. Potter (eds) *The Companion to Development Studies*, London: Arnold.
Desai, V. and Potter, R., eds., 2002, *The Companion to Development Studies*, London: Arnold.
Dicklitch, S., 1998, *Elusive Promise of NGOs in Africa: Lessons from Uganda* New York: St. Martin Press.
Dicklitch, S., 2000, 'The Incomplete Democratic Transition in Uganda' in R. Bensabat-Kleinberg and J. Clark (eds) *Economic Liberalization, Democratization and Civil Society in the Developing World*, London: Palgrave.
Diejomaoh, V., 1988, The crisis of African development and Lagos plan of action in Glickman, H. (ed.) The Crisis and Challenges of African Development. New York: Greenwood Press. Pp 338-396.
Du Toit, Pierre, 1995, *State Building and Democracy in Southern Africa: A Comparative Study of Botswana, South Africa and Zimbabwe*, Pretoria: HSRC.
Duffield, Mark, 2001, *Global Governance and the New Wars: The Merging of Development and Security*, London: Zed.

Dunn, K., 2001, 'MadLib #32: The (Blank)African State: Rethinking the Sovereign State in International Relations Theory' in K.C. Dunn and T.M. Shaw (eds) *Africa's Challenge to International Relations Theory*, London: Palgrave.

Dye, T., 1998, *Understanding Public Policy*, Upper Saddle River: Prentice Hall.

Economic Intelligence Unit (EIU), 1995, *Country Profile: Uganda 1995–96*, London: EIU.

Edge, W., 1998, 'Botswana: A Developmental State' in W. Edge and M. Lekorwe (eds) *Botswana: Politics and Society*, Pretoria: Van Schaik.

Edge, W. and Lekorwe, M., eds., 1998, *Botswana: Politics and Society*, Pretoria: Van Schaik.

Edwards, M. and Hulme, D., eds., 1996, *Beyond the Magic Bullet: NGO performance and accountability in the Post-Cold War World*, West Hartford: Kumarian.

Ehrhart, C. and Ayoo, S., 2000, 'Conflict, Insecurity and Poverty in Uganda: Learning from the Poor', *UPPAP Briefing Paper #4*, Kampala: MFPED and Oxfam UK.

Ellison, K., 1990, *Report and Recommendations of the District Development Plan 4 Consultancy*, Prepared for Government of Botswana, Ministry of Finance and Development Planning and MLGLH.

Emmanuel, A., 1976, *Unequal Exchange: A study of the imperialism of trade*. New York: Monthly Review press.

Evans, P., 1995, *Embedded Autonomy: States and Industrial Transformation*, Princeton: Princeton University Press.

Evans, P., 1998, 'Transferable Lessons? Re-examining the Institutional Prerequisites of East Asian Policies', *Journal of Development Studies*, 34 6, August.

Ferguson, J., 1999, *Expectations of Modernity: Myths and Meanings of Urban Life on the Zambian Copperbelt*, Los Angeles: University of California Press.

Fine, B., 1999, 'The Developmental State is Dead—Long Live Social Capital', *Third World Quarterly*, 30 1.

Florini, A., ed., 2000, *The Third Force: The Rise of Transnational Civil Society*, Washington, DC: Carnegie Endowment.

Food and Agriculture Organization, 2000, *The State of Food and Agriculture 2000*. Rome: FAO.

Fowler, A., 2002, 'NGDO-donor Relationships: The Use and Abuse of Partnership' in V. Desai and R. Potter (eds) *The Companion to Development Studies*, London: Arnold.

Fox, J. and Brown, D., eds., 1998, *The Struggle for Accountability: the World Bank, NGOs and Grassroots Movements*, Cambridge: MIT Press.

Friedrich Ebert Foundation, 1995, *Women's Landmarks in the Democratisation Process in Uganda* Kampala: Friedrich Ebert Foundation.

Furley, O., 2000, 'Democratization in Uganda', *Commonwealth and Comparative Politics* 38(3), November.

Gariyo, Z., 1994, 'NGOs and Development in East Africa: The View from Below', paper presented to a workshop on 'NGOs and Development: Performance and Accountability in the New World Order', University of Manchester 27–29 June.

Gariyo, Z., 2002, 'Civil Society and Global Finance in Africa: The PRSP Process in Uganda' in J. Scholte and A. Schnabel (eds) *Civil Society and Global Finance*, London: Routledge.

Gasper, D., 1990, 'Development Planning and Decentralisation in Botswana' in P. De Valk and K.H. Wekwetse (eds) *Decentralising For Participatory Planning*, Aldershot: Gower.

Gerrishon, K. and Coughune, P., 1988, *Industrialisation in Kenya in Search of a Strategy*, Nairobi: Heinemann Kenya.

Ghosh, J., 1999, 'Openness, Deficits and Lack of Development' in M. Khor (ed.) *Rethinking Industrialisation and Reshaping the WTO*, Penang: Third World Network.

Gibbon, P., 2001, 'Civil Society, Locality and Globalization in Rural Tanzania: A Forty-year Perspective', *Development and Change* 32(5).

Gills, B., ed., 2000, *Globalization and the Politics of Resistance*, London: Palgrave.

Glasius, M., Kaldor, M. and Anheier, H., eds., 2002, *Global Civil Society 2003*, Oxford: OUP.

Glickman, H., ed., *The Crisis and Challenges of African Development* New York: Greenwood Press.

Good, K., 1993, 'At the Ends of the Ladder: Radical Inequalities in Botswana', *Journal of Modern African Studies*, 31 2.

Good, K., 1994, 'Corruption and Mismanagement in Botswana: A Best-Case Example', *Journal of Modern African Studies*, 32 3.

Gosovic, B., 2000, 'Global Intellectual Hegemony and the International Development Agenda', *International Social Science Journal* 166.

Government of Botswana, 1982, *A Study Undertaken for Industrial Affairs*, Gaborone: Government Printers.

Government of Botswana, 1997, *National Development Plan 8*, Gaborone: MFDP

Government of Botswana, 1998, *Industrial Development Policy for Botswana*, Gaborone: Government Printers.

Government of Botswana, 1999, *District Planning Handbook*, Gaborone: Ministry of Local Government Lands and Housing.

Government of Botswana and UNDP, 1997, *National Gender Programme*, Gaborone: UNDP.

Government of Botswana and UNDP, 2000, *Botswana Human Development Report: Towards an AIDS-Free Generation*, Gaborone: UNDP.

Government of Uganda, 1995, *Background to the Budget, 1995-96*, Kampala: Ministry of Finance and Economic Planning.

Grahame, I., 1980, *Amin and Uganda*, London: Granada.

Greig, A., Kimmel, M. and Lang, J., 2000, *Men, Masculinities and Development: Broadening Our Work Towards Gender Equality Gender and Development*, New York: Gender and Development Programme.

Griffiths, A. and Wall, S., 1999, *Applied Economics: An Introductory Course*, New York: Addison Wesley Longman.

Grindle, S. and John, T., 1990, 'After the Decision: Implementing Policy Reforms in Developing Countries', *World Development*, 18 8.

Gulbrandsen, O., 1996, *Poverty in the Midst of Plenty*, Bergen: Norse Publications.

Hampson, F., ed., 2001, *Madness in the Multitude: Human Security and World Disorder*, Toronto: OUP.

Hampson, F., Hillmer, N. and Molot, M., eds., 2001, *The Axworthy Legacy*, Toronto: OUP.

Hansen, H. and Twaddle, M., eds., 1991, *Changing Uganda. The Dilemmas of Structural and Revolutionary Change*, London: Villers Publications.

Hansen, H. and Twaddle, M., eds., 1988, *Uganda Now: Between Decay and Development*, Oxford: James Currey.

Hansen, H. and Twaddle, M., eds., 1998, *Developing Uganda*, Oxford: James Currey.

Harker, J., 2001, *Human Security in Sudan: The Report of a Canadian Assessment Mission*, Halifax: Centre for Foreign Policy Studies.

Harvey, C., 1991, 'Botswana: Is the Economic Miracle Over?', *Journal of African Economics*, 1 3.

Harvey, C. and Lewis, S., 1990, *Policy Choice and Development Performance in Botswana*, New York: St Martin's Press.

Hauser, Ellen, 1999, 'Ugandan Relations with Western Donors in the 1990s: What Impact on Democratization?' *Journal of Modern African Studies* 37 (4).

Herring, R., 1999, 'Embedded Particularism: India's Failed Developmental State' in M. Woo-Cumings (ed.) *The Developmental State*, New York: Cornell University Press.

Heyzer, N., Riker, J. and Quizon, A., eds., 1995, *Government-NGO Relations in Asia: Prospects and Challenges for People-centred Development*, London: Macmillan.

Hill, C. and Mokgethi, D.N., 1989, 'Botswana: Macroeconomic Management of Commodity Booms, 1975-86' in *Successful Development in Africa*, Washington DC: World Bank.

Hobona, B, 1995, 'Local Government Financing in Botswana' in A. Briscoe (ed.) *Local Government Financing in Southern Africa*, Gaborone: SADC.

Holm, J., 1985, 'The State, Social Class and Rural Development in Botswana' in L. A. Picard (ed.) *The Evolution of Modern Botswana*, London: Rex Collins.

Holm, J., 1996, 'Development, Democracy and Civil Society in Botswana' in A. Leftwich (ed.) *Democracy and Development*, Cambridge: Polity Press.

Holm, J., 2000, 'Curbing Corruption Through Democratic Accountability: Lessons from Botswana' in R. K. Hope and B.C. Chikulo (eds) *Corruption and Development in Africa: Lessons from Country Case-Studies*, Hampshire: Macmillan.

Holm, J. and Molutsi, P., 1992, 'State-Civil Society Relations in Botswana' in G. Hyden and M. Bratton (eds) *Governance and Politics in Africa*, London: Lynne Rienner Publishers.

Holm, J. and Molutsi, P., ed., 1989, *Democracy in Botswana*, Gaborone: Macmillan.

Holm, J. and Darnolf, S., 2000, 'Democratising the Administrative State in Botswana' in Y. Bradshaw and S. Ndegwa (eds) *The Uncertain Promise of Southern Africa*, Bloomington: Indian University Press.

Holmgren, T., Kasekende, L. et al, 2000, 'Uganda' in S. Devarajan, D. Dollar and T. Holmgren (eds) *Aid and Reform in Africa: Lessons from Ten Case Studies*, Washington, DC: IBRD.

Hood, C., 1994, *Explaining Economic Policy Reversals*, Buckingham: Open University Press.

Hope, K., 1996, 'Growth, Unemployment and Poverty in Botswana', *Journal of Contemporary Studies*, 14 1.

Hope, K.R. Sr. and Kayira, G., 1996, The economic crisis in Southern Africa: some perspective on its origins and nature. Development Southern Africa, Vol. 13 (6) Pp 881-894.

Hope, K.R., and Chikulo, B.C., (eds.), 2000, Corruption and Development in Africa: Lessons from Country Case-Studies, London: Macmillan.

Hountondji, P.J., 1992, *The crisis of the state in Africa in Auroi, C. The Role of the State in Development Processes*. London: Frank Cass. Pp 239-246.

Hubert, D., 2000, *The Landmine Ban: A Case Study in Humanitarian Advocacy*, Providence: Watson Institute, Occasional Paper no. 42.

Hudson, D., 1991, 'Boom and Busts in Botswana', *Botswana Notes and Records*, 23.

Hughes, T., Mills, G., Grobbelaar, N., Hebert, R., Mabena, W., Shaw, M. and Sidiropoulos, E., 2003, *Southern Africa Scenario 2015 Renaissance, Asymmetry or Decline and Decay?*, Johannesburg: South African Institute of International Affairs

Hulme, D. and Edwards, M., eds., 1997, *NGOs, States and Donors: Too Close for Comfort?*, London: Macmillan for SCF.

Human Rights Watch, 1999, *Hostile to Democracy: The Movement System and Political Repression in Uganda*, New York: Human Rights Watch.

Human Rights Watch Report, 2001, *Just Die Quietly: Domestic Violence and Women's Vulnerability to HIV in Uganda*, New York: Human Rights Watch.

Hyden, G., 1997, 'Foreign Aid and Democratisation in Africa', *Africa Insight*, 27 4.

IFAD, 2001, *Rural Poverty Report 2001: The Challenge of Ending Rural Poverty*, Oxford: OUP.

IFPRI, 1995, 'Foreign Assistance to Agriculture: A Win-Win Proposition', *Food Policy Report*, Washington: IFPRI.

Iheduru, O., 1999, *The Politics of Economic Restructuring and Democracy in Africa*, Westport: Greenwood Press.

International Commission on Intervention and State Sovereignty, 2001, *The Responsibility to Protect*, Ottawa: IDRC.

International HIV/AIDS Alliance, 2003, *Working With Men, Responding to AIDS: Gender, Sexuality and HIV—A Case Study Collection*, Brighton: Progression Design.

International Monetary Fund, 2000, *World Economic Outlook 2000*, New York: IMF.

Bavan, J. Collier, P., Dercon, S. and Gunning, J., 1994, *Some Economic Consequences of the Transition from Civil War to Peace*, mimeo, CSAE, Oxford University.

Jefferis, K., 1998, 'Botswana and Diamond-Dependent Development' in W. Edge and M. Lekorwe (eds) *Botswana: Politics and Society*, Pretoria: Van Schaik.

Jefferis, K. and Kelly, T.F., 1999, 'Botswana: Poverty Amid Plenty', *Oxford Development Studies*, 27 2.

Jenkins, R., 2002, 'The Emergence of the Governance Agenda' in V. Desai and R. Potter (eds) *The Companion to Development Studies*, London: Arnold.

Johnson, C., 1981, 'Introduction: The Taiwan Model' in J.S. Hsiung (ed.) *Contemporary Republic of China: The Taiwan Experience, 1950-1980*, New York: Praeger.

Johnson, C., 1982, *MITI and the Japanese Miracle*, Stanford: Stanford University Press.

Johnson, C., 1993, 'Comparative Capitalism: The Japanese Difference', *California Management Review*, Summer.

Johnson, C., 1999, 'The Developmental State: Odyssey of a Concept' in M. Woo-Cumings (ed) *The Developmental State*, New York: Cornell University Press.

Johnstone, H., 1902, *The Uganda Protectorate*, London: Hutchinson.

Jones, D., 1998, 'The Economic Effects of Privatization: Evidence from a Russian Panel', *Comparative Economic Studies*, 40.

Kaberuka, W., 1990, *The Political Economy of Uganda (1890–1979)*, Kampala: Vantage Press.

Kabwegyere, T., 1995, *The Politics of State Formation and Destruction in Uganda*, Kampala: Fountain Publishers.

Kalema, W., 1969, 'Private Enterprise in Uganda,' in P. Thomas (ed.) *Private Enterprise and the East African Company*, Dar-es-Saalam: Tanzania Publishing House.

Kaplinksy, R., 1991, 'Industrialisation in Botswana: How Getting the Prices Right Helped the Wrong People' in C. Colclough and J. Manor (eds) *States or Markets? Neo-liberalism and the Development Policy Debate*, Oxford: Clarendon.

Karugire, S., 1996, *The Roots of Instability in Uganda* Kampala: Fountain Publishers.

Kasfir, N., 2000, 'No-Party Democracy in Uganda', *Journal of Democracy* 9 (2).

Kasfir, N., ed., 1998, *Civil Society and Democracy in Africa: Critical Perspectives*, London: Frank Cass.

Kassimir, R., 1998, 'Uganda: The Catholic Church and State Reconstruction', in J. Villalon and L. Huxtable (eds) *The African State at a Critical Juncture*, Boulder: Lynne Rienner.

Katz, B., 1992, 'Public Enterprises in Sub-Saharan Africa' in B. Katz and A. Aliene (eds) *Privatisation and Investment in Sub-Saharan Africa*, New York: Praeger.

Kayizi-Mugerwa, S., 1997, *Uganda 1996: Security, Credibility and Market Development (Macro economic Report, 1997)* Stockholm: SIDA.

Kayizi-Mugerwa, S., 1998, *Uganda: Towards Results-oriented Economic Management? (Country Economic Report 1998)* Stockholm: SIDA.

Kearney, R., 1990, 'Mauritius and the NIC Model Redux: Or, How Many Cases Make a Model?', *Journal of Developing Areas*, 24 (2).

Keck, M. and Sikkink, K., 1998, *Activists Beyond Borders: Transnational Advocacy Networks in International Politics*, Ithaca: Cornell University Press.

Kevane, M. and Englebert, P., 1999, 'A Developmental State Without Growth: Explaining the Paradox of Burkina Faso in Comparative Perspective' in K. Wohlmuth, H. Bass and F. Messner (eds) *African Development Perspectives Yearbook 1997/98*, Munster: Lit Verlag.

Khadiagala, G. and Lyons, T., eds., 2001, *African Foreign Policies: Power and Process*, Boulder: Lynne Rienner.

Khadiagala, L., 2001, 'The Failure of Popular Justice in Uganda: Local Councils and Women's Property Rights', *Development and Change* 32 (1).

Khama, S., 1980, 'Addressing the Nation on the Occasion of the Tenth Anniversary of Independence—30 September 1976', in G. Carter and P. Morgan (eds) *From the Frontline: Speeches of Sir Seretse Khama*, London: Rex Collings.

Kindleberger, C.P., 1958, Economic Development (2nd ed.), Tokyo: McGraw Hill Kogakusha Ltd.

Klein, N., 2000, *No Logo: Taking Aim at the Brand Bullies* London: Flamingo.

Knight, B., Chigudu, H. and Tandon, R., 2002, *Reviving Democracy: Citizens at the Heart of Governance*, London: Earthscan.

Koelble, T., 1999, *The Global Economy and Democracy in South Africa*, New Brunswick, New Jersey: Rutgers University Press.

Kwesiga, J., 2000, *Women's Access to Higher Education in Africa: Uganda's Experience*, Kampala: Fountain Publishers.

Langseth, P., ed., 1995, *Uganda: Landmarks in Rebuilding a Nation* Kampala: Fountain Publishers.

Leftwich, A., 1995, 'Bringing Politics Back In: Towards a Model of the Developmental State', *The Journal of Developmental Studies*, Vol. 31, No.3.

Leftwich, A., ed., 1996, *Democracy and Development*, Cambridge: Polity Press.

Leftwich, A., 1996, 'On the Primacy of Politics in Development' in A. Leftwich (ed.) *Democracy and Development*, Cambridge: Polity Press

Leftwich, A, 1996, 'Two Cheers for Democracy? Democracy and the Developmental State' in A. Leftwich (ed) *Democracy and Development*, Cambridge: Polity Press

Leftwich, A., 2000, *States of Development: On the Primacy of Politics in Development*, Cambridge: Polity Press.

Leith, C., 2000, 'Why Botswana Prospered', unpublished paper, November.

Lekorwe, M, 1998, 'Local Government and District Planning' in W. Edge and M. Lekorwe (eds) *Botswana: Politics and Society*, Pretoria: Van Schaik.

Lengseth, P., 1996, 'Civil Service Reform: A General Overview', in F. Lubanga and S. Villaden (eds) *Democratic Decentralisation in Uganda: A New Approach to Local Governance*, Kampala: Fountain Publishers.

Lewis, D. and Wallace, T., eds., 2000, *New Roles and Relevance: Development NGOs and the Challenge of Change*, West Hartford: Kumarian.

Lewis, S., 1993, 'Policymaking and Economic Performance: Botswana in Comparative Perspective' in S. Stedman (ed.) *Botswana: The Political Economy of Democratic Development*, Boulder: Lynne Rienner.

Lindberg, S. and Sverrisson, A., eds., 1997, *Social Movements in Development*, London: Macmillan.

Lister, S. and Nyamugasira, W., 2003, 'Design Contradiction in the New Architecture of Aid? Reflections From Uganda on the Roles of Civil Society Organisations', *Development Policy Review* 21 (1).

Lubanga, F., 1996, *The Process of Decentralization in Uganda: A New Approach to Local Governance*, Kampala: Fountain Publishers.

Macdonald, L., 1996, *Supporting Civil Society: The Political Role of NGOs in Central America*, London: Macmillan.

MacLean, S., Quadir, F. and Shaw, T., eds., 2001, *Prospects for Governance in Asia and Africa*, Aldershot: Ashgate.

MacLean, S. and Shaw, T., 2001, 'Canada and New 'Global' Strategic Alliances: Prospects for Human Security at the Start of the Twenty-first Century', *Canadian Foreign Policy* 8 (3).

Madisa, M., 1991 'Women in Politics' in M. Molomo and B. T. Mokopakgosi (eds) *Multi-Party Democracy in Botswana*, Harare: Southern African Political Economy Series.

Mahajan, A., 1990, 'Pricing Expropriation Risk', *Financial Management*, 19.

Makara, S., 2000, 'Decentralisation for Good Governance and Development: Uganda's Experience' *Regional Development Dialogue*, 21 (1).

Makgatlhe, S., 1995, 'Disadvantages of Central Planning and Financial Control with Particular Reference to Botswana' in A. Briscoe (ed) *Local Government Financing in Southern Africa*, Gaborone: SADC.

Makhan, V., 2002, *Economic Recovery in Africa: The Paradox of Financial Flows*, London: Palgrave.

Makova, S., 2000, 'Decentralization for Good Governance and Development: Uganda's Experience' *Development Policy Review* 18 (1).

Makumbe, J., 1998, 'Is there a Civil Society in Africa?', *International Affairs* 74 (2).

Mamdani, M., 1976, *Politics and Class Formation in Uganda*, London: Heinemann.

Mamdani, M., 1983, *Imperialism and Fascism in Uganda*, London: Heinemann.

Mangat, J., 1969, *A History of the Asians in East Africa: 1886-1945* Oxford: Clarendon Press.

Mannathoko, C., 1992, 'Feminist Theories and the Study of Gender Issues in Southern Africa' in R. Meena (ed.) *Gender in Southern Africa*, Harare: Southern African Political Economy Series.

Manor J., 1999, *The Political Economy of Democratic Decentralization*, Washington D.C: World Bank.

Martinussen, J., 1997, *Society, State and Market: A Guide to Competing Theories of Development*, London: Zed.

Matembe, M., 2001, *Women and Constitution Making in Uganda*, Kampala: Fountain Publishers.

Matsheka, T. and Botlhomilwe, Z, 2000, 'Economic Conditions and Election Outcomes in Botswana: Is the Relationship Spurious?', *Pula: Botswana Journal of African Studies*, 14 (1).

Maundeni, T., 2001, 'Gender Based Violence Against Women and Children and HIV/AIDS' in Ministry of Labour and Home Affairs *Report of The First National Conference on Gender and HIV/AIDS 21–23 June, 2001, Boipuso Hall, Gaborone*, Gaborone: Ministry of Labour and Home Affairs, 73 - 84.

Maundeni, Z., 2001, 'State Culture and the Botswana Developmental State', paper presented to the Department of Political and Administrative Studies, University of Botswana, January 25.

Maundeni, Z., (no date), 'The Public Policy Process in Africa: The Case of Botswana', paper prepared for 'Botswana Leadership Development Programme', co-ordinated by the Department of Adult Education of the University of Botswana.

Mawhood, P., 1983, *Local Government in the Third World*, New York: John Wiley and Sons.

Mazonde, I. and Sigwele, H., eds., 2001, *The Operations of Multilateral Trade Organisations—Towards a Policy on Agricultural Trade Within SADC: Focus on Botswana*, Gaborone: University of Botswana.

Mbabazi, P., 2002, 'Governance for Reconstruction in Africa: Challenges for Policy Communities and Coalitions', *Global Networks: A Journal of Transnational Affairs*, 2 (1).

Mbabazi, P., Maclean, S. and Shaw, T., 2002,. 'Governance for Reconstruction in Africa: Challenges for Policy Communities and Coalitions', *Global Networks 2*.

Mbabazi, P. and Shaw, T., 2000, 'NGOs and Peace-building in the Great Lakes Region of Africa: States, Civil Societies and Companies in the New Millennium' in D. Lewis and T. Wallace (eds) *New Roles and Relevance: Development NGOs and the Challenge of Change*, West Hartford: Kumarian.

Mbaku, J.M., 2004, 'Fighting Poverty and Deprivation in Africa: The Continuing Struggle', in: Mbaku, J.M. and Saxena, S.C. (eds.), Africa at the Crossroads: Between Regionalism and Globalization, Westport, Connecticut: Praeger.

McGee, R., 2000, 'Meeting the International Poverty Targets in Uganda', *Development Policy Review* 18 (1).

McGraw, A., 1992, 'The Third World in the New Global Order' in T. Allen and A. Thomas (eds) *Poverty and Development in the 1990s*, Oxford: Oxford University Press.

Meier, G., 1984, *Leading Issues in Economic Development*, New York: Oxford University Press.

Meisenhelder, T., 1997, 'The Developmental State in Mauritius', *Journal of Modern African Studies*, 35 (2).

Mfundisi, A., 1998, 'The Formation and Structure of Central Government and its Institutional Relationship with Local Government in Botswana' in W. Edge and M. Lekorwe (eds) *Botswana: Politics and Society*, Pretoria: Van Schaik.

Mhone, G., 1996, 'Botswana Economy Still an Enclave', *Africa Development*, 21 (2 and 3).

Mijumbi, Peter B, 2001, 'Uganda's External Debt and the HIPC Initiative', *Canadian Journal of Development Studies* 22 (2).

Ministry of Finance and Development Planning, 2003, *National Development Plan 9 2003/04 – 2008/09*, Gaborone: Government Printer.

Ministry of Health, 1998, *Men, Sex and AIDS: Addressing Male Sexuality, A Pilot Study*, Gaborone: Aids/STD Unit.

Ministry of Industry and Technology, 1989, *Proposals for District Industrial Planning for Jinja*, Kampala: Government Printers.

Ministry of Industry and Technology, 1991, *Industrial Sector in Africa countries – Economic Commission for Africa*, Uganda Government Kampala: Government Printers.

Ministry of Labour and Home Affairs, 1995, *Policy on Women and Development*,Gaborone: Government Printer.

Ministry of Labour and Home Affairs, 1998, *Report On A Review of All Laws Affecting The Status of Women in Botswana*, Gaborone: Government Printer.

Ministry of Trade and Industry, 1981, *Strategies for Spearheading Small Scale Industries in Uganda*, Kampala: Government Printers.

Ministry of Trade and Industry, 1994, *Uganda Industrialisation policy framework (1994-1999)*, Kampala: Friedrich-Ebert-Stiftung.

Mittelman, J., 2000, *The Globalization Syndrome: Transformation and Resistance*, Princeton: Princeton University Press.

Mkandawire, A., 1998, 'Thinking About Developmental States in Africa', Paper presented at the UNU-AERU Workshop 'Institutions and Development in Africa' UNU Headquarters Tokyo, Japan, October 14-15, 1998.

Mkandawire, T., 2001, 1998, 'Thinking About Developmental States in Africa', *Cambridge Journal of Economics*, 25.

Mkandawire, T. and Soludo, C., 1999, *Our Continent, Our Future: African Perspectives on Structural Adjustment*, Dakar: CODESRIA, Africa World Press and IDRC.

Mkandawire, T. and Olukoshi, A., (eds.), 1995, *Between Liberalisation and Oppression: The Politics of Structural Adjustment in Africa*, Dakar: CODESRIA Books.

Mogalakwe, M., 1997, *The State and Organised Labour in Botswana: 'Liberal Democracy' in Emergent Capitalism*, Aldershot: Ashgate.

Mokhawa, G. and Osei-Hwedie B.Z., 2003, 'Africa Growth Opportunity Act (AGOA) Trade Regime: Opportunities and Challenges For Botswana', paper presented to the Department of Political and Administrative Studies Seminar, University of Botswana, November 2003, Gaborone.

Mokhawa, G, 2003, The Problematic Case of Textile Industry as an Instrument for Diversification in a Diamond Dominated Economy: The Case of Botswana, MPA Dissertation, University of Botswana, Gaborone.

Mokopakgosi, B. and Molomo, M., 2000, 'Democracy in the Face of a Weak Opposition in Botswana', *Pula: Botswana Journal of African Studies*, 14 1.

Molomo, M., 1989, 'The Bureaucracy and Democracy in Botswana' in J. Holm and P. Molutsi (eds) *Democracy in Botswana*, Gaborone: Macmillan.

Molomo, M., 2000, 'Understanding Government and Opposition Parties in Botswana', *Commonwealth and Comparative Politics*, 38 (1).

Molutsi, P., 1989a, 'The Ruling Class and Democracy in Botswana' in J. Holm and P. Molutsi (eds) *Democracy in Botswana*, Gaborone: Macmillan.

Molutsi, P., 1989b, 'Whose Interests Do Botswana's Politicians Represent?' in J. Holm and P. Molutsi (eds) *Democracy in Botswana*, Gaborone: Macmillan.

Molutsi, P. and Holm, J., 1990, 'Developing Democracy When Civil Society is Weak: The Case of Botswana', *African Affairs*, 89 356.

Mookodi, G and D. Fuh., 2003 'Finding the 'Missing' Male in Gender Discourses in Botswana' in *Pula: Botswana Journal of African Studies* 18 (1).

Morrell, R., ed., 2001, *Changing Men in Southern Africa*, London: Zed.

Morton, B. and Ramsay, J., 1994, *The Making of a President: Sir Ketumile Masire's Early Years*, Gaborone: Pula Press.

Mugaju, J. and Olaka-Onyango, J., eds., 2000, *No-Party Democracy in Uganda: Myths and Realities*, Kampala: Fountain Press.

Mugambe, B., 1996, 'Are Women Afraid of Seeking Elective Office?', *Arise*, 32 (2).

Mugyenyi, M. R, 1998, 'Towards the Empowerment of Women: A Critique of NRM Policies and Programmes', in H. Hansen, and M. Twaddle (eds) *Developing Uganda*, Oxford: James Currey.

Mulyampiti, T., 1994, 'Political Empowerment of Women in the Contemporary Uganda: Impact of Resistance Councils and Committee', M.A Thesis, Women's Studies, Makerere University, Kampala.

Murindwa-Rutanga., 1991, Nyabingi Movement: *People's Anti-Colonial Struggles in Kigezi 1910–1930*, Centre for Basic Recherch Working Paper No18, CBR, Kampala.

Murphy, C., ed., 2001, *Egalitarian Politics in the Age of Globalization*, London: Palgrave.

Murray, A. and Parsons, N., 1990, 'The Modern Economic History of Botswana' in Z. Konizacki, J. Parpart and T. Shaw (eds) *Studies in the Economic History of Southern Africa, I: Frontline States*, London: Frank Cass.

Museveni, Y., 1992, *What is Africa's Problem?* Kampala: NRM Publishers.

Museveni, Y., 1997, *Sowing the Mustard Seed: The Struggle for Freedom and Democracy in Uganda*, London: Macmillan.

Mutibwa, J., 1992, *Uganda Since Independence: A Story of Unfulfilled Hopes*, London: Hurst.

Nankani, H., 1990, 'Lessons of Privatization in Developing Countries,' *Finance and Development*, 27.

Nanzi, V. and Hamid, D., 1998, 'Roads to Nowhere: How Corruption in Public Investment Hurts Growth', *IMF Journal of Economic Issues* 12.

National Council of Women (NCW), 1991, *Directory of Women Groups in Uganda: Results of a Survey Conducted Under the UNDP/NCW/NGO Project 'Partners in Development*, Kampala: NCW.

Nelson, P., 1995, *The World Bank and NGOs: The Limits of Apolitical Development*, London: Macmillan.

Nelson, P., 2002, 'The World Bank and NGOs' in V. Desai and R. Potter (eds) *The Companion to Development Studies*, London: Arnold.

Ngwato, T., 1990, 'Factors Behind Ineffective District Development Planning and Poor Implementation in Botswana: Central District Case Study', Masters thesis, Institute of Planning Studies, University of Nottingham.

Noppen, D., 1982, *Consultation and Non-Commitment: Planning Without the People in Botswana*, Leiden: African Studies Centre.

NRM Secretariat, 2001, *Consolidating the Achievements of the Movement, 2001 Election Manifesto* Kampala: NRM.

Nsibambi, A., ed., 1998, *Introduction Decentralization and Civil Society in Uganda: The Quest for Good Governance* Kampala: Fountain Publishers.

Nsouli, S. and Le Gall, F., eds., 'Globalization and Africa', *Finance and Development* 38 (4).

Nteta, D., Hermans, J. and Jeskova, P., eds., 1997, *Poverty and Plenty: The Botswana Experience* Gaborone: Botswana Society.

Nyamnjoh, F.B, 2005, 'Fishing in Troubled Waters: Disquettes and Thiofs in Dakar', *Africa*, Vol.75(3).

Nyamnjoh, F.B., 2000, 'For many are called but few are chosen' Globalization and popular disenchantment in Africa. *African Sociological Review* Vol. 4 (2) pp 1-45.

Nyamnjoh, F.B., 2001, 'Delusions of Development and the Enrichment of Witchcraft Discourses in Cameroon', in: H.L. Moore and T. Sanders (eds.), *Magical Interpretations, Material Realities: Modernity, Witchcraft and the Occult in Postcolonial Africa*, London: Routledge, pp. 28-49.

Nzongola-Ntalaja, G., 2002, *The Congo from Leopold to Kabila: A People's History*, London: Zed Books.

O'Brien, R., Goetz, A.M., Scholte, J.A., and Williams, M., 2000, *Contesting Global Governance: Multilateral Economic Institutions and Global Social Movements*, Cambridge: CUP.

Obote, M., 1969, *The Common Man's Charter*, Kampala: Milton Obote Foundation.

Odhiambo, E.S.A., 2004, 'Africa's "Brain Gain": Whose Shibboleth?', paper prepared for Africa's Brain Gain Conference, Nairobi, December 19-22, 2004.

Öni, Z., 1991, 'The Logic of the Developmental State', *Comparative Politics*, 24 1, October.

Onyango, O., 2000, *A Political History of Uganda: The Origin of Museveni's Referendum 2000*, Kampala: Monitor Publications.

Osei-Hwedie, B., 2001, 'The Political Opposition in Botswana: The Politics of Factionalism and Fragmentation', *Transformation* 45.

Owusu, F. and Samatar, A., 1997, 'Industrial Strategy and the African State: The Botswana Experience', *Canadian Journal of African Studies*, 31 2.

Oyugi, W., 2000, 'Decentralisation for Good Governance and Development: Concepts and Issues' *Regional Development Dialogue*, 21 (1).

Parpart, J. and Staudt, K., eds., 1989, *Women and the State in Africa* Boulder: Lynne Rienner.

Parpart, J. and Shaw, T., 2002, 'African Development Debates and Prospects at the turn of the Century', in P. McGowan and P. Nel, eds., *Power, Wealth and Global Equity: An International Relations Textbook for Africa* Cape Town: OUP.

Parson, J., 1981, 'Cattle, Class and the State in Rural Botswana', *Journal of Southern African Studies*, 7 (2).

Parson, J., 1984, *Botswana: Liberal Democracy and the Labour Reserve in Southern Africa* Boulder: Westview Press.

Parsons, N., 1985, 'The Evolution of Modern Botswana: Historical Revisions' in L. Picard (ed.) *The Evolution of Modern Botswana*, London: Rex Collings.

Parsons, N., 2000, *Botswana History Pages* 'Economy', October, http://ubh.tripod.com/bw/bhp13.htm#

Parsons, N., 2000a, *Botswana History Pages* 'Ethnicity', http://ubh.tripod.com/bw/bhp13.htm#ethnicity

Parsons, N., Henderson, W. and. Tlou, T., 1995, *Seretse Khama, 1921-1980* Gaborone: Macmillan/Botswana Society.

Payne, A., 1999, 'Reframing the Global Politics of Development', *Journal of International Relations and Development* 2(4).

Picard, L., 1980, 'Bureaucrats, Cattle and Public Policy: Land Tenure Change in Botswana', *Comparative Political Studies*, 13 (3).

Picard, L., ed., 1985, *The Evolution of Modern Botswana* Lincoln: University of Nebraska Press.

Picard, L., 1987, *The Politics of Development in Botswana: A Model for Success?*, Boulder: Lynne Rienner.

Ponte, S. and Gibbon, P., 2004, *Globalization and Economic Change in Africa*, London: Palgrave.

Preece, J., 2001, 'Gender Power Relations and the HIV/AIDS Crisis in Botswana: Some Food For Thought' in *Pula: Botswana Journal of African Studies* 15(2).

Quadir, F., MacLean, S. and Shaw, T., 2001, 'Pluralisms and the Changing Global Political Economy: Ethnicities in Crises of Governance in Asia and Africa' in F. Quadir, S. MacLean and T. Shaw (eds) *Crises of Governance in Asia and Africa*, Aldershot: Ashgate.

Ray, D., 1998, *Development Economics*, Princeton, New Jersey: Princeton University Press.

Reddy, P., ed., 1999, *Local Government Democratisation and Decentralisation: A Review of the Southern African Region*, Kenwyn: Juta.

Reilly, W., Craig, J. and Tordoff, W., 1981, *Studies in Decentralisation: Papua New Guinea, Botswana, Sri Lanka*, Manchester Papers on Development, Department of Administrative Studies, University of Manchester, Issue No. 3.

Reinikka, R. and Collier, P., 2001, *Uganda's Recovery: The Role of Firms, Farms and Governance*, Washington DC: IBRD.

Reno, W., 2002, 'Uganda's Politics of War and Debt Relief', *Review of International Political Economy* 9(3).

Republic of Botswana, 1970, *National Development Plan II 1970 – 1975*, Gaborone: Government Printer.

Republic of Botswana, 1985, *National Development Plan VI 1985 – 91* Gaborone: Government Printer.

Republic of Botswana, 1994, Directorate on Corruption and Economic Crime Act Gaborone: Government Printer.

Republic of Botswana, 1996, *Presidential Task Group—A Framework for a Long Term Vision for Botswana* Gaborone: Government Printers.

Republic of Botswana, 1997, *National Development Plan 8 1997/98 – 2002/03* Gaborone: Government Printer.

Republic of Botswana, 2001, 'Economic Snapshot', http://www.gov.bw/economy/index.html

Republic of Botswana, 2002, *Presentation Speech on Draft National Development Plan 9 2003/04 – 2008/09* by B. Gaolathe, Minister of Finance and Development Planning Delivered to the National Assembly on the 21st November 2002, Gaborone in www.gov.bw.

Republic of Botswana, 2003, *Budget Speech* by B. Gaolathe, Minister of Finance and Development Planning Delivered to the National Assembly on the 3rd February 2003, Gaborone.

Republic of Uganda, 1972, *Speeches by His Excellency the President General Idi Amin Dada*, Entebbe Government Printers.

Riley, S.P, 2000, 'Western Policies and African Realities: The New Anti-Corruption Agenda' in R. K. Hope and B.C. Chikulo (eds) *Corruption and Development in Africa: Lessons from Country Case-Studies*, Hampshire: Macmillan Press Ltd.

Robi, M., 1994, 'Economic Policy for the 21st Century' in S. Brothers, J. Hermans and D. Nteta (eds) *Botswana in the 21st Century*, Gaborone: Botswana Society.

Rupesinghe, Kumar, ed., 1989, *Conflict Resolution in Uganda*, London: James Currey.

Ray, D., 1998, Development Economics, Princeton, New Jersey: Princeton University Press.

Samatar, A., 1997, 'Leadership and Ethnicity in the Making of African State Models: Botswana Versus Somalia', *Third World Quarterly*, 18 (4).

Samatar, A., 1999, An African Miracle: State and Class Leadership and Colonial Legacy in Botswana's Development Portsmouth: Heinemann Press.

Samatar, A. and S. Oldfield, 1995, 'Class and Effective State Institutions: The Botswana Meat Commission', *Journal of Modern African Studies*, 33 4.

Sandbrook, R., 2000, *Closing the Circle: Democratization and Development in Africa* Toronto: Between the Lines.
Schapera, I., 1955, *The Tswana*, London: Kegan Paul.
Schapera, I., 1994, *A Handbook of Tswana Law and Custom*, Gaborone: Botswana Society.
Schatz, S.P., 1988, 'African Capitalism and African Economic Performance' in Glickman, H. (ed.) *The Crisis and Challenges of African Development*. NY: Greenwood.
Schechter, M., ed., 1999, *The Revival of Civil Society: Global and Comparative Perspectives*, London: Palgrave.
Schneider, B., 1999, 'The Desarrollista State in Brazil and Mexico' in M. Woo-Cumings (ed.) *The Developmental State*, New York: Cornell University Press.
Sharer R.L., 1995, *Uganda: Adjustment with growth, 1987 – 94* Washington DC: IMF.
Sharma, K, 1999, *Integrating 'Top-Down' and 'Bottom-Up' Planning: The Nature of Decentralised District Development Planning Botswana*, paper for Departmental Seminar, 25 November 1999, Department of Political and Administrative Studies, University of Botswana.
Shaw, T., 1997, 'Prospects for a 'New' Political Economy of Development in the Twenty-first Century' *Canadian Journal of Development Studies* 18 (3).
Shaw, T., 2002, 'Peace-building Partnerships and Human Security' in V. Desai and R. Potter (eds) *The Companion to Development Studies*, London: Arnold, 449-453.
Shaw, T., 2003, 'Africa' in M. Hawkesworth and M. Kogan (eds) *Routledge Encyclopaedia of Government and Politics*, London: Routledge
Shaw, T. and Nyang'oro, J., 2000, 'African Renaissance in the New Millennium? From Anarchy to Emerging Markets?' in R. Stubbs and G. Underhill (eds) *Political Economy and the Changing Global Order*, Toronto: OUP.
Simukonda, P., 1998, 'The Role and Performance of the Parastatals' in R.K. Hope and G. Somolekae (eds) *Public Administration and Policy in Botswana*, Cape Town: Juta.
Singh, K., 1999, *Rural Development: Principles, policies and management* (second edition) New Delhi: Sage Publications.
Siwawa-Ndai, P., 1997, 'Some Facts and Figures about the Quality of Life in Botswana' in D. Nteta, J. Hermans, and P. Jeskova (eds) *Poverty and Plenty: The Botswana Experience*, Gaborone: Botswana Society.
Smillie, I. and Helmich, H., eds., 1999, *Stakeholders: Government-NGO Partnerships for Development*, London: Earthscan.
Smith, I.D., 1997, *The Great Betrayal: memoirs of Ian Douglas Smith*. London: Blake Publishing Ltd.
Somolekae, G., 1993, 'Bureaucracy and Democracy in Botswana: What Type of a Relationship' in S. Stedman (ed.) *Botswana: The Political Economy of Democratic Development*, Boulder: Lynne Rienner.
Somolekae, G. and Lekorwe, M., 1998, 'The Chieftaincy System and Politics in Botswana, 1966-95' in W. Edge and M. Lekorwe (eds) *Botswana: Politics and Society*, Pretoria: Van Schaik.

South Commission, 1990, The Challenge to the South. Oxford: Oxford University Press.
Stedman, S., ed., 1993, *Botswana: The Political Economy of Democratic Development* Boulder: Lynne Rienner.
Stein, H., 2000, 'The Development of the Developmental State in Africa: A Theoretical Inquiry', Occasional Paper Centre of African Studies University of Copenhagen.
Stein, Howard, ed., 1995, *Asian Industrialization: Lessons for Africa* London: Macmillan.
Stiles, K., ed., 1999, *Global Institutions and Local Empowerment: Competing Theoretical Perspectives* London: Macmillan.
Tamale, S., 1999, *When the Hen's Begin to Crow; Gender and Formal Politics in Contemporary Uganda* Boulder: Westview Press.
Tangri, R., 1999, *The Politics of Patronage in Africa: Parastatals, Privatisation and Private Enterprise* Kampala: Fountain Publishers.
Taylor, I., 1999, 'South Africa's Promotion of "Democracy" and "Stability" in Southern Africa: Good Governance or Good for Business?', Centre for the Study of Globalisation and Regionalisation annual conference 'After the Global Crises: What Next for Regionalism?', University of Warwick, England, September 16-18.
Taylor, Ian, 2001, 'Hegemony, Neo-Liberal "Good Governance" and the International Monetary Fund: A Gramscian Perspective' in M. Bøås and D. McNeill (eds) *The Role of Ideas in Multilateral Institutions*, London: Routledge.
Taylor, J,. 2001, 'No Mathatha (?) Botswana's strategies for Gaborone's Place in the Global Economy', A paper prepared for the conference 'Sate/Society responses to globalisation: Case Studies from Japan and Southern Africa' Stellenbosch, South Africa, August 2-3.
Taylor, I., 2003, 'As Good as It Gets? Botswana's 'Democratic Development', *Journal of Contemporary African Studies*, 21 (2).
Taylor, I., 2003a, 'The Developmental State in Africa: The Case of Botswana', paper prepared for the CODESRIA workshop on the 'Potential of Developmental States in Africa', Gaborone, Botswana 15-16 April 2003.
Taylor, I., 2003b, 'Botswana and Uganda as Developmental States (?): A Discussion paper. A paper prepared for the CODESRIA workshop on the 'Potential of Developmental States in Africa', Gaborone, Botswana 15-16 April 2003.
Taylor, I. and Nel, P., 2002, '"New Africa', Globalisation and the Confines of Elite Reformism: Getting the Rhetoric Right, Getting the Strategy Wrong', *Third World Quarterly* 23(1).
The Economist, 2004, 'How to Make Africa Smile: A Survey of Sub-Saharan Africa', January 17, pp.1-16.
The International Bank for Reconstruction and Development/ The World Bank, 2002, *Global Economic Prospects and the Developing Countries*. Washington DC: IBDR/ World Bank.

Theobald, R. and R. Williams, 1999, 'Combating Corruption in Botswana: Regional Role Model or Deviant Case?', *Journal of Commonwealth and Comparative Politics*, 37 (3).
Thomas, C., 2000, *Global Governance, Development and Human Security* London: Pluto.
Thumberg-Hartland, P. (1978) *Botswana: An African Growth Economy* Boulder: Westview Press.
Tinkasimire, T., 1996, 'Women and Decision Making within the Catholic Church in Uganda', *Arise*, July-September.
Tlou, S, Rantona, K and N. Phaladze., 2001 'Health Care, Gender and AIDS: Prevention Treatment and Care' in Ministry of Labour and Home Affairs *Report of the First National Conference on Gender and HIV/AIDS 21st to 23 June 2001, Boipuso Hall, Gaborone* Gaborone: Ministry of Labour and Home Affairs.
Tlou, T. and Campbell, A., 1984, *History of Botswana* Gaborone: Macmillan Botswana.
Todaro, M.P., 1992, *Economics for a Developing World: An introduction to principles, problems and policies for development* (third ed.), New York: Longman Publishing.
Tripp, A., 2000, *Women and Politics in Uganda* Kampala: Fountain Publishers.
Tripp, A. and Kwesiga, J., 2002, The *Women's Movement in Uganda, History, Challenges, and Prospects* Kampala, Fountain Publishers.
Tsie, B., 1984, 'Industrialisation Policy and Regional Cooperation in Southern Africa; The Case of Botswana', PhD Thesis Submitted to the Department of Politics, University of Leeds.
Tsie, B., 1995, *The Political Economy of Botswana in SADCC* Harare: SAPES Books.
Tsie, B., 1996, 'The Political Context of Botswana's Development Performance', *Journal of Southern African Studies*, 22 (4).
Tsie, B., 1998, 'The State and Development Policy in Botswana' in R. K Hope and G. Somolekae (eds) *Public Administration and Policy in Botswana*, Cape Town: Juta.
Tukahebwa, G., 2000, *Participation and Good Governance*, Addis Ababa: ILO.
Tumwesigye, J., 1997, 'Public Declaration of Wealth as a Weapon of Fighting Corruption in Uganda', paper presented at the 8th IACC, Lima, Peru.
Twaddle, M. and Hansen, H., 1991, *Changing Uganda, East African Studies*, James Currey: London.
Uganda Investment Authority, 1992, *A Guide to Investing in Uganda*, Kampala: Ministry of Planning and Economic Development.
UNDP, 1994, *Human Development Report 1994*, New York: OUP.
UNDP, 1997, *Human Development Report 1997*. New York: Oxford University Press.
UNDP, 1998, *Human Development Report on Uganda*, Kampala: UNDP.
UNDP, 1999, *Human Development Report 1999*, New York: OUP.
UNDP, 1999, *Uganda's Human Development Report*, New York: UNDP.
UNICEF, 1989, *The Women and Children of Uganda: A Situation Analysis*, New York: UNICEF.
UNIDO, 1999, *Rehabilitation of Industrial Enterprises in Tanzania, Uganda and Zambia: Interim Report on Blenders Uganda Ltd*, Kampala: Amanath Kamath.

UNDP, 1993, *Uganda: Development Co-operation, 1991 Report*, New York: UNDP.
United Nations Conference on Trade and Development, 2001, *Economic Development in Africa: Preformance, prospects and policy issues*. New York and Geneva: United Nations
Van Rooy, A., 1998, *Civil Society and the Aid Industry: The Politics and Promise* London: Earthscan.
Van Rooy, A., 2002, 'Strengthening Civil Society in Developing Countries' in V. Desai and R. Potter (eds) *The Companion to Development Studies*, London: Arnold
Vengroff, R., 1977, Botswana: Rural Development in the Shadow of Apartheid London: Associated University Presses.
Wade, R., 1990, *Governing the Market: Economic Theory and the Role of Government in East Asian Industrialisation*, Princeton: Princeton University Press.
Wade, R., 1996, 'Japan, the World Bank, and the Art of Paradigm Maintenance: *The East Asian Miracle* in Political Perspective', *New Left Review* 217.
Washington, R., 1988, 'Development and deviance? A situational perspective on African governmental corruption'. Glickman, H. (ed.) *The Crisis and Challenges of African Development*. NY: Greenwood Press
Weiss, J., 1988, *Development and Industrialisation in Developing Countries*, London: Croon Helm.
Weiss, L., 1998, *The Myth of the Powerless State: Governing the Economy in a Global Era*, Cambridge: Polity Press.
Weiss, L. and J. Hobson, 1995, *States and Economic Development: A Comparative Historical Analysis*, Cambridge: Polity Press.
Weiss, T., 2000, 'Governance, Good Governance and Global Governance', *Third World Quarterly* 21(5).
Weiss, T. and Gordenker, L., eds., 1996, *NGOs, the UN and Global Governance* Boulder: Lynne Rienner.
White, C., 1973, 'The Role of Women as an Interest Group in the Ugandan Political System', M.A Thesis, Makerere University, Kampala.
White, G., 1984, 'Developmental States and Socialist Industrialisation in the Third World', *Journal of Development Studies*, 21 (1).
White, Gordon, ed., 1988, *Developmental States in East Asia*, Basingstoke: Macmillan.
Wiseman, J., 1977, 'Multi-partyism in Africa: The Case of Botswana', *African Affairs* 76 (302).
Wiseman, J., 1995, 'Notes on Recent Elections: The October 1994 Elections in Botswana', *Electoral Studies*, 76 (1).
Woo-Cumings, M., ed., 1999, *The Developmental State*, New York: Cornell University Press.
Woo-Cumings, M., 1999b, 'Introduction: Chalmers Johnson and the Politics of Nationalism and Development' in M. Woo-Cumings (ed.) *The Developmental State*, New York: Cornell University Press.
World Bank, 1981, *Accelerated Development in sub-Saharan Africa: An Agenda for Action*, Washington DC: World Bank.

World Bank, 1989, *Sub-Saharan Africa: From Crisis to Sustainable Growth*, Washington DC: World Bank.
World Bank, 1993, *The East Asian Miracle: Economic Growth and Public Policy*, Washington DC: World Bank.
World Bank, 1993, *Women and Development in Uganda*, Washington DC: World Bank.
World Bank, 1994, *Adjustment in Africa: Reforms, Results, and the Road Ahead*, Washington DC: World Bank.
World Bank, 1999, *Botswana: A Case Study of Economic Policy Prudence and Growth*, Washington: World Bank.
World Bank, 2001, *Can Africa Claim the 21st Century*, Washington DC: World Bank.
World Bank, 2002, *Global Economic Prospects and the Developing Countries*, Washington DC: World Bank.
World Bank, 2002b, *World Development Report: Building Institutions for Markets*. Oxford University Press.
Zeleza, P.T., 1997, *Manufacturing African Studies and Crises*, Dakar: CODESRIA.

www.ingramcontent.com/pod-product-compliance
Lightning Source LLC
Chambersburg PA
CBHW031552300426
44111CB00006BA/287